The true story of two Appalachian Trail southbound hikes—one the adventure of a lifetime, the other ending in tragedy—and how they came together twenty years apart.

unsheltered

NANCY J. REEDER

No AI was used for any part of this book

UNSHELTERED

A UBiQ PRESS BOOK

North Carolina, USA

nancyjreeder@gmail.com

Cover Art by Lonnie Busch

ISBN: 978-1-964024-21-9 (hardcover)

ISBN: 978-1-964024-20-2 (paperback)

First Paperback/Hardcover Editions, April 2026

Library of Congress Control Number: 2026908701

DEDICATIONS

Dedicated to Jim LaRue
And to the memory of his daughter
Molly Ann LaRue

And to Glenda Hood
And to the memory of her son
Geoffrey Logan Hood

CONTENTS

FOREWORD

Written by Molly's father
Jim LaRue

When my cousin, Nancy Reeder, shared with me her intention to think of Molly and Geoff as she and Lonnie hiked the Appalachian Trail and finish the hike for them, I was immensely grateful for their thoughtfulness.

When they encountered the man who had discovered the bodies of Molly and Geoff while hiking the A.T., it was as if the whole venture was made to be. I hope you, the reader of Unsheltered, will celebrate the wonderful storytelling of Nancy. Molly and Geoff would want you to celebrate the A.T. and never let their deaths hold you back from enjoying it as much as they were.

A construction worker from Georgia had camped with Molly and Geoff at the Delaware Water Gap, "They were so quiet, such humble-type people," he said. "They felt if they tried, they could make a change in the world."[1]

---

1. Deb Kiner, *"They could make a change in the world': But they were murdered 30 years ago on the Appalachian Trail"* penlive.com, Sept. 13, 2020

unsheltered

PART I

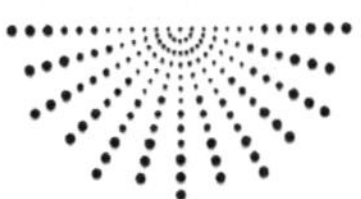

EMBRACING THE UNTAMED

On November 8, 2010, we were eating lunch at a road crossing when a man stopped in his car and asked if we had seen his son, who was hiking southbound. Lonnie and I were backpacking the Appalachian Trail and hadn't seen anyone this gray, blustery day. The man told us he was meeting up with his son and that they planned to hike together for a few days. His son, who had just graduated high school the previous spring, was hiking the entire A.T. The trail had been free of other hikers for nearly a week, but that might have been because we were hiking south and northbound hikers had already finished by now. The man, who was considerably younger than us, probably in his mid-forties, told us that he and his wife hiked the trail in 1990, but they'd had to get off and finish the following year. He wasn't sure where he and his son would camp that night, then added that he was fairly certain they wouldn't make it to the Thomas Knob Shelter, which was over twelve miles from this road crossing. We hoped to make it through Grayson Highlands by nightfall and had planned to camp near Thomas Knob.

It was dark when we arrived. Weary from the strenuous twelve-mile climb, and the cold, we still needed to search for a campsite. At an elevation of 5400 feet, we were nearly at the highest point in

Virginia, with a kaleidoscope of stars shimmering across the black sky. Figuring that the dad and his son would not hike this far, and us having no luck finding a decent spot to camp, we set up our tent inside the Thomas Knob Shelter, hoping to avoid the brutal winds that can blast across this rocky, unprotected mountaintop.

Nearly ready for bed, we were surprised and a bit shocked when two hikers ambled up to the three-sided shelter and dropped their backpacks on the raised wooden floor. We spoke little to them other than to offer to move our tent. They declined saying there was plenty of room for them to set up.

After they unpacked their gear, one of them said, "Sorry to bother you. We were going to stop at the previous shelter, but felt we could make it to this one. I'm here with my son." Though I couldn't see them through our tent, it sounded as if they were eating, and I questioned to myself if this could be the man who stopped and asked about his son earlier when we were having lunch.

The man went on to say, "My wife and I hiked the trail twenty years ago, but we had to leave the trail because a couple was killed." They continued whispering to each other with their headlamps splashing through the walls of our tent. I couldn't believe my ears. Did he say twenty years ago, a couple killed? They sounded as if they had finished eating and were settling into their sleeping bags.

After a charged, protracted silence, I just had to ask, "The couple, were they…" I paused, almost afraid of the answer, but needed to know Molly LaRue and Geoff Hood?"

"Yes," he answered. He went on to tell us that he'd found their bodies about ten hours after they were killed.

I could never have imagined my desire to finish the hike for my cousin's daughter Molly could possibly have led to this encounter. I'm sure Lonnie was equally perplexed by the meeting. By now the man and his son had stowed their gear and were settled into their sleeping bags on the plain plank floor. The world was suddenly, impossibly silent. And fragile.

Lonnie, unzipping his sleeping bag, sat up in the tent. I said, "What are you doing?"

"I have to just go outside and sit..."

By the tremulous edge to his voice, it was obvious he was troubled. When he turned to seal the entrance to the tent, I said, "I'll get it."

"Thanks," he said absently. A second later he was gone.

I thought about joining him, but in that moment, we didn't need to be in each other's space. A chill, not from the cold, had settled into my sleeping bag like a thin sheet of frost. I reached across and zipped the tent closed, wanting not only to keep out the frigid night, but also, if possible, to shut out the memory of what the stranger had just told us of Molly's death. But it didn't work. Sitting in the stillness, I couldn't pull myself from thoughts of Molly, and the bizarre slant of the evening. The man's words hung in the air like solid, unbreakable objects, circling my mind, he and his son lying in the darkness only five feet away. They were supposed to have spent the night at the previous shelter. That's what the man had told us at the road crossing. By all reckoning, we should never have seen him again.

Unable to sleep, I watched headlamps glare through the thin walls of our tent when the son, or his father, it was impossible to tell which one, rattled around looking for something, or maybe performing some task he'd forgotten to do before bed. Yet even with the distraction, my mind would not stop struggling with thoughts of Molly, and what had happened to her so many years before in a shelter just like this one.

~

As I reviewed the next day's lessons for my kindergarten students on the evening of September 14, 1990, the phone rang. It was my mother. "Nancy," she said, "You know Jimmy LaRue's daughter, Molly. She was killed on the Appalachian Trail up near you. Edie just called me."

Aunt Edie was one of my mom's six sisters. Aunt Iris was another and her oldest son was Jimmy, fifteen years older than me. He had married and moved to Ohio when I was little, so I had had very little contact with him. I knew he had two children, a son, and Molly, his daughter. My mother had such a large family that I never really connected with most of my cousins.

"That's awful. What happened?" I had heard of the Appalachian Trail, but really didn't have any idea where it was.

"Edie said she was killed, she and her boyfriend, near a town called Duncannon, up near you."

Living and teaching in the Bald Eagle Valley, on the other side of the mountain from State College, home of Penn State University, I would drive past Duncannon, often stopping at the truck stop there to use the bathroom, or buy gas and grab a snack, on the four-hour drive back to my hometown of Lansdale, Pennsylvania, to visit my parents.

"That's just terrible!" I said, unable to find the word that best described my shock. "How old was she?" I wasn't even sure why I asked the question. Maybe it was my way of trying to make sense of something so abstract that I was having difficulty finding a place for it in my brain.

"She was twenty-five. Edie says Iris is a mess. Is Duncannon near you?" my mother asked.

"Not real close. It's near Harrisburg, about a two-hour drive from here," I answered, then paused, images shuffling through my head, finally asking, "Mom, did I ever meet her? I don't remember seeing her at any reunions." Even before I was born, my mother's family— her parents along with her six sisters and three brothers and their families—gathered together every year. Maybe I had met her and couldn't even remember. Molly was much younger than I was, so maybe I didn't pay attention to her back then. Or maybe they just never came because they lived in Ohio and it was too far to drive. I didn't know, and in that moment, it was impossible to unravel the past.

"Edie didn't have all the details, cause Iris just called and said they just heard, but I think they were murdered in their sleep on the Appalachian Trail. I'm sure Jimmy and his wife, Connie are in shock, too. Remember they live in Ohio."

"Isn't Jimmy a minister?"

"Molly was at one of the last reunions. I have a photo of her and

Iris somewhere here," my mother said. "It's just not safe out there anymore."

...and there it was, Molly's death while hiking the trail—planted inside me—this extremely sad and tragic event that would blossom quite profoundly two decades later.

~

Since moving to the mountains of North Carolina in 2001, my friend Lonnie and I had been day hiking to waterfalls, especially to take photos. As a professional illustrator and artist, he dabbled in photography, enhancing and manipulating the pictures in Photoshop to create conceptual imagery for stock sales.

Taking these walks with Lonnie to see waterfalls, I wanted to do more hiking, even overnight, and possibly, by myself. Being out in the woods all day alone sounded exciting, even though the thought of bears, snakes and lightning made me fidgety. But if I kept hiking all day, by nightfall, I'd be too far from my car to hike back, so I'd have to set up the tent and make the best of it. I imagined myself climbing into my sleeping bag in the dark of night, lying awake, staring into a formless black void, yearning for morning. Sleeping outside in a tent wasn't new to me, but doing it by myself was.

Before I embarked on a solo-backpacking adventure, I figured I should walk the woods around our home. Lonnie and I lived in a mountain community with macadam roads, some only gravel-packed dirt, twisting up and around several mountains. Many of the homes were vacation spots, built on several acre lots strewn with enormous boulders, poplars, hickories and loblolly pines. It was spring, new leaves bursting with lime-green brilliance. I strolled down a dirt and gravel road still covered with fallen branches and limbs from the previous winter's storms.

Just then, something rustled in the weeds alongside the road. I spun toward the sound. There, watching me, was a large, wild turkey. It was staring, then advancing. I stepped back, but it didn't stop, its beak poking toward me, its four-foot wingspan spread wide in a posture of aggression. I was cornered. I had to get around the huge bird to head back up the road to my home. If I continued to go the way it was chasing me, I would be trapped, since the road dead-ended, and the climb up the mountain was too steep. I didn't even have time to pick up a stick. I kept moving backward.

Then I saw them. One little chick after another climbing over the lower bank onto the road. They were little puffballs, probably only a few days old, each one cresting the dirt berm along the edge, waddling onto the road, their mother still pursuing me. Then I understood, and said, "Oh, don't worry, I won't hurt you or your little ones." She backed off. *Did she understand me?* She left, tending to her charges. They went back to the edge of the path as I ran past on the other side. I practically flew back to the main road, where I once again felt safe.

This encounter didn't stop me from wanting to hike in the woods, but it did make me realize I wasn't ready to backpack a trail on my own. Something would have to change in me.

One afternoon, Lonnie and I stood on our deck looking out over the repeating mountains, when he turned to me. "I want to stand on top of that mountain," he said, pointing across the valley. Soon after that we discovered the Appalachian Trail, which crossed Route 64 at Winding Stair Gap, about twenty miles from our home. On a frosty spring morning in 2006, we left the Winding Stair parking lot and hiked north on the A.T. About a hundred yards in, we crossed a log bridge over a frothy white waterfall. A quarter mile later we rock-hopped a clear flowing stream and started up a steep hill. We had been on the A.T. for ten minutes and already we were becoming hikers. The higher we climbed the more rugged the trail became; thick roots and jagged rocks and slippery sheets of leaves. Immersed in this new realm, we could almost imagine wild boar rooting through the dark rich soil, and huge black bears around every bend. It's hard to convey the exhilaration we felt embracing the untamed outdoors. A short time later the trail leveled out at a small sign that read, Swinging Lick

Gap. I turned toward Lonnie and said, "Whew! I'm so tired. I've got to stop." He agreed. We both felt triumphant with our accomplishment. After sharing a thermos of hot soup, we decided that we'd had enough for one day. Arriving back at the car, neither of us could wait to see how far we'd hiked. I checked the distance in the A.T. guide and turned to Lonnie, "For our very first hike on the Appalachian Trail, our total round-trip miles to and from the car," I said, pausing just a moment. "One mile!" Lonnie smiled and said, "Yeah, it was a great hike."

A few days later we drove back to that same parking area and started up the mountain again. With snow on the ground from a late spring storm, and branches sprouting tiny green buds, we were determined to reach Panther Gap. Even though the trail was challenging, we weren't tired when we reached the overlook at the gap with views of distant peaks including Albert Mountain about seven miles away. Our distance for that day totaled four miles. Now we considered ourselves hikers, even though we had yet to reach the top of a mountain.

On subsequent trips to the A.T. we started seeing more and more hikers. One day we came upon a young man with a heavy 35mm camera dangling from his neck and a huge, bulging pack strapped to his back. "Isn't that a lot of extra weight to carry?" Lonnie asked, looking at the camera hanging at his chest.

"I don't want to miss anything," he said. Then added, "I've already photographed a bear and two deer, so for now, I'm going to carry it."

"Are you going all the way to Maine?" I asked, figuring he was a northbounder, thru-hiking from Springer Mountain, Georgia all the way to Mt. Katahdin in Maine. Today the Appalachian Trail Conservancy, the governing board of the A.T., considers a *thru-hike* walking the entire 2,190-mile trail within twelve months.

"Yep, that's the plan. One day at a time, though." He had that same energy we had seen in other hikers that passed us, but he seemed to have something more, a personal drive tempered with acceptance, free from expectation; just keep hiking. I hoped he would make it all the way, and I told him as much before we parted. But for me, in that moment, I just had to make it back to the car.

Preferring cooler weather, Lonnie and I tended to hike less when the summer heat came to the mountains. I was working a full-time summer job and had started my studies at East Tennessee State University to earn a Master's Degree in Storytelling. By October, we were back on the trail, the fall colors fading, the trees losing their leaves. We started up the A.T. again, passing Panther Gap, this time continuing up the mountain. After four miles, the trail took us to the base of an open field. To our left was a scruffy path leading up a steep hill covered in sedge grass that went to a mountain peak we assumed was Siler Bald. "Not more climbing," I said, looking up the long slope. This path to the top was about a quarter-mile long, with a dog-leg to the right, then climbed again. Lonnie went straight up.

At the dog-leg, he turned around and yelled down to me, "Wait until you see this!" The promise of a fantastic view motivated me. Using my hands like pistons, I pushed down on each thigh thinking it might help me get up there faster. Actually, I believe it did.

Reaching the top of this bald, I let my eyes travel the 360-degree view. "Oh, Wow!" Nantahala Lake to the west shimmered like a jewel in the vast valley below. To the south the repeating mountains of Georgia continued for miles and miles and I felt as though I could see all the way to Atlanta. And right there in the middle was Tray Mountain, pointing toward the sky like some kind of sign. To the east, forests and fields were nestled in a tapestry of mountains. In the distance, about four miles as the crow flies, a ridge sprouting several radio towers cut a silhouette across the northern sky. When I turned toward Lonnie to say something, I noticed him studying the marble marker embedded in the slab rock. I walked over and read it. *Siler Bald, 5,216 feet 1990.* We had reached our first mountain top!

Just then, I was overwhelmed by the notion of being able to follow this one trail all the way to Maine. How was that even possible? But seeing thru-hikers over the past several months heading north from Georgia, I wanted to be part of it, whatever *it* was. The thought of doing a thru-hike suddenly seemed outrageously possible. "Why don't we thru-hike the A.T.?"

"What for?" Lonnie said.

"To hike!" I said, unsure of what he even meant.

"Well…what would we do all day?"

"Hike!" I said again, wondering what part of this concept he wasn't grasping. It would be an understatement to say he wasn't excited. Hikers who started in Georgia in the spring had to hike through the summer months, and maybe it was Lonnie's dislike of the heat, humidity and bugs that was derailing his enthusiasm. But neither of us had ever done such a thing. We both had been on week-long canoeing trips, but never hiked for an entire day, much less months on end. We both had backpacks, and I even had a tent, but neither of us had ever tried backpacking. At the time, even though we discussed it, we weren't ready to commit to such an undertaking. It would be another year before we ventured out to give it a try.

It was the day before Thanksgiving, 2007. We decided to try a three-day hike over Standing Indian Mountain, a part of the A.T. in North Carolina, to see what it would be like. We headed up Kimsey Creek Trail for four hard miles. It ended at Deep Gap where the Appalachian Trail crosses. There we headed north on the A.T. to the Standing Indian Shelter halfway up the mountain. When we arrived, there was no one around, and we were beat! This was a stupid way to acclimate to the trail. First time carrying full packs, and we decide to hike up a total elevation gain of almost 1500 feet. It looked like it could be a cold night, so we pitched our free-standing tent in the shelter. We were on one side, so there would be room for someone else if anyone came. But it was the night before Thanksgiving, already dark out, so we did not expect anyone.

To our surprise, about eight-thirty, we saw two light beams approaching the shelter, an eerie thing when you see lights and you have no idea who they might be, especially being our first overnight.

Two people with headlamps walked into the shelter area. They started setting up their tent, saying they were fine outside the shelter. They didn't have a free-standing tent, so it worked best for them. Then they built a little fire and ate their dinner. It was a father and son, who were out over the holiday for a few days' adventure. They were going to stay at the last shelter, but it was pretty early in the day, and they both thought they could get to this one before dark. (There was no way to know at the time that three years later, while Lonnie and I were hiking the A.T., another father and son would trek beyond their original destination and end up staying at the same shelter as us. Only the latter father and son would share the story of Molly and Geoff's deaths. I wouldn't recognize *this* synchronicity until many years later.)

Anyway, that night at the Standing Indian Shelter, the temperature dropped below freezing. By morning there was snow and ice on the ground and trees. The guys were up early and the father put his boots near the fire to thaw them. Lonnie suggested using their stove to thaw them out, but the father didn't listen. He had them too close, and they caught fire. The tip of one boot melted. It was still smoldering. They didn't argue with each other, but then again, it seemed they weren't having much fun. It's hard to bond when your boots are melted and it's freezing out. They said it was their first time backpacking together, so I wondered if they would ever be back. We packed up and were heading out, while they were still trying to get their gear organized. I sure hoped they'd have a better day than how their morning started. But maybe they've had a good time laughing about their adventure.

Lonnie and I left the shelter and headed up Standing Indian Mountain, the mountain named from a Cherokee myth. It tells of a flying monster that swooped down and took a young child. The people speculated the monster's lair was on top of Standing Indian. When other children were taken, a warrior was sent to the top to keep lookout for the winged creature. The Cherokee asked the Great Spirit for help with this monster, who answered them by sending thunder and lightning, destroying the monster and its lair. The bright light from the sky frightened the warrior. Some say he was turned to stone from the light, while others believed his fear led him to abandon his post, and thus he turned to stone for his cowardice. The mountain became known to the Cherokee as *Yûñ'wï-tsulenûñ'yï*, or *Where the man stood*.

Today we know it as Standing Indian, with a rock outcropping on top of the mountain, where it was said the warrior had kept watch. There is only a little bedrock left, most of the rock broken off some time ago. The Native people consider this mountaintop sacred, and home to the remains of this Cherokee warrior.[1] Rising to 5,498 feet, Standing Indian stands out among all the mountains in the area.

We hiked toward the summit where the trail leveled out just before reaching the peak, with tree limbs and branches encased in ice. As the sun warmed the air, ice broke loose from the limbs, the clear, brittle fragments hitting the ground with the ping of crystal glass. We stopped and rested, watching and listening to nature unveiling itself. I believe this magical moment was when we both fell in love with back-packing. This kind of feeling you can't find when you are scraping ice off your windshield just to go out and get milk. But could we do this for an extended period? The average time to complete a thru-hike is six months.

Many years earlier I had stopped teaching to devote myself fully to telling stories. I never completed my master's degree in education, so when I learned that East Tennessee State University, a school close enough for me to take a class each semester, offered a master's program in storytelling, I said, "Sign me up!" Since 2004 I had been taking classes, planning to complete my thesis by the summer of 2009. That's when we could start our long-distance hike.

The idea of hiking the entire trail in one trek was never the A.T.

---

1. James Mooney, History, Myths, and Sacred Formulas of the Cherokee, Bright Mountain Books, Asheville, NC, 1992, Pg. 409; Deena C. Bouknight, (Contributing Writer), "Standing Indian is testament to living history and modern recreation", Macon County News, March 21, 2019.

planners' goal in 1937 when they connected the various sections of the trail, creating the entire 2,050-mile length (at that time this was the length, but it changes almost yearly when parts of the trail are rerouted). No one thought a person could hike the complete trail in one stretch. But Earl Shaffer did it in 1948, the first, walking the entire length from Mt. Oglethorpe, Georgia which was the southern terminus at that time, and completing his hike at Mt. Katahdin in Maine. Thru-hiking then became a commonly heard phrase. In 1949, National Geographic magazine published a twenty-one page article describing the Appalachian Trail, explaining, "He [Earl Shaffer] was the first, so far as the record shows, to traverse that Olympian footpath in a single, continuous journey." When asked how many pairs of shoes he had to wear, Shaffer said, "One pair of boots lasted the whole way. But they were in tatters at the end."[2]

By the spring of 2008, we decided to hike a seventy-three-mile section of the Appalachian Trail, a *shake-down* hike, to see if we really wanted to plan a thru-hike. At the time, seventy-three miles sounded overwhelming, maybe impossible. We left one car at the end point, Hot Springs, North Carolina, then drove a second car to Erwin, Tennessee. There we stayed at a hotel near the Erwin trailhead. The next morning Lonnie dropped me by the trailhead beside a hostel. "I'll be back shortly. You okay?" Lonnie said as I set my backpack on the ground next to his. I nodded, nervous, worried about the things we probably forgot. Lonnie would drive the mile back to the hotel, then walk back to meet me.

There was an older woman rocking on the front porch of the hostel where I stood waiting for Lonnie to return. Over the years, as the trail grew in popularity, people living near it would open part of

---

2. Andrew H. Brown, "Skyline Trail from Maine to Georgia", The National Geographic Magazine, August, 1949, pg. 249.

their homes or outbuildings as hostels. Often with minimal essentials, the owners charged low prices for a night's lodging.

Before Lonnie returned, the wind picked up. It looked like rain.

"You headed up the trail?" the elderly woman asked.

"Yes… hope to," I said, still not sure I could even make it up the first mountain.

"Gonna' get nasty out later. Storm comin' in," she said.

Great, I thought, extremely fearful of thunderstorms, especially on tops of mountains.

When Lonnie returned, and with nothing else to delay this crazy venture, we put on our backpacks.

Buckling his pack, Lonnie said, "You have everything?"

"I must," I said, fastening mine, "because my pack is so heavy, I can't carry anything else. How 'bout you?"

"Mine's heavy, too. But we need all this stuff, right?" We both knew our packs were overloaded, but we wanted to be prepared—hiking clothes, bulky heavy coats, stove and extra gas, water filter, first aid kit, sleeping bags, huge tent and enough food for probably two weeks rather than the one week we estimated it would take to hike seventy-three miles.

The climb southbound out of Erwin was rugged and steep.

"There is no way I can haul this pack up this mountain," I said. Lonnie, though, seemed to have no problem. He was soon out of sight, while I heaved myself from one foot to the other repeating, "One more step to the top; One more step to the top," pausing to rest, catch my breath and get a drink. Something had awakened inside me, though, and I wasn't going to let a heavy pack stop my journey. I caught up to him at an overlook of the Nolichucky River. He stood there, resting, taking a big drink. Far below us, a diesel train with numerous cars and caboose chugged along next to the river. From this vantage point it reminded me of the Lionel trains my father and older brother set up each December, part of our holiday celebration. The conductor blew the whistle, as if he knew we were watching, cheering us on. Though the day had turned chilly, the strenuous climb warmed us. We stripped off outer garments and continued. But that meant we had to carry them in our packs, adding weight to my thirty-plus-pound load, Lonnie's pushing over forty. Reaching the mountaintop, we beamed with success, until we hiked a little farther on only to find ourselves at the base of another mountain! But what a victory, no matter how brief.

By evening we had hiked eleven miles. We crossed Route 19, that cuts through the mountains at Spivey Gap, and found a nice campsite just inside the woods. Camping next to a highway made us uncomfortable, but neither of us could climb the next mountain, so we set up the tent. With snow falling, Lonnie fired up the stove, as I fixed our sleeping bags and gear inside. It wasn't long before I saw him *dancing* around flames! He was stamping out leaves that caught fire from the stove. A relative had bought it for him as a birthday gift. The brand is well-known, and we were assured it was easy to use. Despite the falling snow, we both panicked with the thought of burning down the forest. By the time I jumped from the tent, he had it under control. "I guess I pumped a little too much gas!"

"I thought this stove was fool-proof," I said.

"Not for this fool," he chuckled. Lonnie's humor calmed tense times. We prepared bean soup with couscous, but he wasn't a bit hungry, so I ate most of it.

The next morning a thin dusting of snow covered everything. We had both been cold in the night, so it wasn't a surprise; it seemed the woman at the hostel was right, a storm had passed through. Even so, the light snow managed to brighten our hike. My pack wasn't feeling as heavy; my body acclimated to the weight. I was eating a lot during the day, though Lonnie still had very little appetite.

We rested, eating a snack at Bald Mountain Shelter, which was built in 1988, one of the highest on the A.T. at 5100 feet. A hiker, probably having started at Springer Mountain in Georgia, prepared his breakfast inside the shelter, dumping three packs of oatmeal into a huge bowl, then topping it off with a heaping amount of powdered Tang. He stirred the gloppy mess for a few seconds with his spoon, then proceeded to gobble it down. He beamed with pride, telling us this is what he had for breakfast every day. It looked disgusting, but then we hadn't been on the trail as long as he had. Just between Lonnie and me, we named him *Mush*, a fitting trail name, but we never told him. Hikers, after being on the trail a while, *earn* a trail name, or one is foisted upon them, a sort of nickname, that can spring from a positive attribute, but mostly from stupid stuff they did that was witnessed by other hikers. Although the hiker doesn't have to accept it, they often do. Hiking south, Lonnie and I were never around enough people for us to *earn* a trail name, even though we did enough stupid stuff, so we each just gave ourselves one.

Big Bald, at 5,516 feet, was the first open mountain top we hiked across in Tennessee. With no trees and very little brush, the relatively flat bald had the feel of a pasture. It took us twenty minutes to cross Big Bald, with amazing views in all directions, a skyline of successive mountains rolling one into another. In the Southern Appalachians, balds like this are not uncommon. Scientists aren't sure why some mountain tops are mostly grasses, hence the term, balds, while other mountain tops host a dense spruce and tree population.

On the fourth day, wind gusted out of the north, and the cold kept us moving. A car came by as we crossed Rector Laurel Road. A young man yelled out the window, "Get a car!" We both kind of laughed, having our own doubts about the hike. A half-mile later the trail moved into North Carolina. From here the trail followed the border between Tennessee and North Carolina, moving in and out of each state paralleling Route 212. A middle-aged couple driving by stopped and told us they had just opened a new hostel off Log Cabin Drive. The woman added, "We have great ice cream sundaes!"

We both yelled back, "We'll definitely be stopping by!"

As the couple pulled away, Lonnie said, "How far is Log Cabin Drive?"

"I have no idea," I said, watching the anticipation on Lonnie's face droop.

The rest of the morning, we hiked in numbing cold, bitter wind and rain. Needing a break from this lousy weather, we stopped at the

Flint Mountain Shelter for lunch. I rummaged through my pack standing under the roof of the shelter, finding the meal we would cook for lunch. Lonnie stood near me unpacking gear until he found the stove, both of us using the elevated floor of the shelter like a counter top for our stuff. The stove we chose for our hike was a compact steel device, the base a canister for the fuel, the top a circular cooking grate with the burner-flame assembly in the center; a bit heavy for backpacking, but highly recommended by seasoned outdoor enthusiasts. In order to ignite the stove, Lonnie had to pump the plunger in and out several times to create pressure in the liquid fuel canister. Then, holding a match to the burner cap with his right hand —where the pressurized gas would escape—he reached down with his left and turned the generator valve a couple turns, the pressurized gas hissing out, waiting for the flame to ignite. But it didn't. The match went out and Lonnie had to start all over. He twisted the generator valve back to the closed position, then started pumping the plunger again, creating more pressure. In and out. In and out. In and out. After several seconds, he lit another match and held it to the burner cap, then carefully reached down to twist the generator valve to the open position, pressurized gas escaping again, waiting for the stove to ignite.

And ignite it did! The entire stove was engulfed in flames. In a white panic Lonnie hastily tried to shut down the stove, knocking it over on the wooden platform, liquid fuel shooting across the wood, flames hungrily chewing along the old weathered boards. *"Holy shit! Nancy!"* he screamed, probably imagining himself making the *A.T. Trailway News* as the guy who burned down the Flint Mountain Shelter. At that point, he swept the stove to the ground with his hand, then leaped up into the shelter, stomping out the flames with the soles of his hiking shoes.

When it was all over, we had peanut butter sandwiches for lunch. Other than singeing the hair on his hand, and being somewhat emotionally wrecked by the experience, Lonnie came away unscathed. "That was a close call," I said, chewing my sandwich. He just sat there, staring at his peanut butter and jelly.

In the melee, I had been ready to haul water, imagining the dried-out beams of this antiquated structure going up like a pyre. As it ended up, there was no real damage other than some black scorching along the wood. From then on, I began to notice charred marks on the floor of shelters and understood that our camp stove mishap wasn't the first.

If hiking was going to become an actual pastime for us, we would definitely need a different stove. We'd been told this particular piece of equipment was easy to operate, so maybe the averted disaster was due to our own inexperience, coupled with the cold weather, or maybe just bad luck.

The rain continued, so before leaving the shelter, we put on our rain gear. All hikers carry some form of foul-weather wear, but when it's pouring, nothing stays dry. I decided on a poncho for this trip, but hadn't considered wind. With this huge green thing surrounding me, it worked, just not very well. When the wind blew, the poncho flew out to the sides and my pants got soaked.

Later that afternoon, the sky milky-gray, we came to the approach of Big Firescald Knob. There were two trails; one that traveled across the top of the knob, which was just completed five years earlier—a narrow rocky unprotected ridge exposing hikers to storms and strong winds. And the other trail, called the *Bad Weather* trail, which traveled down along the side of the knob and stayed in the trees, offering protection from less desirable weather. We figured we'd be fine crossing the ridge on the newly constructed trail; the sky was merely cloudy, the wind calm. The trail cut across the ridgetop, taking us over and around huge boulders. To our left, exposed rock dropped more gradually with stunted growth of rhododendron and blueberry shrubs lining the edge.

Crossing the northwest side of the ridge, at an elevation of 4500 feet, with a steep drop down off the crest, the wind picked up, occasionally grabbing our packs and knocking us off balance. We shambled forward, wondering if crossing the crest had been the right choice. Carefully navigating ups and downs, small outcrops, piles of rocks, precarious footing, the wind our constant nemesis, we were treated to the most amazing 360-degree views. Just as we came down off Firescald, a hard rain swept across the mountain. Fortunately, we made it down into the trees before the storm hit.

A few miles later, like a reward for conquering Firescald, we spotted the signpost for Log Cabin Drive. Another sign directed us to the new hostel. The woman welcomed us and showed us to our cabin, which sat beside a small creek. Our cozy accommodations came with a dresser, small table, double bed and a microwave. We pigged out on frozen pizzas and burritos we bought at the hostel office and cooked in our microwave. For dessert, the owner served us whopping ice cream sundaes, just as she had promised. Of course, it meant we weren't eating the meals we'd brought, but we didn't care. It poured all night. We were grateful to be in a warm, dry bed.

Two days later, after coming down our last steep, rock-crusted mountain face, we were headed into Hot Springs. Our seven-day adventure had taught us three things about backpacking. One, we loved it! Two, dump all our gear! Three, buy equipment that was easier to use, lighter, more efficient and safer, even for fools! On the way back to my car at Erwin, I laughed till I had tears, Lonnie and I reliving our escapades, talking non-stop about our adventure.

The next step in planning our thru-hike was deciding when to hike. The idea of starting in 2009 excited both of us, but first, I had to finish school. I was nearing the end of my thesis work with only two classes left, which would be completed in the next eighteen months, no problem. Except there was a problem; hiking through the spring and summer meant heat, humidity and bugs, none of that sounding good to either of us.

Most thru-hikers hike north, hence the name, northbounders. Each spring they start at Springer Mountain, Georgia, the southern terminus of the trail. Marching north, they hope to reach Katahdin before wintry weather hits Maine. We knew about the big crowds, which, in 2009, could range anywhere between ten and twenty thru-hikers starting at Springer each day. These throngs congealed into pockets of hikers which could number twenty or more, often referred to as the herd. They bunched up, then spread out, often reconnecting in towns, sometimes breaking into smaller groups, only to gather again. Scattering, then coalescing, always changing. It was like a living, breathing, ebb and flow of hikers. These were—the *north-bounders*, or GAME hikers: *GeorgiA to MainE*, hiking steadily through the fourteen states encompassing the A.T. until they reached the summit of Mount Katahdin in Maine, usually sometime in September, covering nearly 2100-plus miles on their northbound trek.

Southbounders, or MEGA hikers, *MainE to GeorgiA*, begin some-time in June or July, starting at Baxter State Park in Maine, summiting Mount Katahdin first, then hiking south with hopes of reaching Springer Mountain by December or January, risking a frigid and uncomfortable finish to their journey if winter comes early to the Southern Appalachian Mountains.

Considering these alternatives, I recalled my cousin, Molly, and her partner Geoff, who started at Mount Katahdin in Maine in 1990 and hiked south. I said to Lonnie, "Why don't we hike south like they did. For us, it would be like hiking home."

"Actually… hiking south sounds much better," Lonnie said. "Maybe we can even avoid the black flies in Maine." Molly and Geoff started in early June, which is when most southbounders began. We were reluctant to start that early; it meant we would hit more bugs in New England. In January, 2009, Lonnie talked with a couple from New Zealand who were hiking south. They had eighty miles until Springer. With a late July start, the New Zealanders avoided the bugs and wet conditions in the northeastern states. When Lonnie told me about them, I checked their online trail journal and saw they had started at the end of July. That's when July 29th, 2009 became our start day. We would attempt to follow their timeline, which gave us seven months to prepare.

We purchased an MSR Hubba Hubba two-person lightweight tent, which weighed only three pounds, half the weight of the tent we took on our shake-down hike. For sleeping, I decided on a lighter weight ten-degree goose down bag. I had always heard that goose feathers, if wet, become matted and no longer provide warmth. But I found once they are completely dry, they are fine. The salesperson assured me that down bags were best for backpacking due to their lighter weight and warmth, something Lonnie, unfortunately, would later learn the hard way. Many hikers use lightweight inflatable mattresses under their sleeping bags, but I preferred the foam rubber Z-pad, not wanting to plow into camp dead tired and have to sit there blowing up my sleeping cushion. Lonnie agreed.

But now, what to eat? We knew we wanted it simple. Oatmeal for breakfast sounded good, a nice hot way to start the day, then peanut butter and jelly roll-up burritos for lunch. Trail mix of assorted nuts, raisins, cranberries and M&Ms would keep us going between meals, and a CLIF bar for the pocket, making it possible to nibble without stopping. At camp in the evenings, we wanted no-hassle cooking, deciding on freeze-dried meals for our main course, simple, yet nutritious, requiring only boiling water. The titanium Jet-Boil stove was the perfect solution—easy to use, compact, safe, lightweight, and super-fast, boiling two cups of water in under a minute. Pour the boiling water in the freeze-dried pouch, stir, seal the top, and wait eight to fifteen minutes, and voila, time to eat! Right from the pouch. No bowls or pans to clean.

The next item; backpacks. They had to be lightweight, plenty of room for sleeping bag, clothes, food and medical supplies, with exterior pouches and straps for gear like the tent and poles, which at times could be soaked and best carried on the outside of the pack. At three and a half pounds, with comfortable but sturdy back support, the Granite Gear Nimbus Meridian became the best choice. The Nimbus Meridian also came with a top pouch, that could be removed from the pack and strapped to the waist like a fanny pack, or left on top, a convenient and secure pouch to stow gear for easy access.

Trekking poles were not an absolute necessity for all hikers, but they were for us. We had tried hiking without them, but found it dangerous at times when crossing streams and hiking on rough, uneven tread, or traversing steep grades, especially down. The poles provided a third foot, even a fourth at times. We bought lightweight telescopic poles that could be easily collapsed to less than eighteen inches, and strapped to our packs when heading into towns.

Our Katahdin water pump was the one piece of equipment that worked well on our shake-down hike; no need to replace it. We'd heard it was a good idea to have a down coat for camp; we found one with a zipper pouch built into the lining, making it possible to stuff the coat *into itself* and zip the pouch closed for a nice, compact parcel which fit neatly into our packs. I also wanted a lightweight jacket for hiking on cold days, discovering one with removable sleeves and poly-filling. For windy, chilly days, a lightweight fleece with hood did the trick. We each purchased hiking pants, shirts, sun visors, merino wool socks, boots, sock hat, rain jacket and pants.

Based on hiking ten to fifteen miles per day, we calculated how many days it would take between towns along the trail, figuring we'd need to carry seven to eight days of food. Working backwards, we determined where to send resupply boxes. By knowing how many days between towns, we could also determine what food and supplies to put in each box. At that point it felt like it would be so complicated trying to keep track of everything while we were hiking, we created a chart with the name of each town, mileage, and box contents. We carried this chart with us, as well as a list of what was in each box.

Our twenty-four resupply boxes included freeze-dried meals, oatmeal, vanilla-flavored Carnation Instant Breakfast for our oatmeal, Band-Aids, mole skin, ace bandages, cream for cuts, Motrin, Tylenol, vitamins, toothpaste, dental floss, and trail notes and maps for each section. Items like peanut butter, burritos, toilet paper, and granola bars, we would purchase when we needed them, while supplementing our perishables in grocery stores along the way. With our boxes organized, our lighter, more efficient gear, and our maps and trail notes divided into the correct town resupply boxes, we were set. Preparing for our hike got me thinking of Molly and Geoff, and about all the resupply boxes they must have prepared for their journey, but ended up never using.

Molly and Geoff met while working at a youth camp in Kansas helping kids who were having trouble coping with school and family problems. Taking small groups of young adolescents on three-week backpacking trips, they taught them the value of cooperation, and introduced them to the beauty and tranquility of the outdoors, something many of these students may never have experienced on their own. Molly told her dad that on one outing, the group broke the windows in the van. Instead of getting angry, Molly told the group, "Well, now we'll just have to endure the weather!" The kids were shocked, thinking this would have ended their adventure, but it didn't faze the pair. The ten to twelve-year-old students experienced the result of their actions: driving in a van with no air conditioning, no heat, and no way to keep out the rain. In May of 1990, after working with students for a year, the couple, finding themselves unemployed, decided to do something they both had always dreamed of: hike the Appalachian Trail.

They left Kansas and headed to Molly's parents' place in Ohio to begin their preparations. Molly used her savings to help fund their journey. They purchased the gear they needed. Their biggest task was figuring what food to pack in all the resupply boxes and where to mail them. They hoped to average eighteen miles each day and have Molly's parents send them a resupply box every eleven days or so.

In 2004, a year after my father died, my Mom and I were going through papers and photos when we discovered newspaper articles about Molly and Geoff, and what had happened to them. They'd been hiking the Appalachian Trail southbound when they were murdered at the shelter near Duncannon, Pennsylvania. My Mom gave me the newspaper clippings, along with a photo of Molly with her grandmother, my Aunt Iris, taken at one of the family reunions. Several years later, while Lonnie and I were planning our own hike, I got the idea: *Why not finish the trail for Molly?* I decided to carry that photo with me, though I could never have imagined that my decision to finish Molly's hike for her could possibly have led to the events Lonnie and I would encounter on our A.T. journey.

Molly with her grandmother at a family reunion. (Nancy's Aunt Iris) (Photo: family relative)

PART II

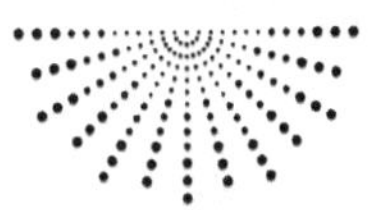

2

BUSES, TRAINS AND AUTOMOBILES

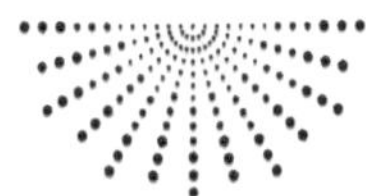

By July 2009 we were ready. I had finished my thesis at East Tennessee State University; the professor and I scheduled the defense of my paper for the week before Lonnie and I were to start our hike. After defending my paper, which went very well, I was relieved and ready to go. We had everything planned, our twenty-four resupply boxes sitting in our living room, sealed, addressed to the various post offices, marked General Delivery, with our name under it, and labeled in big letters with magic marker: *Hold for thru-hikers, ETA*, with the various approximate dates we expected to arrive. Lonnie added some colorful designs on the sides of our boxes to make them more memorable for the postal workers, making them stand out from all the other hiker boxes.

Here's how it would work. My brother, Dick in Pennsylvania agreed to mail the boxes for the northern half of the trail. Lonnie's daughter, Britt in Virginia would handle the southern ones. A few days before we would start the trail, we'd drop boxes with his daughter, then drive to my brother's home with the northern boxes, and leave my car in their driveway. From there we would take the train to Bangor, Maine, then a bus to Medway where we'd meet Paul, the shuttle driver and hostel owner. He would drive us to his hostel in

Millinocket where we'd spend the night, seventeen miles from Baxter State Park.

The plan was nearly perfect, until we encountered a major setback! I didn't realize at the time, but my thesis defense was just for the Department of Curriculum and Instruction. The Graduate School also required completion of any revisions to the thesis before my paper could be entered into official university files. Once the document review was finished, I would be given time to make any corrections before returning it to the university, all via the Internet. If I didn't have this process completed by the end of August, I would have to pay tuition for another semester. This complicated things. We needed to reconsider our hike and decide if we should postpone it for another year.

"Maybe we should wait and hike the trail next year," Lonnie suggested. I didn't like that idea. I knew he was probably right, but felt I could make the changes easily if I had access to a computer when we went into towns. I just didn't want to wait another year. Perhaps as things turned out, we really weren't supposed to wait. Lonnie agreed to send his laptop to Monson, the first town we'd come to after hiking the 100-Mile Wilderness—a stretch of trail we'd heard was without road access and completely cut off from civilization. We bought a special computer box for mailing, then sent off box and laptop from my brother's place before leaving on the train. Hoping this process of corrections wouldn't drag on and on, I still had to make room for the possibility that it could, giving me second thoughts about the potential of all this *shipping*—sending Lonnie's expensive MacBook Pro from town to town seemed to be begging for disaster—the whole process feeling more idiotic and convoluted by the second! In my growing anxiety, I was coming to the conclusion that we should call the whole thing off until 2010. But, for some inexplicable reason, I just couldn't.

〰

After dropping boxes with Lonnie's daughter, we headed to my brother's home in Pennsylvania. On July 28th, my brother, Dick and his wife, Bonnie dropped us at the train station. We said our good-byes, ready to embark on the first leg of our adventure; the forty-five-minute train ride to Philadelphia. Arriving at the main terminal around ten-thirty pm, we started for the stairs to make our next connection, when I heard my name, "Aunt Nancy," echoing through the ground terminal. Lonnie and I both looked around. Across the tracks was a young woman with brown hair; my niece, Jessica who lived in Philly and came to see us off. We hurried up the stairs to meet her. What a lovely gift, her surprising us with such a warm send-off. We had a snack together, her enthusiasm for our hike almost as great as our own. The cool summer air wafted through the partially open terminal as we stood chatting, until Lonnie and I boarded the train.

After an eighteen-hour train ride to Bangor, Maine we arrived at the station late the following afternoon, then boarded a bus for the short drive to Medway where we met Paul. It was hard to believe that in less than twelve hours, we would be at Baxter State Park, and Mt. Katahdin, beginning a hike we had been planning for three years.

Nineteen years earlier, Glenda Hood, Geoff's mom, drove Molly and him from Ohio to the trailhead in Maine. The three of them stayed at a back-woods campground at Baxter State Park. The young couple were undoubt-edly excited to finally start their A.T. adventure. They set up their tent, checking and rechecking their gear, making sure they had everything they needed. They made their first trail meal and ate at the picnic table by the campsite, enjoying this intimate farewell moment together. Molly and Geoff summited Mt. Katahdin the next day, then returned to the campsite at Baxter Park, where Glenda waited for them to return. The next morning she watched them head out from the campsite in a drizzly rain. She recalled later, "I saw them hiking south on the trail, hiking hand in hand. That was the last

time I saw Geoff and Molly." It was June fourth, a Monday, 1990.[1]

---

1. Mike Feeley, *"Mom describes last day with slain trail hikers"*, Sunday Patriot-News, May 19, 1991.

3

PAMOLA'S REALM

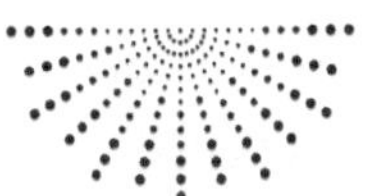

*P*aul picked us up from the Cyr Bus Station in Medway and drove us to his hostel in downtown Millinocket. After showing us to our room, he said, "My café is right across the street. It opens at five. Great sandwiches and hot food. I'll pick you up 6:30 tomorrow morning in front of the café." We just looked at him, both thinking that after our long train and bus ride, we had hoped to sleep in.

Studying the simple furnishings and the comfortable-looking bed, we realized this would be the last night we'd be on an actual mattress for some time. We emptied out a few things from our packs then crossed the street to the café to have dinner.

The next morning, July 29, 2009, we both woke up early, eager and excited to start, had breakfast at 5:30, then returned to the room, packed our gear, then met him promptly at 6:30. We had a chance to talk as he drove us to Katahdin. Paul perceived his life as a series of opportunities. In Vietnam, Paul survived a massive explosion when he stepped on a land mine. Though severely injured, he amazingly came away with all his limbs. Years later, hiking the Smokies, he stepped on a baseball-sized rock and shattered his ankle, and had to be carried out. He later attempted a second thru-hike on the A.T. and it too was cut short by injuries. Paul was no stranger to adversity and pain, and now dedicated his life to helping fellow hikers. He also had a theory about thru-hiking. After his own experiences, Paul felt it made more sense to section hike; that way a person could pick the best time of year and conditions to hike each section. After he dropped us off and drove away, our backpacks sitting on the ground, our hiking poles by our side, we were finally here, our preparations leading to this day, this moment.

Our first task—climb the five miles to the top of Katahdin. At Baxter Park, the ranger gave us site #19. "Up a little hill, one of my favorite sites, just before the trailhead," she told us, handing us tiny little packs. "Here you go, you'll need these for the climb." This must be a rough hike, we figured. Her last words, "Also, be sure you take plenty of water!" It was customary, whether you were northbound or south, to leave your gear—your full backpack, tent, sleeping bag and meals, at the base of Katahdin. In our case it meant we'd spend the night in our tent at Baxter State Park after summiting Mt. Katahdin and coming back down.

For northbounders, climbing Katahdin is the end of their journey; for southbounders, the big mountain is just the beginning. Mount Katahdin is 5,267 feet, the highest peak in the state. Our elevation gain for this hike was 4100 feet, through forests, past waterfalls, over boulders, and up rock staircases. Heading to site #19, *"just before the trailhead,"* we got confused. The last campsite we passed was #16, but there were no campsites after that, so being impatient and feeling like we were running out of time to get up the mountain, we set up the tent and parked our gear at site #16. In a short while, we were heading up Hunt Trail. I now understand why people don't say, "I hiked Katahdin." Instead, they say, "I climbed Katahdin."

Girl Scouts ahead of us climbing Katahdin. [See circles]. (Photo: Nancy Reeder)

The trail was an obstacle course of huge boulders, granite walls and rock scrambles. We soon found ourselves climbing with a group of Girl Scouts, all of us helping each other to get up this crazy, difficult climb. Eventually they passed us by and were quickly out of sight. A short while later I looked up the mountain and saw tiny dots moving up the steep face, the sides of Katahdin dropping off sharply. It was then I realized the *dots* were actually the little white shirts and green shorts of the Scout group way, way up the trail on a winding, slithering ridge like the tail of a dragon.

The wind whipped across the open slab rock as we followed the white blazes painted on stone, scrambling up and over rocks and massive boulders, open ledges falling away all around us. The slinking backbone of Katahdin rose sharply and continued for over a mile. Even with the strong winds and treacherous climbing it was a gorgeous day. When we reached the *Tableland,* a unique and nearly flat alpine terrain near the top, clouds started gathering, steam billowing up from below as if Katahdin was making its own weather. It was quite desolate as we finished the last mile and came to the sign, *Katahdin Mountain, Baxter Peak – Elevation - 5,267 ft. Northern Terminus of the Appalachian Trail.* At that point the clouds were stacking across the summit with less than thirty feet visibility, making it impossible to see anything below. As more hikers arrived, we took a couple of quick photos by the sign, then hustled back across the *Tableland,* starting our descent around one pm.

Molly and Geoff kept a journal of the first 86 days of their hike that she had sent home to her parents. I have included various entries from this journal within the book. Here is their first entry:

6-3-90 Day One ...hiked up Katahdin today, what a beast. On the way down we passed a man & his daughter. He had injured his knee, we did our first good deed consoling them. Later the rangers had to go up for them...(we) are out of shape & we're extremely sore... ML & GH

Molly, climbing Mt. Katahdin. (Photo: Geoff Hood)

It was just starting to spit rain when we arrived back at the campsite. To our shock and dismay, our tent and gear were in a pile at the edge of site #16, a family with camping gear and car occupying the space where our tent had been, along with a note from the ranger explaining nicely, that, *Squatters are not welcome.* Really, it wasn't that bad. After telling the ranger that we couldn't find site #19, we were told that site #19 came *before* #16, set back off the road, close to the approach to the trailhead. Oh well! Our names will forever be mud with the Baxter Park Rangers.

Before we made camp that evening, we finally found the illusive *site #19!* Waking to rain the following morning, we rushed packing up and hurried to a nearby pavilion to regroup. Lonnie was still suffering from a knee injury the day before. During the climb down Katahdin, Lonnie's boot had inadvertently slipped just a bit on slab rock, then caught again, sending a keen shock through his right knee. At the time he wasn't too concerned, until he woke up in the middle of the night unable to move his leg. Lonnie broke out the Tylenol, and then in the morning we had to address the issue again when he was barely able to stand. This was not a good start to our six-month, two-thousand-mile hike, and suddenly it seemed our adventure was in jeopardy. I thought of Pamola, a thunder god and protector of the Penobscot First Nation, who inhabited Mt. Katahdin. Henry David Thoreau said after his 1846 exploration of Mt. Katahdin, "Pamola is always angry with those who climb to the summit of *Ktaadn*."[1] I wondered if it was Pamola who tripped Lonnie up, causing his injury. Traversing the *Tableland* the day before, I had also hurt my knee, but it was feeling much better.

By 8:30 that morning, the rain stopped and we started the trail, planning to camp at the Abol Bridge Campground ten miles away. We only made it about a hundred yards when Lonnie stopped. "I can't carry all this weight!" Lonnie was carrying more than I was, but for my size, I was already over the recommended load. Plus, our gear was soaking wet from the night before, making it heavier than normal. I said, "I can take a little more." After shifting some gear between us, Lonnie draped the tent over the outside of his pack so it would dry faster.

Fortunately, a little rest, Tylenol and a knee brace got Lonnie going again. Even though the rain had stopped, we were reluctant to take off our rain suits, which would have to be stowed in our packs, adding even more weight on our backs. So we trudged on, only walking a short distance before we had our first encounter with bogs, water and mud. I went down face first, landing on my knees. "I'm okay," I shouted to Lonnie, but I don't think he heard.

When he finally looked back, he said, "Are you okay?"

"Yeah," I said, mostly okay, but was beginning to wonder about this trail.

Then he yelled back, "It's like what I saw on the sign at the café: *No pain, No rain, No Maine.*" I hadn't seen the sign, but I was getting its meaning. We continued slogging through boggy swamps, traversing

---

1. Henry David Thoreau, "Ktaadn," *The Book of the Mountains*, pg. 439, A.C. Spectorsky, Ed.

slippery wooden puncheons, and bumbling over rocks. Around five pm, the trail followed Golden Road a short distance into the Abol Bridge Campground, tucked right beside a stream. Including Katahdin, we had trekked our first twenty miles of the A.T.

We easily found our reserved campsite #27 with a full view of Katahdin overlooking the fairly wide West Branch of the Penobscot River. The day was hot, so after our meal, we bought ice cream at the campground store, followed by a quick splash in the cool river, refreshing our feet and legs. The stars shone brightly that night, and we ended our day with hot showers, hot chocolate and what would be our first and only campfire of our entire hike.

ONLY SOUND HORN ONCE!

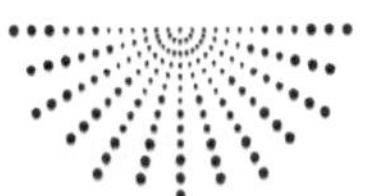

riday morning, July 31st, greeted us with sun and a light breeze; a perfect day for hiking. We met Dave, a Maine ridgerunner, while crossing the Abol Bridge after leaving the campground. Ridgerunners are trained volunteers who patrol the trail during peak season. They perform trail maintenance, but mainly assist and converse with hikers, sharing the *Leave No Trace* principles: 1. Plan ahead & prepare. 2. Travel and camp on durable surfaces. 3. Dispose of waste properly. 4. Leave what you find. 5. Minimize campfire impact. 6. Respect wildlife. 7. Be considerate of others. In this way ridgerunners act as a *voice* for the trail.

Dave held up his hand toward Katahdin, "See that little pointy spot? That's the top of Katahdin. Check it out with my binoculars."

I held them up and looked as he added, "With those you can see the pile of rocks that hold the sign."

"I see it, at least I think I do." Unbelievable that just two days ago I was standing beside that sign.

Dave said, "Just this year some fellow Katahdin climbers and I were there putting up that new sign."

"Well, thank you, Dave," we both told him.

Then he said, "You're pretty lucky. Other SOBO's (southbounders) who started in June never saw Katahdin because of cloud cover and rain."

We said good-bye to Dave, finished crossing the bridge, then entered the woods where the trail led into the 100-Mile Wilderness. Dave yelled back to us, "And don't worry about bears here in Maine. Hunters use doughnuts to attract them, so bears have learned to stay away from anything to do with humans!" That shocked us both, and we wanted to believe him, but still hung our food bags at night.

Our packs were heavy, but we figured they would get lighter each day as we consumed the food. We went a few yards when I said, "Do you hear that? It sounds like a truck?" We looked back to the bridge and saw logging trucks rolling by. "Do you believe this? There's supposed to be nothing for a hundred miles." Throughout the wilderness, we often heard trucks, and even crossed their roads. Apparently, logging was allowed, and the *wild*erness was not quite as *wild* as we were led to believe.

After hiking up to Rainbow Ridges, we came to Hurd Brook. This was a twenty-yard wide, fast-moving stream that appeared difficult to cross. We knew there would be no bridge crossings over streams and rivers in the wilderness, yet we had no real experience with fording. We both had fairly new boots, only hiking in them enough to break them in, but certainly didn't want soaked boots and socks the rest of the day.

"How are we going to get across?" I asked Lonnie as I came up behind him. He was already searching up and down the bank looking for a way. There weren't enough big boulders to rock-hop, and no logs for footbridges. After about twenty minutes we decided the only way to get to the other side was to get wet. It didn't look too deep, so we took off our packs, sat down, removed our boots and socks, rolled up our pant legs and were getting our plastic camp shoes on when two hikers heading north came up and plowed right across, boots, socks and all. They didn't even stop to think about it. I was shocked! Obviously, they were trail veterans!

So now it was our turn. Holding onto a downed tree for support, our boots lashed on top of our packs, we walked across wearing only our camp shoes, some simple Crocs. At first, the water was frigid, but slogging in the cold soon became invigorating, or maybe it was mastering our first stream crossing that left us feeling jubilant and heroic.

Just before we came to the Rainbow Ledges, with stunning views of surrounding mountains, it started to drizzle. In the 1920's, a fire destroyed the forested area of the ledges, leaving behind huge slabs of granite. Over time, some conifers grew back, but sporadically. We were halfway across when the drizzle turned to rain. Continuing for another mile, I said, "It doesn't look like it's going to let up. What do you think?"

"Do you want to make camp?" Lonnie asked me.

I looked at my watch. It was only three o'clock. "I suppose we could. This seems like a good place." We had just arrived at the southeast corner of Rainbow Lake. The area seemed to have a lot of *Rainbows*, maybe because of all the rain!

As we set up camp, the rain eased somewhat, but we decided, even though it was still early, to take the rest of the day off. This was our first official day in the wilderness, both of us hoping to make more miles. Soon as we got in the tent, we both conked out until dinner, then ate a quick meal in the tent and went back to sleep. Clearly, we needed the rest.

~

6/4/90 Spent our first day hiking in soggy socks and battling the bugs. Being the hearty souls that we are we endured just fine though we didn't make any incredible mileage. We set up camp about five miles from Katahdin stream campground near a beautiful waterfall. Crunchy beans in dinner—still haven't mastered outdoor cuisine—Ah well 180+ days to do so. We both dreamt of losing our teeth!? ML & GH

~

We left early in the morning, tromping through bog after bog. "Look at this," I shouted, holding up my boot for Lonnie to see; the bog had sucked it right off my foot! He yelled back, "Have you fallen yet?"

"Three times… but I'm okay." Most of the time, with our trekking poles functioning as stabilizers, it was possible to prevent a fall. But not always. Fortunately, the quagmire sections were mostly void of rocks, so inadvertent trips into the sludge were less likely to result in injury. We wore knee-high gators—heavy vinyl shin wraps designed to keep small stones out of one's boots—which helped to keep our pants a little cleaner, and our shins protected. While traversing mud, creeks and bogs had become easier, or at least more tolerable, we were still uncomfortable in this untested world.

By early afternoon, the sun was glaring hot. I came around a bend to find Lonnie's backpack, but no Lonnie. I looked up and down the trail, then caught movement from the corner of my eye, down the bank. Lonnie had his shirt off, his head and shoulders above the surface of Rainbow Lake, his hair dripping wet.

"That looks like fun!" I said.

"Come on in," he said.

I sat on the ground and took off my left boot. As I worked on the right, my left one rolled down the bank, splashing into the water. "Oh no!" I shouted, believing this was the worst thing that could have happened: *Wet boots!*

He looked back and said, "What's wrong?"

"My boot rolled into the lake."

Crawling down the bank to retrieve it, I feared the worst. And my *worst* was realized. My boot was soaked! I was mortified. I carried it up the bank and set it in the sun, then stripped down to my shorts and tank top, determined not to let it ruin my swim. I eased out into the lake and joined Lonnie. It was a refreshing break from the hot afternoon. After a fun time paddling around, we got dressed, packed up and headed back on the trail, me with one wet boot.

There wasn't much of an elevation change hiking to the Rainbow Stream Lean-to, a small rickety shelter with three drafty wood walls and barely enough room for six people. It wasn't that inviting, so we ate a quick lunch and decided to keep moving. We climbed a short distance up to the summit of our second mountain, *Nesuntabunt.* There we saw a great place to pitch the tent. Lonnie suggested we camp there, but even with the sky clear, I was concerned about being on the crest—a sudden change in weather could leave us exposed— even though the area was wooded and protected. Still pondering the possibility of severe weather, I thought I heard a mobile phone, quickly chalking it up to my imagination. A moment later two men without backpacks approached the summit carrying hedge clippers. It seemed an odd time for trail maintainers to arrive, since it was already six pm and they would have to be off this mountain before dark. They saw our tent and told us someone else made camp there the night before and flattened it out for us. I asked if the weather would be clear, and they acknowledged it was supposed to be. After finishing their trimming, they said goodbye and headed back down the mountain, the weather update leaving me a bit more at ease.

Sitting on a rock outcrop overlooking *Nahmakanta* Lake far below, with Katahdin beyond, Lonnie saw something moving across the water and said, "Look at that boat down there."

Searching the lake, I finally spotted what he was looking at and thought, is that really a boat? The lake looked pretty inaccessible, not really a *boat* kind of place. "Lonnie, look again," I said. Then he smiled, and said, "Oh, jeez, is that a moose? My first moose! Anybody could make the same mistake." Now we clearly saw the antlers as it swam past a few hundred feet below.

That evening, I doctored a huge blister on my left heel, which caused a stabbing pain with every step. During the day I tried not to think about it, focusing instead on just moving forward, but it was hard, the persistent discomfort.

Lonnie looked at it and said, "I could open it up to relieve the pressure, at least then it may not hurt as much." The blister had formed a hard, white husk. He added, "I'm not sure you'll even feel me cut it open, but it should help." When he took out his pocket knife, I looked the other way. I didn't really feel the blade, as Lonnie suspected, but when we continued our hike the next day, the blister pain was still my constant companion.

Early the next morning, we descended a series of stone steps down *Nesuntabunt* Mountain, with *Nahmakanta* Lake frequently visible to the north. The trail then paralleled *Nahmakanta* Lake. A strong breeze blew across the water, keeping us cool. Lonnie could not help wondering what kind of fish were out there. We learned later that *Nahmakanta* had landlocked salmon and brook trout. Just before lunch the trail passed a beach, where we took time for another swim; another chance to air out our tired, hot feet. Cool sand squished between my toes as we crossed a narrow beach, the cold water easing the pain of the blister.

6/8/90 A day of rest! We tried to tell ourselves it was too early to take a day off but our bodies told us otherwise, so we did! We don't want to burn ourselves out, knowing that most people quit in the first 90 miles. We took a dip in Nahmakanta Lake and lay out in the sun in our bug gear: nylon jackets and pants. Geoff with a head net and me with a stuff sack over her head. We also rinsed clothes near the lake. Back of the shelter, we spent the afternoon experimenting w/the bakepacker—with very good results. Naps and an early night—hope we're ready for tomorrow and beyond! ...sign off listening to the sound of black flies batting against our rain fly—so many it sounds like rain. ML

Two northbound hikers passed as we were drying off. One of the girls told us about Whitehouse Landing—a hostel on a lake—which they visited three to four miles back.

"Great food," she said. "You can even spend the night."

We chatted about their journey, as they were about forty miles from finishing their thru-hike, and asked if they would do anything differently. Friends told them to only carry things they needed. "But after a few hundred miles," the one girl said, "I decided I *needed* my pillow from home and had my mom ship it to me." We all had a laugh and wished each other good luck, and they were on their way. When they were out of site, I couldn't help but wonder about this White House Landing place they had mentioned, and by the expression on Lonnie's face, he was wondering, too. It seemed odd to us. The 100-Mile Wilderness was notorious for being an uninhabited void, nothing but, well… wilderness! Now we were learning there was a safe haven hostel in the middle of nowhere with great food and lodging! Even though we had more than enough food to make it to Monson, the thought of thick hot pizza and icy cold Coke was tempting.

Slinging our packs on our backs, we grabbed our trekking poles and hiked on with a new focus: White House Landing. But instead we came to a boggy, gnarly ravine of mud, stopping us cold. Two thick logs bridged the fourteen-foot gap between the two steep muddy banks, one log slightly higher than the other. Lonnie darted right across the top log with his pack on, hurrying along it as if it were a bridge. I just stared at him.

We had crossed logs before, but this was too high for me, the drop over ten feet down, the logs way too narrow. I just wasn't that brave. Lonnie waited patiently on the other side, as I searched for another way to cross. The brush was too thick, plus under the logs the bog was murky and nasty. Five minutes later, I headed back to those logs. Time to buck up, I told myself.

When Lonnie saw what I was about to attempt, he moved out on the logs and said, "Here, pass me your backpack." I took my pack off, and put it in front of me laying it on the log. Kneeling at one end of the log, I pushed my pack toward him, suddenly realizing I could sit on the top log, put my feet on the lower one, continuing to push it toward him, while he slid across to meet me. When close enough, he grabbed my pack. Just then the simplicity of crossing this mudhole became clear to me!

I shouted, "I can do it this way!" I felt stupid I hadn't figured it out sooner. Inching across, sitting on the upper log, my feet on the lower, I made it across easily. "I did it!" I said, realizing that what seemed impossible at first, becomes easier when you use your head.

A short while later, we navigated through the muddy side trail that led to the boat landing, which was nothing more than a weathered 8 x 10-foot platform that pitched to one side. Hanging on a post was a big sign that read, *Only Sound Horn Once!* Below the sign was a big air horn. We sounded it once, as instructed, and within a few minutes Bill Ware cut a huge white swath across the blue lake in his motorboat, driving the bow right up to the shore. Thirty minutes later we were gorging ourselves on veggie burgers, chips, pizza, and ice cream. Sitting near a table of young guy hikers, we overheard them sharing their war stories about how many times each of them had fallen that day. One said twice, another three times, and one unfortunate, no less than four. We thought about chiming in with our own perils but just laughed quietly and finished our lunch.

Later that afternoon, we made the decision to spend the night; giving me a chance to rest my foot, the blister still a painful reminder of how much I loved hiking. Plus, neither of us wanted to head back out and find a campsite, especially with all that homemade pizza our hosts were serving for dinner. That evening we sat around talking with our cabin mate, Mike, who was from Bangor, Maine. After a delightful conversation we all went to bed, but Mike became my first trail angel. When I mentioned the blister, he asked what I was using, and I said moleskin. He said he had some thin skin bandages, and he gave me two of them. What a blessing; they really relieved the discomfort.

After a great breakfast from Bill and his wife Linda, we packed up and left our gear at the office, then went out in one of the canoes they had for guests. The camp was on *Pemadumcook* Lake, a remote, crystal blue expanse of water with limited road access. Who would have thought we'd be canoeing on our fourth day of hiking! The wind grew strong, pushing waves over the tops of enormous underwater rocks, some barely poking above the surface, while others rose a few feet from the water. We stopped the canoe at a boulder with two feet of exposed top. Lonnie stepped from the canoe onto the rock, then jumped in the water for a swim, but the air was too cool for me. Paddling back to the lodge, Lonnie said, "Look, there's Katahdin!" And sure enough, you could see it through the clouds. At 5,000 feet plus, it towered over everything.

After lunch Bob motored us across the lake to a point south of where we came in, where the A.T. skirted the lake, only a few feet from the shore. This meant we missed about a mile of trail, but we liked to say we didn't miss it, we blue-blazed it, which meant we traveled that section by water. By Bob dropping us there, we avoided a lot of rough boggy areas and stream crossings. Maybe someday I'll go back and hike that mile. (Not likely, Lonnie says.)

That evening we stopped at another lake to camp. With our tent set up and dinner prepared, we were just about ready to eat when two northbounders, a guy and a girl, plopped down near us. They dropped their gear, brought out ramen noodles and their little stove, cooked their dinner, and ate, talking between bites. The girl told us they encountered high-water streams a few days earlier. The guy said, "Yeah, the water was to my chest. I had to carry my pack above my head. Then I went back for hers."

The couple had met on the trail; she carried a tent, he didn't. One cold night he was outside on the ground in his sleeping bag, freezing. "Just come in here," the girl had said. From then on, they hiked together, even though they had very different styles. She seemed a bit more pragmatic, while he, sitting there on the ground in his ragged tennis shoes with the soles duct taped to the uppers, holes so big his cruddy socks showed through, was emphatic about finishing the trail in the same shoes he'd started in, smiling with satisfaction as he told us. Within what seemed like five minutes of finishing their meal, they were packing up to leave. Less than a minute later they were gone.

Lonnie and I looked at each other as if to say, "What a whirlwind!" We were also shocked they weren't stopping for the night to camp. That's when I recalled the two hikers who had sloshed through the stream without taking off their boots. I couldn't imagine us ever becoming as feisty as those northbound long-distance hikers.

Tuesday, August 4th, our seventh day on the trail, was pleasant, the tread easy and mostly flat. We were cranking out the miles—lots of pine needles, very few rocks, and hardly any bogs. With so many sunny days, and with all the climbs, Lonnie was perspiring throughout the day. He almost hoped for clouds and rain. We stopped at Cooper Brook Falls Lean-to, where we had a nice lunch, then rested on some flat rocks with our feet dangling in the stream. There were a lot of girls there; some kind of self-journaling, reflection spot for them, I figured. Then Lindie, a woman from the United States, but living in New Zealand, arrived and we chatted. We had first met her at White House Landing. She planned to do the entire one hundred miles of the wilderness without getting off the trail, but was low on food. When we asked what she was going to do, she told us there were back roads where she could get a ride into a town. Once again, we were surprised by how *unwild* the wilderness really was.

After lunch we made the decision to move on, hoping to camp on the other side of Little Boardman Mountain. Finding no possible campsites there, we headed to the next lean-to. Crossing the East Branch of the Pleasant River wasn't too bad, the stream narrow, fast, and a little deep, but we made it just fine, not bothering to remove our shoes and socks. With our soaked boots and soggy socks, we were slowly becoming thru-hikers!

At the East Branch Lean-to, there was a large group of French-Canadian high school boys, part of a wilderness group that had spread out everywhere, which made it problematic for finding a tent site. The only place we found suitable was between two four-foot-high boulders. We pitched the tent between them with just enough room for each of us to crawl out our side of the tent. The next morning, we chatted with one of the counselors from the group. After he apologized for his boys taking up so much room, he told us they had several wilderness groups out in the Maine woods.

Around nine am we were just heading out, very late for us, when

Lindie arrived. The night before she had stopped a couple of miles before the lean-to, after finding a nice spot for her hammock. Lindie hiked with us for a while, but she was even slower than I was, so we were soon way ahead of her, thinking we would see her at the next camping spot. But we never did. That's one odd thing about meeting hikers on the trail, spending time with them, maybe a portion of a day or longer, then never seeing them again. Or sometimes running across them many miles or weeks later.

After hiking through a forest of hardwoods and several slab rock ridges, we came to the Logan Brook Lean-to. There we had lunch before climbing White Cap Mountain. Sitting at the picnic table looking at our maps, we heard a commotion, someone hurrying down the trail from behind the shelter where the A.T. continued south. Out of breath, this hiker, an Asian man, plopped himself down across from us and started taking out little bowls for his lunch. He filled the bowls with various food items to complement his main course. This reminded me of how I ate in South Korea, where I taught ESL— English as a Second Language. Then I noticed the South Korean flag sewn on his pack. When we planned our hike, I purchased maps for each section of the A.T. in all fourteen states. Each map included a detailed description, profile and topography of forty to fifty miles of trail. Lonnie and I had map #1, which began at Mt. Katahdin and ended at *Nahmakanta* Lake, spread out on the picnic table. We were celebrating finishing this first section. A few minutes later I unfolded map #2 in order to check out the big climbs ahead of us. The Asian hiker, a northbounder, a man maybe in his fifties, began pointing at the series of mountain tops on the map that we would be climbing after leaving the shelter. He had a pained look on his face, pointing toward his chipped front tooth. I understood that he must have fallen. I said, "Yes," as I nodded my head. "We'll be careful."

Then he started pointing at Mt. Katahdin on map #1, which was still sitting on the table. This map showed moderate climbs over seventy-two miles, except for Katahdin spiking out of this somewhat flat profile line. He pointed to himself, then back at the map, gesticulating as if he wanted me to give the map to him, so I did. He then pointed to us and threw the map on the ground. "Why did he do that?" I thought.

I bent over and picked it up, as he continued pointing to the map, then back to himself. I finally understood what he was trying to say. He must have figured us for southbounders, and knew that we didn't need map #1 anymore. The problem was, I had planned to keep every one of these maps, sending them home when we completed the section—maybe as a reminder of our hike, but mostly because when it comes to maps, I'm a bit of a pack-rat. Folding the map, I thought about this man who had hiked nearly 2100 miles of the A.T., from Springer Mountain, Georgia to within seventy-eight miles of Katahdin, without a companion, unable to speak the language, and so far from home…. I handed him the map. He gave us the biggest smile and I even thought I saw tears in his eyes. He took the map and went to the back of the shelter, holding it up, making a big rectangle on the back wall. I understood, and so… I still have all the notes and every one of the maps from our journey, except map #1, which hangs on this man's wall somewhere in South Korea.

We packed up after lunch and headed up Whitecap Mountain, the highest peak in the 100-Mile Wilderness at 3,650 feet. It felt like there were six hundred stone steps leading to the top. I was exhausted! The Maine Trail Crew with great effort had positioned these hundreds of rock steps using only hand tools and teamwork. Today the continuous rock staircase of 749 steps in the three-quarter-mile section headed south up to the top of Whitecap, the way we were climbing—making it the longest set of rock steps to be found anywhere in Maine. This undertaking took eleven years over a period beginning in 1994 then continuing on and off until 2010. Since then, an extra 169 steps have been added on the West Ridge of White Cap. The final number is 1,049 steps on the A.T. over the entire mountain!

We had a few sprinkles that morning, but the sky cleared, leaving us with a bright, picture-perfect day. From the summit of Whitecap, we viewed mountains, valleys and lakes spreading out endlessly, making it one of the most spectacular vistas for us so far, since we had missed the view from Katahdin due to cloud cover. After leaving the summit, we headed down steep rock slides, which became somewhat technical, requiring care and caution. It took me a long time to navigate these ups and downs, as I moved from White Cap to Hay, and then to West Mountain. I didn't realize how far I had gotten behind Lonnie, and evidently, neither did he. I only stopped once to shoot a photo of lichen that looked like a round piece of pizza. Food must have been on my mind. When I caught up to Lonnie, he'd been waiting almost a half-hour. "I was beginning to wonder what happened to you," he said, standing by the sign for the Sydney Tappan Campsite, then added, "I was just getting ready to start hiking back." It definitely had been a tough day!

We needed water but Lonnie was quick to point out that the water source for Sydney Tappan was two hundred yards past the campsites and down a steep hill. "Are you good to go to the next shelter?" he said.

Studying the notes, I said, "It's only about two miles, and over one more mountain. I can do it."

We were pumping adrenalin as we moved over Gulf Hagas and down another steep slope to the Carl A. Newhall Lean-to. A group of American Boy Scouts, with lots of tents, had made themselves welcome here, but we were still able to easily find a site. Lonnie commented to me how much more *subdued* the French-Canadian boys had been compared to these guys. The Canadians were even *bonding* through song! Regardless, the noise here wasn't going to bother us; another late night mingled with exhaustion was the perfect recipe for great sleeping.

The next morning, we descended through lots of serene pine forests, me about forty or so yards behind Lonnie. "Guess what just went across the trail right in front of me?" Lonnie said when I caught up to him. Before I answered, he said, "A bull moose! I watched it go into the woods beside the trail. But what amazed me was how it just disappeared. Even with those huge antlers! Just gone!"

I finally saw a moose a few days later, a female that moved across the trail about thirty yards in front of me. It went into the woods, and disappeared, just like Lonnie said. How they maneuvered through all those vines and thickets amazed us.

We arrived at the West Branch of the Pleasant River. It looked like a fairly easy crossing. There were some day hikers who took their shoes off to ford, but we waded across in our boots. Such a silly thing feeling my world ended when my boot fell in that lake just a few days before. Thank goodness we brought lots of socks.

After lunch, we started up the next mountain, passing two hikers coming down, one guy carrying his own pack on his back, plus the other guy's pack in front. His friend was hurt, taking every step very carefully. He had injured his knee, and was obviously in a lot of pain, having great difficulty walking. They planned to leave the trail at Pleasant River on some side trail. By the way the one guy moved, his hike was over. They asked if we had any extra water, but we were almost out, and really didn't. We gave them what we could spare. Water is the most important commodity on any trail.

The injured hiker looked like a body builder, lean on fat and bristling with muscle. Out here, climbing these mountains in unrelenting heat, with his muscle mass and injury, he could quickly become dehydrated. We hoped he'd be okay and that they'd easily find a way out of the wilderness. That was one aspect of the *wild* 100 miles; getting help could be an arduous and difficult affair, with few ways out, and not easily accomplished.

A short while later we came to exposed ledges with a view of the mountain directly in front of us, its nearly vertical face stacked high with huge, jagged boulders, some the size of bears, rising steeply toward the top. Chairback! The guide book had talked about this mountain, but I couldn't recall any adjectives like, *Impossible! Ridiculous! Insane!*

There's no way we're climbing that! I thought, recalling the anguished hiker, wondering if maybe this was where he'd screwed up his knee. But then, maybe we weren't even going to climb that absurd mountain. *Maybe that wasn't even Chairback!* Moving forward, creeping through the underbrush, I saw the trail was taking us closer and closer to the base of that preposterous wall-of-a-mountain. Lonnie, who was ahead of me, hollered, "Wait till you see this! Fold up your trekking poles! It's Katahdin with a full pack!"

Almost straight up, a mad ascent, scaling sharp-chiseled boulders with dark, mysterious ankle-breaker spaces between them; this had to be where that guy hurt his knee. I started up, grabbing onto rocks anywhere I could find a handhold to pull myself up, always looking for the next safe place to put my foot. Stealing a quick glance over my shoulder, I saw mountains and lakes far off in the distance. It was breathtaking, but I had to focus, force myself to keep my mind on staying close to the granite and climbing. At one point the rockface became step-like, so we stopped, needing a rest. What a spectacular view; a thousand shades of green melting together as the mountains faded to violet in the distance.

"So, what do you think about this A.T. now?" Lonnie asked with a tinge of his infamous sarcasm, his face stony as the mountain.

Sitting there, I didn't really want to say what I felt, because I had no other choice but to keep climbing. "It's rugged, but beautiful," I said, then after a pause, added, "and a little scary." He said nothing. Sometimes I felt like he wasn't sure we should have undertaken such a journey, but then neither was I in that moment. But this wasn't the time for mining our psyches to get to the bottom of things. We were still trying to get to the top.

Continuing upward, finally arriving at the crest of level bedrock, I took a deep breath. We were both ready for camp, but needed to get to the Chairback Gap Lean-to, a half-mile away. Protected by a smattering of pines, we crossed over rock slabs, able to see in all directions. After a short walk down the side trail, we arrived at the shelter with a wonderful feeling of satisfaction; we conquered the formidable Chairback Mountain.

The Chairback Gap Lean-to was located on the slope of the mountain, which limited the number of tent sites. No one else was there, so we chose the best site, set up the tent, ate our dinner, and tucked into our sleeping bags. Not quite ready to sleep, I sat up, and with my headlamp on, journaled the events of the day, reliving each one. Around seven pm, the sun already down, a couple and their teenage son arrived at the lean-to. I wondered where they would set up their tent, or if they'd sleep in the shelter. Just then, the sound of metal clanging, something heavy hitting the ground with a thud, followed by the father giving instructions on how to set up their hammocks. The sky darkened amidst the clamor of chains and hardware, the tightening of straps, the rustle of footsteps scuffing through dried pine needles. Obviously, they had some heavy-duty tackle for their hammocks. It took them a long time to set up, and I couldn't help but wonder how much heavier that gear made their packs. Dividing the stakes, poles, tent and fly between Lonnie and me, our three-pound MSR Hubba Hubba tent added little to our load, and took about three minutes to set up.

In the morning, we were up and gone by seven-thirty. Our hammock dwellers were still asleep when we left camp. It was a long day hiking up Columbus Mountain, then Third Mountain, the sun bearing down all morning; another unpleasant day for Lonnie. The heat didn't affect me the way it did him, but we hiked on, Lonnie sweating bullets, complaining occasionally about the (insert swear word of your choice) heat! Along the way, we passed a view of the rounded dome of White Cap Mountain, where we had been just two days earlier, and Long Pond, which was actually a huge, oval-shaped lake set like a precious stone in a forest of lush green pine trees. Yet always, interrupting this magnificent beauty, was the irritating buzz of the chain saws. The day before, ascending a steep slope, we were shocked when a huge truck rumbled through the woods with the deafening thunder of a freight train. I never did see it, but when we reached the road crossing at the top, dust still billowed out, spreading along the trail like a creepy brown ghost. It gave me this eerie feeling that a truck could bear down on me at any moment, just like in Stephen King's novel, *Pet Sematary*.

When we stopped for a snack on Third Mountain Monument

Cliff, the drone of chain saws rose around us like a swarm of jumbo killer bees. Finishing our peanut butter and jelly burritos, we noticed steely-green clouds forming to the west, a brewing storm, so we put on our backpacks and headed out. Just as we were crossing the open, rocky ledges, the rain flew. I didn't want to hike over slippery rocks.

"What do you think we should do?" I asked Lonnie. "I'm not keen on going over those ledges in a thunderstorm."

"Well, we could set up the tent here somewhere."

My immediate response was, "Yes, let's do that!" Unfortunately, there was no place to set up, except…

I had the tent up within a minute, breaking our normal three-minute set-up time. We sat inside, dry, and to my imagination, safe. But half the tent was on the trail, never the best policy when hiking, but there were no open spots. The rain crashed against the thin material of our tent, followed by my other arch nemesis, thunder. Before I had much time to worry, a hiker shuffled by, did a little two-step around our tent. We were both mortified, apologizing profusely from the safety of our shelter, camped on the trail like idiots; maybe we'd never truly be thru-hikers. This was our first encounter with heavy rain and thunder on top of a mountain in ten days of hiking, and we hadn't answered the challenge with much dignity. Even so, it was oddly comforting for me to be inside our tent.

After about forty-five minutes, the rain stopped. As quickly as the storm had arrived, it had left just as suddenly, leaving the skies clear. Steam drifted up, rising from leaves and plants as the sun burned along the ground. Considering the mist we just witnessed rising from the ground, I thought it fascinating we were headed to the Cloud Pond Lean-to.

Nearing it, the sky turned bruised and gray again, rain coming in sprinkles at first, turning quickly to a deluge. We were running by that time, clambering over rocks and fallen trees down in a deep trough, trying to get to the shelter before we got soaked. When we finally arrived, we chose to set up our tent inside the shelter, praying no one would show up. We dried out our backpacks and gear, ate a meal, and settled in for the evening, relieved to have the place to ourselves all night.

I'd been noticing the rocks and how they changed as we hike. The rocks since Katahdin were a white, grainy granite, easy to traverse with a nice grit for our shoes. Nearing Monson, the rocks were more of a bluish black slate, smoother, and were most surely slicker in rain.

The following morning, we ate breakfast and left the shelter, knowing we were coming closer to the high, swollen stream the couple from days earlier had told us about. All I could picture was the young man, not very tall, carrying their packs above his head one at a time, the fast, muddy water swirling up around his chest. At various times over the past few days, Lonnie and I had discussed the possibility of bank-swallowing flooded rivers with knee-buckling currents and bottomless holes, Lonnie very uncomfortable with the situation, feeling as if we'd both gotten in over our heads (no pun intended) with our thru-hike. Lonnie loved to fish and day hike, but was quick to point out that he wasn't some kind of National Geographic outdoor explorer, the kind he'd seen in magazines with five inches of ice frozen in their beards. I didn't know what to think. I had never tried crossing a flooded river, water over my head, my backpack acting like an anchor pulling me under. That didn't sound fun at all, but what were our choices. I wanted to think we'd find a safer passage, some kind of kiddie crossing for less experienced hikers, but from what we'd seen so far, the trail didn't grade on the curve. Everyone was truly equal out here; truly okay, or truly screwed; and Lonnie and now I, feared we were in that latter category.

At least for now the rain had stopped, and we were fairly dried out. We reached the cone-shaped top of Barren Mountain, with an abandoned fire tower still standing. A mile down, Barren Ledges had incredible views, but I'm not sure how much I enjoyed them, my mind on the river crossings coming up soon. Both of us were still concerned about Long Pond Stream, especially given the amount of rain we'd been having. Two miles later we were standing on the bank, staring out over white-water swells, riffles and eddies, huge brownish boulders lingering beneath the surface like specters. The stream was flowing pretty fast, but didn't look too much higher than normal, which was knee-deep, according to the notes. When Molly crossed these streams in 1990, there were no ropes.

When Molly hiked the trail, there were no ropes to assist her while crossing. (Photo: Geoff Hood)

But in '09 when Lonnie and I crossed, someone had fastened a rope to trees on both sides of the stream, stretching it across the water's width. We assumed the rope was there to aid in crossing, but of course, no instructions on how that might be accomplished. We learned later that any ropes suspended above the streams are not official installations by the Appalachian Trail Conservancy. They are apparently left by well-intentioned hikers.

Lonnie went first, the rope about shoulder-height above the surface of the stream, and crossed it easily. I wasn't sure how to navigate the rope, which was much higher for me, probably above my head. I started across, trying to figure how to hold the rope.

Lonnie yelled to me from across the stream, "Just let it guide you, don't depend on the rope."

With all the other crossings I had my trekking poles to put down first, then move each foot taking one step at a time. Now they were collapsed in my side pouch. Each step took me into the frothing water, current grabbing at me. One hand over the other, sliding my palms along the rope, and soon I was across. I stumbled four feet from the bank when I let go of the rope, but amazingly didn't go down. I made it!

We encountered someone at another stream who'd told us, "Make sure you undo your pack belt, so if you fall, it won't pull you down, but float up behind you. If not, the weight of your pack could push your face down into the water, or just drag you under." We remembered to undo our pack belt when crossing this fast river. Four miles later, we found another surprise on the trek, railroad tracks for the Canadian Pacific Railroad. No trains came by as we crossed, but it was one more element reminding us of civilization.

Three-tenths of a mile later, we came to our last ford in the hundred miles, Big Wilson Stream, knowing tomorrow we'd be out of the wilderness. We considered ourselves experienced *rope crossers of streams* having just done so at Long Pond Stream. We'd discovered it was best to use the rope as a stabilizing aid, as opposed to a handle for *pulling* yourself to the other side. The current didn't ply its pressure side to side, but rushed down from upstream, swirling over boulders, forming eddies, digging out holes in the river bottom, hurtling toward the ocean. We found it better to have our feet pointed mostly upstream, into the current, body slightly askew, then carefully shuffling to the side, moving one foot, then the other—never crossing our legs—toward the other bank. The rope helped steady our footing when we lifted our lead foot (the current trying to upend the plant foot and sweep us downstream), but only if the rope had no slack on either side. Using the rope to *pull* ourselves across would cause the line to become taut in front of our body, and slack behind, giving too much sway to the current, and down we'd go. Luckily, we never experienced the *down we go*, but came close a few times.

When we reached the other side of Big Wilson Stream, there was a small family of hikers heading north who appeared to be out for a short stint, maybe just hiking the wilderness. They had watched us cross and thought they might get some pointers. Neither Lonnie or myself felt qualified after *two* rope crossings to be ready to give advice, but Lonnie, and maybe to his own chagrin, tried to offer help. "Point your feet into the current... and give yourself to the rope," he had offered, and I knew what he meant, but his instructions were sketchy at best. The young man with the enormous backpack, and who seemed to be leading their trek, cautiously grabbed the rope and slowly entered the stream. He made it about ten feet before he started twirling around, fighting to keep his feet under him, flailing his body, but unfortunately, never releasing the rope. He went down, pack and all, and jumped up quickly, high-kneeing it for the bank, soaking wet, his gear dripping, yelling, "I gave myself to the rope! I gave myself to the rope!" He wasn't happy and Lonnie and I figured that was a good time to be on our way. We wished them luck and hurried down the trail, finding a campsite not too far from the crossing, but far enough.

Setting up camp, we experienced the weirdest thing; tiny bugs flying around us, and yet we couldn't see them, but we kept getting bit. They were *no-see-ums,* teensy flying insects we'd heard about, with a painful, itchy bite, and nearly impossible to spot, and so small they can get through screens. Luckily, we didn't notice them once we were in the tent ready for sleep. Maybe our tent screens were small enough to keep them out. This is where we started to open and close the tent flaps quickly at all times.

The next day, Sunday, August 9th, having eaten the last of our food during lunch, we were boogieing toward the town of Monson, already smelling the pizza and spooning down Ben and Jerry's. We were headed out of the wilderness... finally! We passed an awesome waterfall along the way, Little Wilson Falls, one of the biggest in Maine. I snapped a quick photo and hiked on. Arriving around two in the afternoon at Route 15, after hammering out lots of ups and downs, we found ourselves in a trail angel's back seat headed for Shaw's hostel in Monson.

Starting later than all other southbounders, and with no one to see us do stupid, silly or even strange stuff, Lonnie and I gave ourselves trail names. I had an acquaintance, after learning I was a storyteller, say, *Ahh, One with the Twisted Hair.* I had no idea what he meant, other than I told stories and had natural curly hair. Later I discovered that his reference was to ancient storytellers. I liked the way it sounded, so being a storyteller, I called myself, *Twisted Hair.* When we ran into hikers a second time who couldn't recall my trail name, they'd call me *Wild Hair,* or *Crazy Hair.* After a few days on the trail, the tangles in my hair started to look like *crazy* hair!

Lonnie had no idea why his dad called him Cheesemeyer as a kid. And Lonnie never asked. When we started hiking, he remembered this and soon became: ChzMyr.

Molly and Geoff took their trail names—Nalgene and Clevis—probably from things important to them as hikers. Nalgene bottles were created by the Nalge company in New York. The idea began when Emmanuel Goldberg, a chemist, developed the first plastic pipette jars in 1949. Then he founded the Nalge company, the name coming from his wife's initials, Natalie Levey Goldberg. By the 1960s, Nalge scientists took these jars on Adirondacks hiking trips as water bottles, since they were made from medical grade plastic, were leak-proof and lightweight. In the 1970s, conservationists encouraged hikers not to bury cans and glass containers or burn them in their fire pits which had been the practice. The Nalgene bottle was the solution.

With the first Earth Day on April 22, 1970, the Nalgene water bottle became a symbol of the environmental movement. Over a billion people in more than one hundred and ninety-three countries participate in Earth Day, celebrating environmental protections. Molly was only five when Earth Day began, but maybe she took this name knowing that this almost indestructible bottle was reliable for holding water, and could help save the planet.

Geoff took the name Clevis. Geoff had used a clevis in various adventures with camping and rock climbing. Molly and Geoff had backpacks weighing forty-five to fifty plus pounds, depending on the amount of food they were carrying. They often sent things home they no longer needed—any way to lower their pack weight.

5

CLOWN-FEET AND KNEE-DEEP

We could hear them before we walked up the pathway to the backyard of the Shaw's hostel. There were about ten hikers hanging out, lounging on lawn chairs and sitting at a picnic table. The first thing that caught Lonnie's attention was some guy's feet. The guy, who appeared to be middle-aged, had them propped up on a second chair, both his feet, even his toes, swollen and bright red, oozing pus in places.

"Your room is ready," the hostel hostess called out, ready to check us in. We were fortunate to get our own room. With only a few private rooms, it was nice to be by ourselves. As we unpacked our gear, Lonnie said, "Did you take a good look at that guy's feet? They looked like clown-feet, they were so red and swollen!" Settled in, we headed out to get ice cream. The guy with the feet was still sitting there. Lonnie asked, "How did you mess up your feet so bad?"

He said, "I just came out of that Wilderness."

"When?"

"Yesterday."

We wondered what he could possibly have done. We had just come out as well and our feet were fine. Another guy sitting there seemed to be with him. He introduced himself by his trail name, Whitebeard

Otter. "This is my brother, Luncher. I kept telling him to change his socks, but I don't know what he was doing."

There seemed to be some kind of miscommunication between them, or maybe because they were brothers, it was something deeper. Nonetheless, they weren't able to continue hiking until Luncher healed. For the first time, we introduced ourselves with our newly self-appointed trail names.

6/16/90 We knew last night that we wouldn't be able to make it to Monson in time to get our mail drop. We still woke up early so we'd get to the famous Shaw's Boarding House in time for dinner. We were hiking by 6:45—a record for us. The seven miles to Highway 15 were easy ones. We hitched a ride after just a few cars passed. A really nice guy brought us right to the door of Shaw's. It really is a nice place. Keith Shaw is super. We met George who is hiking ahead of us and several others who were hiking not far behind. Lots of homecooked food and a bed to sleep in. 1st section successfully completed! ML & GH

That evening, a group of hikers who had a car were headed up Route 15 to Greenville, a quiet little town sitting on the shore of a gorgeous, serene lake, about fifteen miles north of Monson. We needed a few things and asked if we could join them. After buying what we needed, we ordered dinner at the restaurant and ate at a picnic table outside, the sun setting over the lake.

The next morning, going over all the corrections that needed to be made to my thesis, I realized that finalizing my paper would be much more work than I had anticipated. Fortunately, the family who owned the hostel had Internet in their home which was just down the road. They were so kind to let me use their Wi-Fi to work on the changes. Lonnie hung out with the other hikers while I spent numerous hours on the computer at their kitchen table. Since I did not finish all the corrections, we stayed another day. Lonnie enjoyed visiting with Luncher and Whitebeard who were around our age. I was just shy of sixty, and Lonnie, a year younger. Whitebeard, from a town near Washington D.C., had been section hiking the trail for nine years. He would finish his hike of the entire Appalachian Trail at the Pinkham Notch Visitor Center at the base of the White Mountains in New Hampshire. Luncher, who lived in New York and had never hiked before, joined Whitebeard for the last leg of his brother's journey.

The following day I emailed my corrected thesis off to the University, hoping I had taken care of everything. Unsure if I was truly finished, we mailed Lonnie's computer to the next town we would come to, Stratton, the postage costing thirty dollars with all the insurance. Maybe Lonnie was right; we should have waited till 2010 to hike the trail. Nevertheless, it felt good to be heading back out in the morning, planning to leave Monson around nine am.

The day started foggy and dreary, but by that afternoon, the sun was out. The terrain was flat, boggy and full of roots. After three stream crossings, with knee-high water, we were getting the knack of it. We finally came to our easiest stream crossing yet… a bridge.

Needing a break, we sat by the bridge with our shoes and socks off, letting the cold-water flow around our toes. With all the hiking, and recalling Luncher's feet in Monson, we realized the importance of our feet. After drying them, we rubbed on Gold Bond powder. That's where Lonnie concocted a bright idea! That night when we were in the tent, he suggested, "What if we lay opposite each other and rub one another's feet."

I asked, "How will that work?"

"You turn around and lie the opposite way, and put your foot on my chest, then I'll rub yours, while I put my foot on your chest, and you rub mine at the same time," he explained. I thought it sounded pretty good. Being small, I did have more maneuverability in the tent, so we tried it. "Oh my," we both sighed at the same time. It did feel good. This became an evening ritual from that night on. It soon became apparent that this foot massage stimulation would be our substitute for sex on the trail; we were just too exhausted for anything else.

At the Moxie Bald Lean-to, we had lunch and a swim in the beautiful Moxie Pond. All the shelters have a journal, usually something as simple as a spiral notebook, for hikers to communicate with other hikers. These journals kept inside a plastic casing or a wooden box, often hung from a nail along the inside wall, giving hikers a chance to leave messages for other hikers, or just thoughts they had, and even drawings. It became a chronicle of all the people who visited or stayed in the shelter.

Molly and Geoff carried a tent, but often slept in the shelters like so many hikers do. They would pick a spot on the wooden floor, roll out their sleeping bags, and place them side by side. They loved writing in the journals. Many hikers who read their entries were so captivated by what they'd read, they wondered who Nalgene and Clevis were, and hoped to meet up somewhere along the trail. In one entry from a Maine lean-to journal, Molly wrote: Last evening I whispered "I think there're less bugs." This morning, BRING ON THE SLUGS. Through the roof of our tent I see their familiar sludge. The stuff that resembles butterscotch fudge. Squish between my toes in my sandal Yuck! This is something I just can't handle. Nalgene.[1]

The idea for shelters and lean-tos began with Benton MacKaye's article in 1921, where he proposed the notion of a long-distance trail. It had always been his vision to have a shelter every ten miles or so. By 1939, trail crews had built thirty-nine shelters, but most of those were in Maine, New Hampshire and Vermont. South of Pennsylvania there were only twenty-five, but by 1943 the number for the entire trail had grown to 169. Currently there are more than 250 shelters on the

---

1. Earl Swift, "Murder on the Appalachian Trail", Outside Magazine, Sept. 2, 2015.

Appalachian Trail. Various communities formed hiking clubs that maintained the trail near them, aided in the construction of shelters, as well as servicing ones that already existed, and building and caring for the privies. There's usually a permanent water source at each one.

In 1955, Grandma Emma Gatewood, the first woman to solo thru-hike the trail, had read in the 1949 National Geographic magazine the trail had a fabulous footway, plenty of lean-tos and shelters, and food easy to come by. It's never been quite that way, but currently, there are many hostels along the trail that provide comfortable, affordable places to stay, and numerous people who will transport hikers in and out of towns.

Sitting in the Moxie Bald Lean-to, I looked in the journal to see what people had recently written…

"I just came down from Moxie Bald, which was awesome, even with its foot-deep mud!" one northbounder wrote.

I said to Lonnie, "Yeah, right. No way the mud was a foot deep."

We left the lean-to and began climbing the 1400 feet over two miles. I took numerous rests, happy when I saw the tree cover thinning out, which meant the summit was near. The trail, with an outstanding 360-degree view, was strewn with waist-high boulders, sections of mud between them, which seemed pretty firm. Until Lonnie dipped sideways, mud sucking up his right leg to the knee, leaving him searching the muck for his boot! Hmm, I guess there was knee-deep mud on Moxie Bald!

NASTY SMELLY WATER

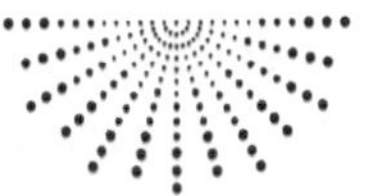

*L*ate that afternoon, walking past the Bald Mountain Brook Lean-to searching for a campsite, I noticed a little white-haired head tucked in a sleeping bag lying on the floor of the shelter. The lady looked at us as we walked past. I figured she must have been really tired, to crawl in her sleeping bag so early.

The next morning, before we headed out, we went to the pond to get water. A few minutes later, the white-haired woman from the shelter came down to get water as well. She looked to be at least eighty years old, waiting patiently for Lonnie, who was perched on a rock near the water's edge. When we moved away from the shoreline to filter it into our bottles, the older woman squatted down on the bank and scooped out water for herself. I hoped when I was her age, that I'd be out there hiking the trail, too. It was weird that we never spoke to each other, as if we were from different worlds. In hindsight, I wish I had talked with her, but at the time, it just didn't seem right, as if she had put out a Do Not Disturb sign.

Two days later, we approached Baker Stream where it flows into Moxie Pond, which was a huge lake like many we had encountered in Maine; nothing like my idea of a pond. Hiking near the southern end of Moxie Pond, we moved through brush and high weeds, with limited views of the lake. The trail ended abruptly where Baker Stream intersected the A.T., with Moxie Pond extending for miles out to the north. On the other side of this twenty-foot wide, deep rushing stream was a tree marked with a white blaze, which meant we had to cross it. The only way we could figure was a rock hop. But these huge rounded boulders, maybe with ten to twelve inches of surface showing above the water, were randomly distributed through the stream. There was no way to jump from one to the other, as I was seeing it, with the huge rocks so far apart. It appeared impossible to me. And the water too swift, too deep, to walk through.

Lonnie went first, making it look easy. Then it was my turn. The water between the rocks was deep enough I couldn't see bottom, and extremely fast. I made it across four of the boulders, halfway to the other side, when my foot slipped, and down I went, falling sideways into the stream. Adrenaline pumping, I gasped, trying to get myself upright, the cold water soaking my clothes to the skin, my pack still pulling me down. Struggling to stand, I jabbed my poles into the stream bed, trying to push myself up, plant my feet on the bottom again, the current jinxing my every attempt. When I finally had my feet under me, I thrashed through the thigh-deep water toward the other side. Making it to the bank, sopping wet, I was certain everything in my pack was ruined; all our food, my extra clothes and down sleeping bag soaked.

I climbed out and took off my pack, setting it on the ground. I hadn't hurt myself, but I was almost afraid to open my dripping pack. My sleeping bag, clothes and the food had been packed in Sea to Summit bags, which were wet on the outside, while everything inside was dry. I was lucky. To be on the safe side, we now line our packs with heavy-duty garbage bags to protect against rain and possible stream mishaps.

The day turned hot and humid, making the four-mile climb to the top of the next mountain nearly intolerable, with no water sources until we arrived on the other side at the Pleasant Pond Mountain lean-to. Because of the heat we were both drinking more. At the lean-to, late in the afternoon, we finished the last of our drinking water, leaving just enough to boil for our meal. We were both so thirsty, that while Lonnie cooked the meal, I went down to the lake to get more water and started pumping. That's when the pump stopped working. Nothing was coming out. I tried pushing the lever down, but it wouldn't budge. After Lonnie tried, we realized the filter was clogged and we didn't have an extra cartridge. There was a replacement in our next resupply box, but that didn't help us in the moment.

We had been using the one from our previous shake-down hiking trips, which was obviously not a good idea, since we hadn't bothered cleaning it before we started our hike. We had been pumping a lot of lake water through it, which can often contain silt and particulates. Despite all our planning, somehow, we had missed this one very important item!

We had iodine tablets in our first aid bag, to be used only if necessary, when we had no other way to purify water. After dropping three tablets into the plastic three-liter bladder filled with pond water, we had to wait four hours until the water was safe to drink. This now became our purification system. Though safe, iodine turns the water slightly brown and has an acidic taste; not nearly as pleasant as drinking fresh, clean spring water. After dinner, we went down to the lake for a swim. There was a dock off the beach, which became a great place to dry off and watch twilight approach. Houses dotted the distant shoreline. People in boats and along the banks laughed and talked. We sat, listening, waiting, and in another three hours, after the iodine did its work, we could drink our nasty iodine water. Pleasant Pond was pleasant, but our water supply was not. Fortunately, we were just a short distance to the next town.

In the morning we hurried down the mountain in record time, arriving in Caratunk by ten, anxious to resolve our filter problem. Neither of us carried a phone on our hike, so the gracious postal worker let us use hers to call numerous places to find more iodine tablets. Since it was Saturday morning, and the post office would close soon, we decided to send our water pump on to Gorham, where our new filter cartridge would be waiting in our resupply box, then continue with the tablets until then. After several phone calls we found tablets in the town of Jackman. Cindy, the postmaster, happened to be going to Jackman that afternoon, a twenty-five-mile drive, to deliver a cake she had baked for a reunion, and said we could drive up with her. About that time a man came into the post office to check his mail. He overheard our problem. "I believe I have the filter you need," the man said, introducing himself as Tom. "Tomorrow morning I'm running the ferry and can bring it with me, if you're heading out then." We said we were, and thanked him and said we'd see him in the morning. There was no way to know if the cartridge Tom had would fit our filter, so we kept our plan to ride with Cindy to Jackman for more iodine tablets.

The only way to leave Caratunk on the A.T. was to cross the Kennebec River, which required a ferry. Wading across the width of the Kennebec—three-tenths of a mile—was hazardous; rocks, strong currents, and fickle water levels that rose quickly, and without warning, when water was released upstream. The ferry service was funded by the Appalachian Trail Conservancy and the Maine ATC, hiring someone to stay at the river bank with a canoe to ferry hikers across during season. A bit of irony, the Native American word, "Kennebec" means "long, quiet water."

Driving north on Route 201 to Jackman, which was sixteen miles from the Canadian border, Lonnie and I saw more of the Maine countryside, plus another huge pond, although I was trying to forget my experience at Moxie. We learned a few local tidbits. Cindy told us people in the summertime collected fiddleheads, a fern plant, dining on the young, curled, edible frond. Also, the local term for a moose was swamp donkey. She told us that moose can be a problem, especially in winter. They stop on the highway, and kneel down to lick the salt off the pavement, surprising drivers coming by.

After Cindy dropped off the cake and we bought the tablets, she took us to the Northern Outdoors Resort back in Caratunk, known for its wild river rafting. The resort had a hostel, but also cabins for rent, with one available, so we paid the extra money for the privacy of having our own place. By the time we settled in, people were everywhere. But it didn't keep us from the hot tub!

The next morning, Tom met us at the ferry next to the highway. He showed us his filter and it was just what we needed, and would fit our pump perfectly. Unfortunately, we had already shipped our pump to Gorham—another goof on our part. We bought the filter from him anyway.

After crossing the Kennebec and thanking Tom, we had a gorgeous hike along Pierce Pond Stream—lots of waterfalls and cascades. It was pretty easy going, moving over nice, fairly flat areas. Walking around East Carry Pond, we found a sandy beach right by the trail. More swimming time since the weather was warm and sunny. During really hot days, swimming brought relief from the heat to Lonnie. By nightfall, the air cooled quickly, which would leave him shivering in his thin, lightweight bag, while my puffy ten-degree down sleeping bag kept me toasty warm. He knew he'd be buying his own down bag sometime soon. He even tried bribing me to let him use mine. It didn't work.

On Long Falls Dam Rd, there was a 2,000-mile marker painted across the road for northbounders. Because the trail changed due to erosion, mud, downed trees, especially in Maine, there was also another 2,000-mile sign a few miles farther, on top of the next mountain. A ridgerunner told us that if someone started the trail today, they would be hiking a different one than what we hiked just starting three weeks before.

When we rounded Flagstaff Lake and saw a nice beach, well, no doubt, we went for another swim. Looking across the lake we could see Little Bigelow, our next mountain.

Three miles later we started up, a slow, steady climb with no reward at the top, completely void of views. At one point, we were on the edge of a narrow rock slab that dropped off on one side. My thoughts about that precipice: "This is a little spooky!"

Just before arriving at the campsite, I said to Lonnie, "Did you look up and see what's ahead?"

He said, "No, I'm just watching the ground, taking the next step." When he did look through the firs and hardwoods, he saw the towering Avery Peak, and wished he hadn't; the formidable mountain rising like a New York skyscraper.

The Safford Notch Campsite, at the base of Avery, was the first time we slept on a tent platform. The wooden stage, propped up with stacked rocks on two corners, the other end on the ground, felt like a water bed, wobbling as we walked across.

Climbing Avery Peak the next morning was tiring, but fun. By taking three-minute rests every half-hour or so, it took us two hours to climb 1800 feet. After Avery Peak came West Peak, both part of Bigelow Mountain. Sitting at the top of West Peak, we saw distant lakes and mountains in various shades of greens and blues, blending into the horizon, spreading out before us in a magnificent swath of color. When we looked back toward Avery, it was hard to imagine we had just been there a short time before. It was noonish, the sun shining brightly with a few cumulus clouds.

We ate a snack, then hiked two miles to South Horn. Haze lingered in the air, making it hard to see the mountains and lakes surrounding us. The wind picked up as we crossed the peak. Looking at the trail ahead, it became obvious we would be totally exposed on the steep edge as we descended from South Horn. Wind gusted across this narrow, rocky terrain, with krummholz and sparse vegetation here and there, the sides dropping off steeply. I was tempted to crawl from rock to rock. Due to my size, Lonnie thought I might get picked up and carried away by a huge gust. Down below I could see Horns Pond and the roof of the lean-to where we were headed. It looked far away, but in reality, was only six-tenths of a mile. When we made it into the pines, not only did the wind die down, but the aroma coming off those trees smelled of Christmas. It was only August, but the fragrance of December wafted all around us.

Ray, the extremely knowledgeable caretaker of the Horns Pond Lean-to, greeted us, directing us to the campsites. We set up the tent, got water, then boiled some for our dinner. While waiting for our meal to cook, we visited more with Ray. Stationed there all summer, he helped hikers understand the need for protecting the delicate alpine ecosystem. He explained how the lean-to was set up for groups to stay the night, then climb the three peaks of Bigelow Mountain—Avery, West and South Horn—then hike back down to the campsite. He discussed the privy, how it was adapted for bio-manageability, so that eventually the material decomposed, and reentered the ecosystem. As I sat in the privy later, I read all about it. The information covered the walls, interesting reading for once. We went for another swim in the pond, a nice evening for relaxing and talking.

7

FIDDLEHEADS & THE ROLLER COASTER

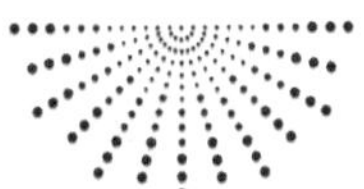

*L*eaving Horns Pond early in the morning, with several steep, difficult descents over the five miles down to Stratton, we arrived by eleven, motivated by the promise of food. At Route 27, we hitched a ride, then went straight to the Stratton Diner. After ordering pizza, Lonnie went to the restroom. When he returned, I told him I also got us a large order of French fries and two large root beers. He just looked at me, "You're pretty hungry, huh?" I guess that was an understatement. When we finished eating, we checked into the Stratton Motel and hostel where we enjoyed talking with Sue, the owner, as well as other hikers.

Wanting to get to the post office before it closed, we didn't dawdle in the room, quickly heading up the road to pick up our food box and Lonnie's laptop. When we came out with all our stuff, a guy driving down the road saw us, obviously figuring us for hikers. "They look heavy, let me give you a ride to the motel." It was only a block away, but we took it. That evening we returned to the Stratton Diner and there on the menu was an appetizer, "fiddleheads." We tried them, and those little curled fronds were pretty tasty.

We hadn't planned on spending an extra day in Stratton, but we were waiting on a FedEx box with Aquamira—a water purifying alternative to iodine tablets—we'd ordered and had sent to the hostel. The delay gave me more time to work on new thesis corrections the university had sent. That evening we learned that Hurricane Bill was moving up the coast, which could dump a whole bunch of rain on the area. Maybe our sunny days were over.

After making my corrections, and receiving our Aquamira, we shipped the computer forward to the next town, then left Stratton around ten-thirty that morning. While heading up Crocker Mountain, an extremely hard climb, clouds started forming, the day growing hotter and more humid, both of us missing our air-conditioned room. We arrived at the Crocker Cirque Campsite. Rain came hard just after we set up the tent. Fortunately, the tent sat on a platform, which meant it wouldn't be sitting in a pool of mud by morning. A thunderstorm moved through, but I wasn't as scared as I had been, my fears diminishing as I became more comfortable living in the woods.

The next morning, we headed to the Carrabassett River and crossed easily. The rain had stopped. Perhaps Hurricane Bill moved on. From the river basin, we climbed steadily up Sugarloaf with no views. At one point, we passed a plaque by a side trail to the summit which had been the original A.T., and the last section to be added in August, 1937 to complete the entire Appalachian Trail.

6/30/90 It rained most of the night. It was subsequently a wet morning w/ slugs everywhere—including two big ones inside of the tent: the alarm went off at 5 and we didn't get moving until after 7. We were a bit sluggish on the trail too, moving very slowly as we climbed up towards Sugarloaf Mtn. gaining lots of elevation. ML & GH

Climbing over the peaks of Saddleback Mountain were the toughest sections in Maine. After leaving our campsite that morning, we began the long ascent, over two thousand feet, our legs becoming acclimated to working hard, our bodies finding their natural rhythm. The trees thinned as we ascended higher, then suddenly, the terrain changed again, just rock ledges with small trees, lichen and moss. Atop the first peak, Little Saddleback, we could see The Horn ahead of us, and Saddleback, which was the highest peak, four miles ahead, all above treeline. From our vantage point, Saddleback didn't look that far, but we were fooled by the illusion; we only saw the mountain tops, not the deep valleys in between. We descended five hundred feet, then back up two thousand to The Horn, then back down. It felt like a very slow and arduous roller coaster, the ups and downs not visible until we had to traverse them. In places along the way there were even ladders to navigate rock faces and stony drop-offs. Nearing the end of day, we were exhausted, but had to keep moving, with menacing clouds gathering in the western sky.

Lonnie arrived first at the top, and stood reading the sign attached to the post spiked into a pile of rocks, *Saddleback Mountain: 4,116 feet*. He had just taken off his pack to rest, when I came up behind him. The clouds were rolling in just above our heads from the western sky, greenish purple, thick and ominous. I had been keeping an eye on them as we continued to move south over the rock ledges. After putting our rain gear on, we pulled out our pack covers and stretched them over our packs. Lonnie said, "Do you want to have something to eat?"

"What about that sky?" I said, my imagination getting the better of me. I guess I wasn't quite finished with my fear of storms.

He said, "What sky?" He glanced over his shoulder, then calmly added, "Looks okay to me, but we can wait to eat." That was all I needed. I didn't even give him time to say anything else. He was back to reading the sign, asking me something, when I took off! He couldn't believe how fast I moved across that mountain top, my yellow pack cover bouncing side to side like a metronome. No way did I want to be caught in that big green monster of a storm, so I hustled the next half-mile across the open mountain like my life depended on it, and didn't stop moving until I began the descent into tree cover. When Lonnie caught up to me, he said, "What happened back there? I was talking to you, and I turn around, you're like a mile away! All I could see was this little dot of yellow rocking back and forth across the mountain!"

Someone told us that coming down off Saddleback was moderately easy, but it turned out to be no picnic either. Lonnie's comment about that, "You take slab rock, put it on a thirty-five-degree slope, then run water down it, and that will be the trail." It was not moderate, to say the least. I told him he earned his mountain climbing badge with that trek. And regrettably, even though I believed I'd conquered my fear of storms, I had to relinquish my badge of courage.

8

A LOT OF DOORS TO KNOCK ON

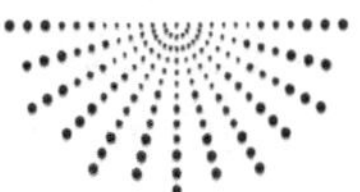

Reaching Route 17, we felt a few sprinkles; a moment later it poured. Lonnie already had his rainwear on, while I was struggling and getting soaked trying to put on my rain pants. From a parking area just across the highway, a woman hollered out her car window, "Do you need a ride?"

With one pant leg on, I grabbed my pack, slung it over my shoulder, and held onto the other dangling pant leg, and ran. Lonnie was waiting in the backseat of their SUV when I threw myself in next to him, the warmth of the car wrapping around me. These trail angels, Anne, and her husband, Bob, who lived in the Midwest, greeted us with smiles and told us to help ourselves to the cooler filled with boxed doughnuts, Gatorade and Little Debbie treats. A few minutes later I realized this was the same couple Sue from the Stratton Motel had introduced us to in Stratton just before we left. I had jokingly said to them, "Well, maybe we'll see you in Rangeley." Little did I know!

Bob and Anne were in Maine helping hikers get to and from the trail. Anne was also doing some hiking of her own, while Bob, who didn't hike at all, spent his time shuttling hikers. During the nine-mile drive to Rangeley, Anne told us her trail name used to be *Slow Girl*, but now *Steady Girl*. Bob said, "Considering she has hiked the three major trails in the U.S., it probably should be *Fast Girl*." I had never heard of the other two trails—the Pacific Crest Trail, or the Continental Divide Trail. Anne explained that both went from the U.S. Southern border to the Canadian border. The PCT followed the mountain crests of California, Oregon, and Washington for 2600 miles. The CDT followed the divide through New Mexico, Colorado, Wyoming, Idaho and Montana, and depending which way a hiker went, and there are many ways, the trail can stretch for 3100 miles. I asked, "Did you hike them, too, Bob?"

"No, I'm more or less the chauffeur; I let her do the hiking."

When they dropped us at the motel in Rangeley, we hoped we'd see them again. After a quick meal at a local restaurant, then picking up our boxes at the post office, I jumped on the computer at the motel to check the changes needed for my thesis. The professor suggested I use the book, *The Chicago Manual of Style* for the corrections. The local library did not have a copy, so I ordered it online and arranged to have it shipped overnight with FedEx to my name and General Delivery at the post office. But what I didn't know was that FedEx doesn't deliver to a post office, no matter how you address the package.

The next morning, I checked with the local FedEx office and they told me it had been sent to an address *somewhere* in Rangeley. They even gave me a street name and house number, but when I looked for the house, there was no such address. I was so frustrated, I wanted to cry. Where could the book be? Rangeley wasn't that big, but even with just less than two thousand homes, that was a lot of doors to knock on. At this point, I questioned if I even wanted to get this *damn* thesis finished.

I searched several streets, basically looking for a FedEx box that may have been dropped off on someone's porch, or was lying on the ground somewhere. I decided to check houses on streets with similar addresses. Mercifully, these streets were within walking distance from the motel. When I knocked on the door of one of them, by some crazy alignment of the stars, I discovered the owners had indeed received it, but had no clue what it was for. I'm not sure which gods reign over the thesis, but was glad they had looked down favorably on me.

All that afternoon and evening I worked on corrections, trying to find the proper format for them in my new book. We planned to head out the following morning, so I did as much as I could before bed. The next town I could send the computer to was Gorham, which by trail was seventy-eight miles away. With only a few days left in the month, there was no way I would get finished by the end of August, which meant I would have to pay another semester's tuition. I couldn't believe what a pain this was becoming, but thankfully, Lonnie didn't rub my nose in it.

We planned to send the style book and the computer onto Gorham the next morning, and I figured the thesis would get finished when it did. I was going to have fun hiking. After a bit more discussion, Lonnie and I decided it might be better to stay an extra day to see if I could finish making the corrections. That extra day of rest worked for him as well, as his feet were giving him trouble when we came into Rangeley.

I worked on it all that next day and into the evening, as Lonnie relaxed and caught up on eating and television time. Though I'd had to make numerous changes throughout the document, the bibliography was my biggest headache, taking extra time to ensure that all commas and periods were in the right places. I went to bed weary, but more ready to hike than ever. Just in case, we decided to send the computer to one more trail town.

Molly received her art education degree from Ohio Wesleyan University, working in many mediums—printmaking, painting, sculpture, drawing and design. Wanting to create a metal sculpture she envisioned as, Junk Yard Dogs, she learned how to weld. Junk Yard Dogs consisted of six separate dogs, each one over six feet tall, welded from metal scraps she collected at a junk yard. The art department so admired her sculptures they displayed them outside their offices. One day the Junk Yard Dogs vanished from the display

area. It wasn't until later that each one was found in the women's dorms and were returned to their original home. Her father told me that the president of the university even had a Junk Yard Dog outside his office door. Molly's work exemplified her joy and exuberance for life, spilling out in surprising ways.

When Molly was a senior in high school, the United States Postal Service launched a stamp competition, open to students of any age. She submitted her idea; a simple outline of a family sketched in three different colors. From over half-a-million students who submitted ideas for the stamp, the Postal Service selected her design, calling it the Family Unity Commemorative Stamp. Her artwork was used on a 20-cent postage stamp, issued on October 1st, 1984. I found it interesting that as a commercial illustrator, Lonnie had created over a hundred commemorative stamps for the Postal Service.

9

OATMEAL ANYONE?

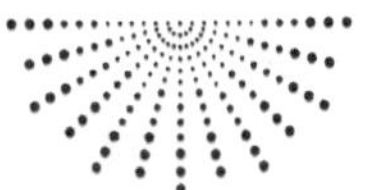

*B*efore leaving Rangeley, we mailed the computer to Gorham, then went back to the room for our packs. Walking by the grocery store, we passed Bob returning to his car. He waved to us, and once again, the trail angel from the Midwest was hauling us to the trailhead. Bob was alone this time; Anne was doing some hiking of her own.

Later that morning, we arrived at a campsite by a pond, where there was a canoe available for anyone to take out. After paddling to the middle of the pond, we ate our lunch, a warm breeze moving us along the water. When we finished, we paddled back and left the canoe where it had been parked, then continued hiking. What a special treat in the middle of our hiking day.

That afternoon at an open field, power lines stretched down the mountain. We stopped, took out our sleeping pads, and laid down in the field, looking up at the sun-drenched sky with the power lines above us. Not the ideal spot, but we welcomed the diversion. These breaks were helpful for our morale, but would we get to Springer before the cold hit? Living in the South, we figured we'd be okay since the winter months were often conducive to outdoor activities, the weather mild and often dry.

Toward the end of the day, Lonnie and I came to the Sabbath Day Pond Lean-to. We decided to pass it by, since the trail supposedly skirted Long Pond in three-tenths of a mile. We were delighted to find a nice, but short, sandy beach with two picnic benches and a little spot just big enough for our tent. In the morning, we waded into the water for a cool, quick dip, then packed up and headed toward the three peaks of the Bemis Range.

The A.T. crossed Route 17, overlooking a stunning vista of mountains and myriad bodies of water reflecting back the blue sky, all part of the Rangeley Lake system. A bench sat next to the road, so we stopped to soak in the view, not wanting to leave.

The Bemis Mountain Lean-to was four miles up the mountain, just before Third Peak. With very little water left, we were dismayed to find twelve people at the shelter telling us there was no water at the spring. Exhausted from the day's hiking, we were almost running on vapors as it was, and still needed more water for the evening; for cooking, and drinks through the night. Staying hydrated was crucial to us maintaining health and preventing injuries. Regardless, there was no other choice but to keep going. We rested a few minutes, then climbed the seven hundred feet over Bemis Mountain to where there was supposedly a stealth camping site near the Bemis Stream Trail. Stealth sites were usually suitable for a tent, but not officially recognized for camping by the ATC. We found a flat place, not that great, but good enough. Lonnie went ahead to find the water source as I unpacked our gear, stowing it in the tent. Two hikers passed while he was gone, talking of a hurricane coming through the next day, probably Hurricane Bill. High winds and possibly three inches of rain were expected. That didn't sound so good. It was dark, when Lonnie returned with water; having found the spring. Concerned by pitching the tent so close to the trail, barely ten feet away, Lonnie hoped no more hikers would come by, but I said, "You just never know!"

Within a few minutes, three girls came up the trail heading north, two with head lamps. The first girl, the one without a light, said, "It's not too dark, I can still see!" We figured they were bound for the shelter, unsuspecting of the rough trail and open ledges going over Bemis, plus the water shortage when they arrived. We told them there was no water at the next shelter, but that we had gotten some from the spring, though it was a fairly long way back for them. They looked at each other, a silent conference, hemming and hawing, then decided to go on, feeling as if they had no choice. We knew the feeling, but still felt bad over what they would encounter at the shelter.

After a night of wind and driving rain, the next morning was more of the same; the day gray and wet, and gusting like crazy. With the tent pole structure supporting both the tent and rain fly, it seemed possible to take the tent down while leaving the fly in place. It was a matter of slipping the tent tabs off at the corners, then reattaching them beneath the rain fly tabs, thereby freeing each corner of the tent. After that, we only had to undo the hooks holding the top of the tent to the main back bone of the pole assembly, then ball the tent into its stuff sack so it would be out of our way. We then worked under the fly, packing our gear into our packs, with everything mostly staying dry. After that, we rushed to take down the fly and store the poles, then headed out.

With the rain and wind still raging, the trees protected us as we headed over Elephant Mountain, which was more of a huge mound, hence the name, than most other mountains we'd been crossing. Two miles later, after climbing the slab rock tread to the top of Old Blue, we rested, even though it was cold, the misty fog an impenetrable curtain. At least the rain had subsided. Decked out in rain coats, fleece underneath, rain pants, leggings and hood, we ate a quick snack. Then heard someone coming up the trail from the south—a guy wearing only a shirt and shorts, most likely a northbounder—soaked through. We were shocked! He had to be freezing, but said nothing as he went by, just continued north over the mountain.

Once he passed, I started moving as well, Hurricane Bill in the throes of a nasty tantrum. The approach to Old Blue had been tricky, but leaving the crest was even worse, steep slab rock slicked with rain, an obstacle course of narrow stone ledges to step down and over, often right on the edge of the mountain. Too frightened to traverse them standing, I chose to sit and go down on my butt. Lonnie stayed upright over the sheer rock, but told me later he had never been so scared in his life.

The climb down from Old Blue to South Arm Road was almost three miles. Even with clouds and rain, and some trees around us, at times I could glimpse the valley below, an eerie image, like a mirage, 2100 feet down. After nearly three hours, we arrived at South Arm Road, glad to be on the flat dirt path, Bill still slinging his wind-driven rain. We walked west toward the campground to pick up the food box my brother had mailed there. This meant we would have to tent camp in rain that afternoon, sitting in it shivering from the cold with nothing to do but wait for night; this idea did not thrill either of us. We were still slogging to the campground through mud puddles, our gear soaked, water pouring off our rainsuit hoods, when our prospects shifted from grim to fantastic!

There had been no traffic on this old weathered road when a guy in a truck stopped and rolled down his window. He was going the opposite way, and said, "You know, you're going the wrong way to town," meaning Andover which was eight miles east. I said, "We know, but we're headed to the campground." There we were, just looking at him, and him looking at us. No one said a word for a moment, then he pulled away. I supposed we looked pretty forlorn, since he went up the road a short distance, and stopped.

I said to Lonnie, "I think he's turning around." I didn't want to look, but I was right.

He stopped again, this time going our way. "Climb in the back. I'll take you to the campground. It's another three to four miles." We climbed in back and soon were on our way. At the campground we expressed our thanks. It felt good to be in the warmth of the office, but the clerk indicated our food box had not arrived. It was Saturday, August 29th. We had hoped to get to Andover somehow and sleep in a motel, but without the food box, we didn't know what to do. Standing in the camp office with all our wet gear, the clerk mentioned that there were some hostels where we could possibly stay and then get our resupply box Monday morning. She let us use her phone.

There was no answer at the first place we called. The clerk

suggested another, but she wasn't sure the proprietors were still taking in hikers. I called anyway. A man answered and I explained our predicament. His trail name was Bear, and he said, "Well, we are somewhat not open as a hostel, but we do still have some guests."

"We're at the South Arm Campground. The woman here said you may have a room for us."

"I believe we could fix you up." I had explained that there were two of us, my friend and myself. Then Lonnie said to ask if they have any private rooms.

"Do you have any private rooms?" I knew this may be asking too much, but I took a chance.

"We don't really have private rooms in the hostel area, but I think we can find you something," he answered.

"Oh, that would be so wonderful. Our box hasn't arrived here at the campground, so we would need a ride back to pick it up on Monday. We'll pay for everything, no problem," I told him.

Bear added, "We can talk about what you need when you get here. My friend and I will be coming to pick you up shortly. Just wait there at the office."

"Thanks so much. We really appreciate it."

Lonnie asked me, "Do they have a private room?" I just nodded and smiled. "You know it's because you have such a sweet voice that he found you a room," Lonnie added.

It wasn't long before Bear and his friend arrived and we were sitting in the back seat of the truck. When we arrived at their home, we met his wife, Honey. They were an older couple and not officially opened anymore, but only took in hikers they knew. We were fortunate Bear had said yes.

Soon after we arrived, Honey and Bear put out dinner for all their hiking guests, so we sat down to a wonderful meal. They even gave us that exclusive private room which was upstairs on the same level as their bedroom. At the huge dining room table there were several other hikers, who were staying downstairs in the hostel. One hiker's legs were bruised and cut, and looked awful. We asked him what happened.

"Just hiking," he said. We didn't have any injuries like that. But then we wore hiking pants and long sleeve shirts, all lightweight, with gaiters up to our knees.

Sunday morning the hikers gathered in the huge kitchen for breakfast. Bear and Honey made pancakes while each of the hikers could make their own scrambled or fried eggs and toast.

After breakfast, Bear dropped us at South Arm Road at the base of Old Blue, where we continued hiking south. Bear planned to meet us at East B Hill Road, ten trail-miles away, around 4:30. This was our first experience as *slack-packers,* which meant we left most of our gear at the hostel, and only carried what we needed for the day.

Moody Mountain was steep and at one point had been rerouted due to a mud slide. The side of the mountain had washed away, and the dirt of the new provisional trail was extremely loose and narrow, making the trek an arduous slog. When the trail switch-backed beside a ravine, Lonnie slipped, then just caught himself before ending up down the mudslide in the tangle of branches and uprooted trees below. Following behind, I took my steps even more carefully. We went over Wyman Mountain with more muddy areas, and even without our full packs, the trail demanded all our attention and a slower speed. When we arrived at the road a little after four, it was nice knowing dinner would be at six that evening.

Bear drove us back to East B Hill Road on Monday for one more day of slack-packing. We began the long, steep climb to the two peaks of Baldpate Mountain on a cold, windy day. Lonnie led, but had gotten so far ahead I could no longer see him. Toward the top, with bigger trees scarcer, the terrain turned mostly rocky with a few scrubby plants. Before long I was above treeline on an open face slab, the wind howling, maybe thirty miles per hour. I could not find the next white trail blaze anywhere. The rock face angled up steeply for about twelve feet, ending abruptly at the sky, as if there was no more mountain beyond that point. I crouched down for a few moments, unable to move, trying to muster the courage to climb the rock cliff in front of me. For whatever reason, I turned my head toward the vastness of the valleys below, and felt as if I was seeing all of Maine at once; it was overwhelming. I was scared, the wind ripping around me. I said a little prayer. Up to my left, a few feet away, was a skinny two-foot-tall sapling. I crawled to it, then crept up a little farther to the next tree, where a rock cairn—a short tower of stacked stones to guide you across slab rock—became visible, but the cairn had been knocked over, I assumed by the wind. I edged myself up to it, where the granite slab wasn't quite as steep, and was able to stand.

That's when I saw the trail, which curved around the cliff edge as I had imagined. It actually did have a drop on the other side, but only about three feet. Lonnie stood nearby waiting for me. He looked about how I felt, wondering what the heck were we doing up here! It was a moment I will never forget. I was scared, and realized I had been scared a lot of the time, climbing and descending mountains, but didn't know what to do about it; there would always be more to climb. We didn't stay very long on top, with it being so windy, and fiercely cold. I was so afraid (it would be one more day before I could let go of the fear gripping me). We headed down the backside of Baldpate, the winds not as strong, making our hike much easier. Near the bottom, we passed a family hiking the Table Rock/A.T. loop trail. The mother asked where we were headed, while her little girl just stared. I told them we started at Katahdin a month before. The mother said to the girl, "They've been living out here in the woods."

The girl asked, "They've been sleeping outside for a month?"

And the mother nodded, "Yes." Little did they know we weren't always roughing it—hot tubs, Jacuzzis, motels, hostels, great food—but Lonnie and I just smiled, not bothering to set them straight. I still feel guilty about that!

We arrived at the meeting spot at Grafton Notch where Route 26 intersected the A.T. After Bear picked us up, he drove us to the post office in Andover where our box had been rerouted. Bear had talked with the postal clerk that morning to let him know not to send our drop onto the campground. Being a small town, the clerk knew everyone, and didn't have a problem.

Andover, with about eight hundred people, has a bit of historical distinction. In 1960, it was selected to be the location of one of the first live transatlantic television signal broadcasts, known as Andover Earth Station. Built by Bell (today AT&T), a white inflated dome housed a huge, sensitive antenna built to pick up signals from the first communications satellite, Telstar 1, launched July 10, 1962 and then Telstar 2, launched May 7, 1963. The station allowed fast telephone and television communications via the Telstar satellite to and from Europe, beginning in 1962. Although no longer functional, the satellites still orbit Earth.

Staying at Honey and Bear's hostel, we weren't eating the meals we had in our packs. So, upon opening our resupply box we'd just picked up, it was rudely obvious we now had way too much food! At some point, we would need it all, but until that time, we didn't really want to carry unnecessary supplies. But there we were, all these extra meals, too many energy bars, oatmeal packets and trail mix which would only add weight and take up space in our packs. Luckily for us, a retired military couple, both long-distance hikers, had been visiting Honey and Bear while traveling in their RV. They were headed to the White Birches Campground and hostel in Gorham, New Hampshire where they planned to stay for a while. Since that was the next town we would come to, they offered to take our extra food so we didn't have to carry it. That sounded perfect to us.

But before we left the hostel, we happily deposited all fourteen oatmeal packs in the *hiker box*. After two weeks, we were sick of oatmeal! At hostels and gear stores along the trail, hikers often encounter *hiker boxes*, where they can leave stuff they no longer want, or maybe find something they need. All kinds of items—packages of non-perishable food, old shoes, backpacking gear—find their way into these boxes.

❧

Molly's parents tended to all the resupply boxes that she and Geoff had planned for their hike. She would call her parents, and ask them to mail the next box, as opposed to how we were doing it, writing the mail dates on the boxes so my brother would know when to ship them. Someone had told Molly and Geoff that a great thing to have for breakfast was couscous, which is a type of North African semolina in granules made from crushed durum wheat. It was easy to prepare, placing it in boiling water with added spices, then letting it steam for five minutes. But after two and a half weeks, Molly told her parents, "Take all the couscous out of our boxes! We can't stand it anymore!" Another problem that plagued the pair was their clothes and gear wearing out. "Please send more socks. I've got holes in all of mine," Molly sent home to her parents. By 2009, numerous outfitters carried hiking socks that lasted much longer than what was available in 1990.

10

A PLAYGROUND FOR ADULTS

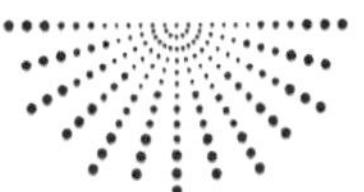

After our last breakfast with Honey and Bear, we left the hostel, thanking them for all their kindness. Bear drove us back to Grafton Notch, where we entered the last section of Maine; our next climb, Old Speck Mountain. Long, steep, 2500 feet up from Grafton Notch, we climbed ladders, grasped roots and tree branches on the rock face, often with water streaming straight down the pathway. The joke became, "If you can't find the trail, just look for where the water's flowing!"

Even though crossing Baldpate had frightened me, by the time we went over Old Speck, for whatever reason, the fear was gone. The trail was steep and spooky, but for the first time, surprisingly, I felt safe and confident. I could climb and descend anything this trail offered.

Coming down the Mahoosuc Arm, the southern peak of Old Speck, we dropped 1600 feet over a mile and a half; a tiring, seemingly endless, and sometimes steep descent. At the bottom was a stream and campsite, where we sat, rested, and ate a snack. Excited, but nervous, we were both quiet, reflective, knowing we were about to enter what some had deemed the hardest mile of the entire A.T. The Mahoosuc Notch. I had read about it in the guide book, and stories from online trail journals; a single mile that had taken some hikers over five hours and more.

We were still sitting when a northbound hiker passed by. "That Notch…" he said. "It was tough. It took me four hours to get through it!" Because it was already 4:00, we debated whether we should attempt the notch this late in the day. Four hours meant we could end up hiking the Mahoosuc Notch in the dark. Not something either of us wanted to experience.

~

7/7/90 The day of "The Notch"! We hiked the Mahoosuc Notch today—"The hardest Mile of the AT." It took us about 2 hours to make it through this nefariously wonderful section of trail. We camped at Full Goose Shelter. ML & GH

~

The notch is a mile-long gorge walled-in by two steep mountain sides, filled with car-sized boulders, often with trees in between them, and an elevation gain of two hundred and fifty feet from the northern end to the southern. Glacial activity over centuries had exposed the vertical talus slopes to the elements, which caused them to crumble and fall, creating the jumbled boulder field filling the Mahoosuc Notch. This curiosity, known as a Cold Air Talus Slope, resulted from cold air drainage which formed ice chunks around some of the boulders, ice which could last throughout the summer months. We observed ice in the crevices, chunks of it ten feet below. Following numerous white blazes painted on trees and rocks throughout the gorge (there were multiple routes hikers could follow), we climbed over boulders, jumped over crevices between massive rock formations, and crawled through a narrow passage, about twelve feet long, under enormous stacked rocks, where we took off our packs and pushed them ahead as we crawled on our bellies.

Throughout it, I lagged behind Lonnie. He was bounding along the high road, up and over, hopping here and there, negotiating the boulders with ease, while I took the low road, deliberating right or left, this way or that, stymied by the network of my own thoughts and indecision. Or we could say, I was careful and Lonnie was reckless! Regardless, when I glimpsed him, Lonnie appeared to bounce along the tops of the boulders, reminding me of something another hiker had told us, calling the notch a *playground for adults.*

But at least I was still moving, until I met my match at a chest high ledge, and no place to put my foot to push myself up. There had to be another way around this huge rock, and there was, but it required a leap across a four-foot span with an eight-foot drop straight down between the boulders; doable, but was it worth the risk? I went back to the ledge to find a way to climb up. Lonnie was about four boulders ahead of me. I yelled, "Wait, I can't get up on this rock face. There's no place for my foot." I could only see his head at this point.

He yelled back, "Use your upper body strength!"

"I don't have any upper body strength!" I screamed back, frustrated with myself, or him, or both. However, the anger proved to be just the ticket, propelling me up the rock so I could continue on my way. There have been a lot of divorces among married couples hiking the A.T.; luckily, Lonnie and I aren't married.

After an hour of rigorous hiking, we were finished. And in record time! "Yeah! We did it!" Lonnie even said, "That wasn't too bad." But we had trouble finding the way out. There seemed to be no trail through trees, bushes or drainage areas. I was in the lead, both of us looking for blazes. When we rounded a bend, it became abundantly clear that the Mahoosuc Notch was not finished with us, huge boulders, and more boulders beyond those, just ahead. It took us another hour to complete the entire notch. When we came out to where the trail headed up a mountain, we knew we had made it; and, in two hours!

Unfortunately, the notes stated there was water at this end, and we assumed that if there was water, there would be camping, but neither was the case, just high grass, and nothing else. There was a side trail, but we didn't know how far it would be to find a campsite or water.

Only one thing left to do, keep hiking, which meant a thousand-foot climb up the steep grade of Fulling Mill Mountain. Once on top, we didn't hang around to observe any views, wanting only to finish the last half-mile to the Full Goose Shelter. Even though there was plenty of daylight, both of us were glad to finally arrive, with a nice tenting area of several platforms. After choosing a spot, we set up camp, had our dinner, then celebrated with cookies, both deciding we'd take it easy the next day.

LAZY HIKER PHILOSOPHY

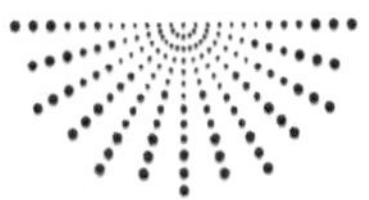

Even though we wanted to sleep in, we both woke early. Four young guys had camped on another platform about thirty yards away up a slight hill. They must have come in after dark.

When Lonnie went to get our food bag, he spoke to them and found out they were heading north.

Relaxing in our sleeping bags, I noticed they were doing some kind of calisthenics. I said, "Wow, those guys are stretching. We probably should be doing that." I figured they'd easily master the Mahoosuc Notch.

Turned on my side, I was trying to doze a few more minutes when the unmistakable aroma of pot drifted through the tent. The four hikers, who had been stretching, were packed up ready to go, sitting on their platform passing a joint between them. We were surprised, but not shocked that these guys were going to tackle the Mahoosuc Notch stoned!

I whispered to Lonnie, "Can you believe that?" I couldn't imagine traversing the notch high; I had enough problems sober, but then figured those guys, as young as they were, would sail over those boulders, and have a rip-roaring time doing it.

We packed up, headed onto the trail, remembering we would be finishing Maine, our first state, the next day. There were more rough climbs ahead, clambering up and over boulders as we headed up Goose Eye, the top with a mile between the two peaks, both above treeline. This section of trail, with its phenomenal views, was aesthetically pleasing, while at times taxing and tough. By the time we reached the second peak, which was only about two miles from the shelter, we were drained, feeling completely used up.

Lonnie and Nancy relaxing on their Z pads atop Goose Eye Mountain. (Photo: another hiker)

The wind was blowing, sun shining, and we could see for miles, a constant repeat of mountains painted across the horizon. We pulled out our Z foam sleeping pads, and tucked them against a rock, savoring our last big mountain in Maine. This open mountain face of slab rock enabled us to see in all directions: 360-degreee view. A perfect place to rest. Facing north, with the sun at our backs, we could see hikers a far distance off still ascending the mountain. For about forty minutes, I watched a guy navigating the climb as he moved in and out of sight. "I think that's Whitebeard Otter," I said to Lonnie. "Remember him from Monson?"

"I think you're right," Lonnie said.

As the hiker crested the final stretch, I could see that it *was* Whitebeard Otter. He was as surprised to see us as we were him. Soon, his brother, Luncher caught up and stopped next to him.

Their style of hiking was very different from ours, almost military-like. Whitebeard and Luncher never stopped to rest, except for a simple bar at lunch, which they often ate standing, or on the move, and hardly ever took their packs off during the day. For them to see us with boots and socks off, our pads out, must have looked to them as if we'd given up hiking altogether.

Yet, just as foreign to me—knowing Whitebeard was a geologist—was that he never stopped to examine rocks and various minerals along the trail. He and his brother were probably making more miles per day, with their straight-ahead, non-stop approach to the trail, but I felt we were having more fun.

Even so, they did partake in our lazy hiker philosophy, sitting for a while, having a snack and talking. We had a really nice visit with our two new friends, and then we all headed out together.

At camp that evening, the four of us sat on rocks, waiting for our meals to cook, getting to know each other better. It was the last shelter in Maine, the Carlo Col. I learned a new word while hiking, "col," which means: the lowest point of a ridge or saddle between two peaks, typically affording a pass from one side of a mountain range to another.

The four of us tented together that night, where a lifetime friendship began. Even though it was chilly, none of us bothered with a campfire, everyone too tired to gather wood, then make sure it was completely out before going to sleep. Lonnie and I weren't big on campfires, and only had the one, our second night on the trail, at the Abol Bridge Campground. Apparently, Whitebeard and Luncher weren't into campfires either, preferring, as we did, the extra sleep instead of the warm glow of crackling wood.

After our meal finished cooking, we ate together, the conversation turning to why Lonnie and I were hiking south. During my explanation, I showed Whitebeard the photograph I was carrying of Aunt Iris and Molly, telling him I was finishing the hike for Molly, and her hiking partner, Geoff. I shared that they were southbounders, too, but had been murdered on the trail near Duncannon.

Whitebeard had no response, and even seemed a bit uncomfortable with my disclosure. Sensing his unease, I placed the photo back in the small plastic bag I kept it in, deciding not to share or talk about Molly and Geoff with anyone else on the trail. The next morning, Whitebeard and Luncher headed out before us, so we weren't sure if we'd see them again.

12

RESUPPLY FIASCO

half-mile from the shelter, Lonnie and I celebrated at the *Welcome to New Hampshire* sign with big smiles and photos. It was Saturday, Sept. 5th. We had one more night on the trail before we headed into Gorham, a smallish resort town of about 2700 people nestled in the White Mountains. Heading into town was usually a good thing, but on this trip, we knew we had a surplus of food to take care of. There was no way to carry the items from the box we would pick up in Gorham from my brother, as well as our resupply box with Honey and Bear's RV friends. And slack-packing those two days meant we didn't eat all the food in our packs, leaving us with lots and lots and lots of extra food to deal with.

After walking out of the woods, just before we crossed the Androscoggin River bridge, we caught up to Whitebeard and Luncher. An older man, just getting into his truck in the trail parking lot, said, "Do you need a ride into Gorham? I'm going that way. You can ride in the back." We were ready to jump in, but Whitebeard said he wanted to walk across the bridge.

Lonnie, Luncher and I agreed to join Whitebeard, but then the guy said, "Want me to take your packs? I'll wait for you on the other side of the bridge?" That sounded fine, so we piled our packs into the back of the truck except for Whitebeard, who was a *purist*. He was fanatical about hiking every inch of the trail, with full pack, and no slack-packing. Even if a shelter had two entrances, one from the northern side of the trail, and one from the southern side, Whitebeard went out the one he had come in, rather than taking the shorter pathway and missing some of the trail.

The four of us strolled alongside the road over to the bridge, Whitebeard carrying his pack, the driver heading out with all our gear. As the truck rumbled away, a thought flashed through my head. "What did we just do? We let a perfect stranger drive away with our packs!" We had gotten so used to trusting people, that we never gave it a second thought. I was going to mention something to Lonnie, but what was the point; it was already too late.

Talking and laughing, we headed onto the bridge, Whitebeard recounting how he hadn't skipped any part of the trail during his nine-year section hike. When we reached the other side, to my great relief, the gentleman was waiting at the parking area.

From there, we piled into the truck bed, next to our packs, and he drove us to the post office for the computer and our resupply box. Then this generous soul took us to the White Birches Hostel and campground. Before dinner, Lonnie and I headed over to the RV section, and easily found our trail helpers from Honey and Bear's, who had graciously brought our extra resupply box.

That evening, Whitebeard and Luncher joined us on our walk into town for dinner. Passing a drugstore, Whitebeard and Lonnie decided to see if they could find something for their sore knees, each of them wearing a brace for the discomfort, Luncher and I following them in. The clerk suggested an ointment that was a little better than Bengay, saying, "Strong as a prescription drug. Really works well."

Watching the swirling currents of the Androscoggin River, we enjoyed the outdoor seating at Crabby Jacks restaurant, a delightful, breezy evening. While we waited for our meal, Lonnie and Whitebeard decided to check out their *better than Bengay* ointment, lathering up their knees, down to their calves. They both agreed: "This stuff feels wonderful."

After dinner and a pleasant walk back to the hostel, Lonnie and I still had our work cut out, emptying all the boxes and sorting through the food: left-over meals from our pack, the box from our RV friends, and the box my brother had sent, with oodles of oatmeal pouches. After spreading all of this on the table in the upper room of the hostel, we attempted to determine what we needed to take with us in our packs, what we needed to send forward to the next town, and what we needed to send home. It developed into quite a fiasco.

Figuring the days to the next town—as well as what we no longer wanted at all, like oatmeal—was taking much longer than we had expected. Other hikers were heading downstairs to the bunkroom to go to bed, while we were still organizing. With packages lying everywhere, we were shocked when the hostel caretaker came into the room and said, "I'm ready to close up. You have to head downstairs. This area is locked from ten until six am."

For a moment, we stared at him, then at all of our stuff. We scrambled, shoving everything together, cramming it haphazardly into the boxes, then schlepped it all down the stairs where hikers were already asleep, quietly plopping this mess at the foot of our bunks. Given the current state of our food situation, there was no way we would be getting back on the trail first thing in the morning.

Whitebeard and Luncher were already in their bunks. That night, not long after we'd gone to bed, Lonnie and Whitebeard, who had been asleep for a while, hurried down below to the hostel bathroom facilities. That magical stuff for their inflamed knees was now creating fire up and down their legs, as well as some weird, prickly current along their skin, not limited to where they had applied the cream! It seemed to hit both of them at the same time, and they ended up in the downstairs bathroom together, running water from the showers over their legs, trying to cool things down. Needless to say, they didn't sleep well that night, and being in a hostel wasn't the nicest place to experience this.

The next day their legs were doing better, and we all had a good laugh about it at breakfast. At times, they experienced some *phantom* effects, tingling and heat, from *this really works well* compound. Lonnie and I still had all the food packages to deal with, so we stuffed everything into our backpacks, and decided we needed a night at a motel. Whitebeard and Luncher also decided they needed one more day to rest, so we all went to the same motel.

Plus, I still hadn't finished my thesis. The back-and-forth process, with me making corrections, then being informed something else was wrong and needed attention, was becoming a distraction. As it worked out, I ended up having to pay the tuition for another semester after all. The decision to not wait a year to start our hike was really buzzing in my mind. We finally figured out what food to take with us, what to send ahead, and what to send home. And our instant oatmeal supply, which now had grown to over thirty-five packages went straight into the hiker box at the hostel.

13

I HIKED THE ENTIRE A.T. AND ALL I GOT WAS THIS CRAPPY T-SHIRT

Finding a ride back to the A.T., Whitebeard, Luncher, Lonnie and I left the Gorham motel around eight-thirty in the morning, and started the long five-mile climb to the top of Mt. Moriah, the beginning of the Carter-Moriah Range. Hiking with Whitebeard and Luncher had been delightful and fun, but we knew Whitebeard's journey would end at Pinkham's Notch, twenty-one miles away, the culmination of a nine-year odyssey of section hikes. Whitebeard's brother, Luncher, was still undecided if he would continue after his brother got off the trail.

At the summit of Mt. Moriah, with the air so clear, we could see the prominent White Mountains in the distance, a rugged chain named in 1524 when an early explorer saw them from the coast with their brilliant snowcaps, and the name stuck. Also visible from Mt. Moriah were automobiles as small as ants crawling up the serpentine Auto Road to Mount Washington. I'd always heard that the Mt. Washington Auto Road was a little spooky, with its sheer drop-offs down the mountain. My daughter, who has driven the treacherous thoroughfare, has a bumper sticker on her car that boasts, *This car climbed Mt. Washington.* I wanted one that said, *I saw the Mt. Washington Auto Road from Mt. Moriah.*

The seven-and-a-half-mile Auto Road first opened on August 8th, 1861, wending up to the top of the highest peak in the Northeastern United States. At that time it was known as the Mt. Washington Carriage Road. Guests made the four-hour journey to the summit in specially built horse-drawn Abbot Downing Mountain Wagons. Though the wagons are gone, the road is still America's oldest and continuously operating attraction.

Climbing Carter Mountain, with its four peaks, we were still able to see the Auto Road. Our next rough climb was over Haight Mountain, a long, torturous descent wreaking havoc with our knees. Farther down the mountain we could see the *Carter Notch Hut*, built in 1877. Still with its original log and bark construction, it was the first shelter built by the Appalachian Mountain Club. In 1877, the AMC came into existence with one mission: to protect the mountains and forests of the Northeast. That decision led members to build and maintain shelters throughout the White Mountains. Today the AMC continues to maintain numerous trails, and a complete system of shelters known in the Whites, as *huts*.

Instead of staying at the Carter Notch Hut, we stealth camped with Whitebeard and Luncher, finding a spot near the trail to pitch our tent. The next morning, we headed out before Whitebeard and his brother, and started our long descent down Wildcat Mountain. If we thought Haight Mountain was a tough drop, Wildcat was even worse. Rougher. Steeper. Wilder, living up to its name.

Moving down Wildcat, the trail zig-zagged back and forth along a sharp, vertiginous grade. These zigzags, known as switchbacks, help prevent water erosion on steep slopes by turning the trail back on itself utilizing hairpin turns, forming a zig-zag pattern down the face of the mountain. Lonnie, in the lead, was somewhere below me when Whitebeard and Luncher approached from behind. I told them to go around, as I wanted to take my time on this tricky descent. They passed me, leaving me on my own.

Eventually I came to a spot where the trail seemed to scramble straight down the steep slope, mostly loose rock and dirt, but it was evident hikers had been using it, though I didn't think it was the actual trail; it looked dicey. There was also a ledge about a foot and a half wide just in front of me that looked a little chancy, too, and I wondered which way to go. The ledge was maybe ten feet long, but then turned abruptly, the trail disappearing around the contour of the mountain. It didn't look right. Even so, I thought if I went down that rockslide, I might not be able to stop sliding.

I yelled, "Lonnie… !" but before I could add, …*Which way should I go?* he yelled back, not even able to see me, but knowing I would be confused, "Go to the left, over the ledge." I could hear Whitebeard and Luncher laughing, and to them, it must have seemed like Lonnie and I could read each other's thoughts. I looked back at the ledge, this time more closely, noticing notches etched into the rock, the grooves providing better footing, making it safer. Holding my breath, I slowly crossed. Once I passed the bend in the rock outcropping, the trail widened out.

When I caught up to the three guys, who waited near the bottom of the mountain, Lonnie said, "I knew exactly where you were." All four of us had a good laugh over that one as we walked into Pinkham Notch.

This was Whitebeard Otter's special day, a moment to commemorate the finish of his Appalachian Trail adventure. A celebration was in order, so we asked the restaurant to bake him a special cake, and we bought a plain T-shirt at the store. With markers, Lonnie decorated the shirt with the saying, *I Hiked The Entire AT And All I Got Was This Crappy T-Shirt.* It also meant we would be saying good-bye to our friend now that he had done it all! Luncher decided to continue on, not sure how many more miles he would hike.

As for Lonnie and me, we were feeling good and loving every day on the trail. My thesis, though, was a burden to us both, still requiring further tweaking.

We took another day off so I could finalize the thesis and pay the tuition, but I needed to get it done before we left Pinkham Notch. Heading into the Whites, we would have no access to towns for over a week or longer, and I needed a computer since we'd already sent Lonnie's home from Gorham.

In Conway, just a short fourteen-mile bus ride away, there was a motel with a business office, and a Starbucks across the street. The promise of a Green Tea Frappuccino was all that was needed to get Lonnie onboard. Luncher and Whitebeard joined us on our trip, planning to hit the outfitter store in Conway to pick up additional gear for Luncher.

14
DON'T FORGET TO SLAM THE DOOR!

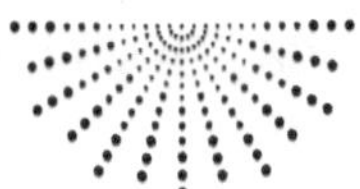

We said our good-byes, waving to Whitebeard as his bus left Conway headed south. Since he lived near Washington D.C., Lonnie and I planned to meet up with him once we arrived at Front Royal in Virginia.

After the bus ride back to Pinkham Notch, we grabbed a bite at the restaurant. Luncher seemed ready to go and decided to start hiking. Later that morning, we began the long awesome climb up Mt. Madison, the first of the Presidential Range. Seven mountains of the Whites are named for presidents. The Appalachian Trail only summits two of them, Mt. Madison and Mt. Washington.

We climbed up and over rocks and boulders; then stood on the Madison peak above treeline, with a 360-degree view. To our surprise, there stood Luncher waiting for us. We hiked down the mountain to our first 'hut' experience; the Madison Hut.

Thru-hikers have always been welcomed at these huts, although in recent years, with the increase of thru-hikers, the hut caretakers have had to limit the number who were allowed to stay. We were fortunate that in 2009 there was no limit.

There are eight Appalachian Mountain Club huts along the A.T.

where day hikers pay to stay overnight, which included a place to sleep, breakfast, dinner and evening entertainment. At the Madison Hut, sleeping quarters were located in two large rooms, one room for men and the other for women, on either end of the building. Bunks made with wooden slats stacked like shelves, and in rows, three high, filled each room. In between was the dining hall, a walkway area, and the kitchen. By the main hall, on the women's side, were the bathrooms.

Thru-hikers stay for *free,* but not in the bunk rooms. Instead, they are allowed to throw a sleeping bag on the floor of the dining room. But *free* has a few strings attached; thru-hikers are expected to perform certain tasks for their keep, which is determined by the care-taker in charge. Meals are also included for hikers, though with a caveat; hikers eat only after the paying customers have finished eating, and only the food left over in the kitchen.

It was fun listening to the caretakers perform the evening presen-tation for the crowd. There were about sixty guests and seven thru-hikers. We gathered in the dining room. Hikers hung out at the back of the room. The caretakers, better known as the *croo,* told ghost stories, jokes, and even sang a song or two. When the entertainment ended, the hikers had a few chores to take care of, such as clean-up in the kitchen, while some guests lingered and others headed off to bed. Having completed the work detail, the hikers sat around waiting until the last of the paying customers toddled off to their bunks. Hikers then spread their pads and sleeping bags out on the dining room floor, staying clear of the main thoroughfare between the bunk rooms and the bathrooms.

With our sleeping area opened to the main hallway, we could hear the men shambling across to use the bathroom. Many of these day hikers were older, obviously well-hydrated, which meant they peed a lot. Each time a guy opened the bathroom door and went in, the door would slam shut. Apparently, the automatic door closer was malfunc-tioning. With so many men needing the facilities, it slammed a lot! Luncher, Lonnie and I were lying there in the dark chuckling each time the door slammed. At one point, Lonnie got up to use the bathroom, and was just going in as Luncher was coming out. Luncher, with his dry wit, said to Lonnie, "Don't forget to slam the door!" I heard him and broke up laughing. Lonnie was still laughing when he came back to the dining room. Even with all the commotion, we finally did get to sleep!

15

WE NEED THE DUNGEON CLOROXED

It was Friday, September 11, 2009, a sunny day to climb Mt. Washington, even though memories of that day eight years before were still vivid in our minds. Mt. Washington is the highest peak in the Northeastern United States, first known by the Abenaki, a First Nation, who called the mountain, *Agiocochook*, which meant, "Home of the Great Spirit."

Surprisingly, the trail did not ascend from the Madison hut as I thought it might. Instead, it plunged twelve hundred feet over a stark landscape void of conifers, the area populated with stunted gnarled trees known as krummholz, which can survive the extreme conditions. Oddly enough, alpine flowers can be found clinging to crevices around rocks, bursting out in myriad colors during blooming season.

Approaching the peak of Mt. Washington, we observed the Cog Railway train, one of the greatest innovations of the industrial age, come around a bend as we neared the top. Sylvester Marsh, suffering from chronic indigestion and needing exercise, invented this amazing piece of machinery. In 1857, Marsh and his companion climbed Mt. Washington and soon found themselves above treeline, caught in one of the numerous life-threatening storms that often besiege the mountain. They had just managed to reach the Tip Top House, a stone hostel (more like a bunker) built in 1853 at the summit of Mt. Washington. Made of rock blasted from the mountain at a cost of seven thousand dollars, Tip-Top House had an observatory on its flat roof where a telescope was set up on clear nights. Today it is a state historic site, having been restored in 1987.

As Marsh recuperated from this near tragic event, an idea came to him. *Why not build a cog railway up to the summit?* People needed a safer and more efficient way to experience the aesthetic and captivating ruggedness of the mountain. The first cog railway was designed and patented in England in 1811 by John Blenkinsop, who used a third rail with a rack and pinion system, making his train effective on low hills, though it was never intended to scale a mountain.

Marsh decided it could be done. He applied for a charter to build a cog railway to the summit of Mt. Washington. The New Hampshire legislature laughed him out of the room, calling him *Crazy Marsh*. But they gave him the charter anyway, saying, "Might as well keep going and *build your railway to the moon.*"

Sylvester Marsh developed his own rack system, different from Blenkinsop's, which made his invention capable of climbing a steep grade. Marsh's first locomotive, *Old Peppersass,* reached the summit of Mount Washington on July 3, 1869, making it the world's first mountain-climbing rail system using a toothed cogwheel to engage the rack between the rails. This cog railway is still functioning to this day.

Watching the Cog Railway train pass, with all its passengers enjoying a pleasant ride in open-air cars to the top of Mt. Washington, Lonnie and I recalled that thru-hikers would often *moon* the unsuspecting train riders, so we thought about it, deciding to take photos instead.

From our current vantage point, the summit of Mt. Washington appeared very close, but the distance was deceiving. We finally arrived two hours later and stood at the highest point of the mountain, 6,288 feet, indicated by a sign, a popular spot for photos.

No one was around when we took each other's pictures. It was late in the afternoon and the crowds had already left the summit. Even before our personal photo op ended, our minds were on food, and more pointedly, the banquet of options awaiting us inside the Mt. Washington food court. We blew past the Tip Top House, headed for the entrance to the Sherman Adams Visitor Center, which had a gift shop, restrooms, a large seating area surrounded by windows with eye-catching views, and an elaborate cafeteria—pizza, soup, drinks of all kinds, whoopie pies and other desserts, ice cream and more.

Most days the visitor center was crawling with people, but maybe with the weather a bit ominous, overcast and breezy, many of the visitors had already left. But the possible impending storm didn't dampen our desire to hang out and keep eating. Returning to the concessions with the regularity of a clock, we were among the very last patrons in the cafeteria, and planned to be there when they shut off the lights.

At the time, we didn't realize that the Mount Washington Weather Observatory's mountaintop weather station was there, housed in the lower level of the building. This facility is a working weather station, with scientists who stay for one-week intervals all year long, staffed continuously since its founding in 1932. One of the rangers, a woman who had been watching the radar screen, said to us, "We've got weather moving in," which we assumed meant, "Why don't you leave, so I can go home, too." It wasn't quite closing time yet, but I understood her concern, since Mt. Washington is well-known for its sudden and treacherous storms. We finally took the hint, and bid the wonderful, calorie-rich environment a sad farewell, and walked the mile and a half to Lakes of the Clouds hut.

Lonnie and I arrived at our second hut experience just before dinner, so it gave us time to relax and wash up. Luncher was already there. The meal that night was a bit skimpier than what we had at the Madison hut, which was fine since we'd stuffed ourselves at the Mt. Washington cafeteria. These hut staffers weren't quite the storytellers as the ones at Madison, but it was still a fun evening.

In the morning, we worked the after-breakfast clean up. When we finished, Lonnie and Luncher were putting on their backpacks to leave when I asked the hut caretaker, "Is there anything else? Or can we get going?" The caretaker, a young fellow with wavy hair, said,

"Well, we're getting ready to end our summer season and we need the *Dungeon* cloroxed."

My mouth dropped. I went over to Lonnie and repeated what the guy had said. Then Lonnie just stared at me, and it was obvious he wasn't happy. And neither was Luncher. "Why did I even ask," I thought, a bit miffed with myself. By now, all the other hikers had left.

The caretaker gave us buckets, rags and a bottle of Clorox, then led us down around the outside of the building to a heavy, stained wooden door below the main floor, like something from a medieval castle, located at the corner of the building. Apparently, this was the *Dungeon*, a small, dank and abysmal room left unlocked year-round, even when the hut was closed, providing a safe haven for hikers who found themselves surprised by a sudden, life-threatening storm.

Built in 1929, the *Dungeon* had two rooms, stone walls and several dark, wooden frames with boards built into the rock to serve as beds. It took us an hour to wash down all the wooden frames and walls. I couldn't tell Lonnie and Luncher that my stupid question had bought us this lovely work detail! We didn't leave until after ten that morning, which meant we'd be scrabbling down Webster Cliffs much later in the day than we had wanted.

Webster Cliffs was another long and tedious descent, the trail hugging the edge of sheer ledges, which plummeted hundreds of feet into the valley below. Spooky at times, especially with a full pack.

When we arrived at the bottom, at Crawford Notch, Luncher was still with us. We planned to stay at the Dry River Campground, two miles from the trail by highway. I didn't think anyone would give the three of us a ride, but when we started hitchhiking, a young couple pulled to the shoulder in a compact car and threw open the doors for us. They were traveling and day hiking themselves, so there was no room in the trunk for our gear. The three of us crammed into the back seat of their little Honda, propping up our backpacks on our laps. We could hear them talking in the front seat, but couldn't see them. They were curious about our hike, so it was pretty funny, as we talked into our packs, right in front of our faces, with them asking questions, unable to see us. Fortunately, it was just a short distance to the campground. We paid the caretaker for our campsite and soon had our tents up, ready for the night.

The next morning, *the three musketeers* hiked out together enjoying a relatively flat, easy terrain. Nearing the Zealand Falls Hut, we lost the trail, and it took us a while to figure out what went wrong. Once we had our bearings, we arrived at the hut, bought a few snacks, then sat on the outdoor porch. After a short rest, we were back on the trail.

Over the next four miles we climbed two thousand feet to the top of Mt. Guyot. There the wind blew so hard I had to stoop over to keep from getting knocked down. A side trail, eight-tenths of a mile across the mountain ridge, led us to two campsites by the Guyot shelter, just as the sky began to darken. The wind howled through the night. Fortunately, we were on the protected side of the mountain.

16

DRESS FOR WIND!

We woke early, to a calmer day, though a bit foggy, stopping at the Galehead Hut, which had no snacks other than what we had in our packs. Luncher was somewhere behind us, having chosen to sleep in that morning. We rested a bit at Galehead, then hiked on, ending that evening at the Garfield Ridge Campsite, having only hiked five and a half miles. Matt, who was the caretaker, resided during season in a huge white tent. Lonnie asked him, "Where should we set up camp?"

"Just go down the trail out in front and take any site you want," Matt said, continuing to lick the spoon he was using to scrape a peanut butter jar. Then he added, "Making everything last! Headed to town soon to resupply." We both understood completely, remembering the last time we were both scooping out a plastic peanut butter jar. We found a nice spot at the end of the trail, near the tip of the ridge.

Matt licking that jar reminded me of a week or so earlier when Lonnie waited at the top of a climb, beginning to worry. He asked me when I caught up to him, "Are you okay?"

"Yeah," I had moaned. "I dropped the last bite of my CLIF bar and couldn't find it. I kept searching for it, but since it was chocolate, I couldn't see it. I know I went way past the ten-second rule, but I didn't care, I wanted it."

There is a popular story on the trail about the difference between a day hiker, a section hiker and a thru-hiker. A day hiker sees food on the trail and walks by without a second thought. A section hiker sees food on the ground, and for a moment, considers picking it up. A thru-hiker sees food on the ground, picks it up, eats it, and looks for more!

We thought our spot would be perfect and private, which it would have been, except we hadn't taken into consideration—the wind! During the night, it started again, blowing so hard, we wondered if the tent would get swept away with us in it, right off the edge of the mountain. It kept us awake a considerable part of the night, and when we needed to go to the bathroom, we knew better than for both of us to do it at the same time. Fortunately, it wasn't raining, just blowing. At one point, with the wind crushing down the front of the tent, Lonnie sat at the entrance gently supporting the main pole above his head, afraid the poles would snap.

In the morning, the wind still roaring through our campsite, I was worried, knowing we had to cross the two-mile long Franconia Ridge; above treeline and very exposed to weather. Before packing up, we decided to check with Matt as to the forecast. Lonnie went, while I stayed in the tent, keeping it from becoming airborne, the wind relentless. When Lonnie returned, he said Matt had been checking on his radio about conditions, and everything was fine. Lonnie had asked him, "What about up on Franconia Ridge? Will we blow off the mountain?" "Nope, you'll be fine. Wind velocity up there is about fifty miles per hour."

"Fifty miles per hour! That sounds like a lot!" Lonnie said. "Are you sure we'll be okay?"

"You'll be fine. Eighty miles per hour could blow you off, but fifty, that'll just knock you to the ground."

Lonnie regarded him a moment, then said, "Any other advice?"

"Dress for wind!"

When Lonnie returned, he told me what Matt said. *"Dress for wind,"* Lonnie said, "whatever that means."

"But what about me?" I asked. "I'm pretty small!"

"Yeah, but your pack's heavy!" Frustrated, Lonnie added, "Jeez, Nancy, I don't know."

I think Lonnie was still struggling with Matt's advice to *dress for wind*, which neither of us understood. We tried to do as Matt suggested, which we took to mean bundling up with our warmest clothes.

We headed out around nine-thirty in misty rain, which, with the wind, was more like high-speed fog. I had on my fleece, raincoat, and rain pants, with a neck gaiter pulled up over my neck and face, and rain hood over my hat. Our first climb was a six hundred-footer over four-tenths of a mile up to the top of Mt. Garfield. This was a lot of scrambling over rocks as we ascended, with roots and small trees to grab as we continued upward, me lagging behind. Lonnie waited, moving around until he saw me, trying to avert a chill, then started walking again.

7/18/90 A real good day for us. We were out of camp at Garfield Campsite before 5:30. A short hike up and we had our breakfast bread on top of Mt. Garfield. We then trekked down to trek up Lafayette Mtn. It was an incredibly blustery day and we were glad we had our heavy packs on to hold us down. Franconia ridge was beautiful & a pretty easy trail... ML & GH

With fog, wind and mist, and maybe fifteen-foot visibility, I stopped long enough to get a drink as we continued upward, climbing closer together, not quite as tedious now. Another three and a half miles, and seven hundred and sixty feet, we arrived at the top of Mt. Lafayette, but wind and misty rain continued to hamper our hike. There were absolutely no views—we were lucky to see each other fifteen feet apart—as we clambered up this ridgeline, the wind screaming. I never felt I would blow off, since there was plenty of vegetation on either side of the trail, but the wind played havoc with my pack, tossing it back and forth, throwing me off balance.

Just ahead, I saw Lonnie standing with his pack off. That was always a good sign, since it meant he had found a place to stop. There was a three-foot-high stone wall on this flat area, maybe an old foundation, so we hunkered down behind it to eat a peanut butter sandwich and chips. The wind roared and circled around us, but we felt safe, though a bit chilled.

Sitting there eating, I questioned why would anyone put a building up here? Were they crazy? Later, I learned that this had been a hotel. Reading more about mountain tops, I began to understand. This was a shelter if a storm started brewing before you could get down off the mountain, similar to the dungeon we cleaned at the Lakes of the Clouds Hut. The White Mountains, including this ridgeline and the entire Presidential Range, were known for their unexpected, and often violent storms, even in the summer months.

We were just grateful to be out of the wind for a few minutes. The fog got so thick at one point it seemed visibility was no more than a few feet. Luncher caught up to us just as we finished eating.

When Lonnie and I planned this hike—trying to make sure we had enough food, the right gear, notes and maps to assist us, all the resupply boxes ready to be sent—I didn't even consider all the awesome scenery we would encounter, with Franconia Ridge purported to be one of the most scenic places on the A.T. And here we were, trudging through the thickest soup I had ever experienced, London kind of fog. Many stellar views along the A.T. were luck of the draw when thru-hiking, because there was no way to plan when you'd cross certain mountains. Evidently, we were going to miss this incredible vista.

We finished the short ascent to the sign at the summit of Mt. Lafayette, 5,249 feet. As I started down from the peak, watching my feet, taking careful steps, the clouds began to loosen a bit. Then, all at once, the dark ominous sky seemed to break apart, sun burning through, leaving huge gaping pools of azure sky at first, until the last few wisps of white clouds disappeared completely, the valleys illuminated below us like a detailed painting.

Nancy crossing Franconia Ridge. (Photo: Lonnie Busch)

We were dumbstruck by the magnificent view, as if the heavens had opened just for us, leaving behind a deep blue sky and about a million miles of visibility. Now we could easily see that the trail snaked for two miles along the rocky, narrow ridgeline, the sides plummeting into valleys alive with rich verdant forests and foliage. Short trees and scrub grasses marked the jagged terrain of the rocky granite path. Hikers coming toward us looked like dots wandering lazily along the trail ahead. It was breathtaking. For several moments we just stood there and took it all in.

The crest went over Mt. Lincoln, the third Presidential peak we crossed, and Little Haystack Mountain, before descending to a nice tenting spot at the Liberty Springs campsite. The next day the trail guided us down the mountain only two and a half miles, about 2400 feet to Route 3 at Franconia Notch. We walked the eight-tenths of a mile to the Flume Gorge Visitor Center, hoping to find a ride into Lincoln, looking forward to resting in a real bed. Throngs of tourists milled about, many who had arrived on tour buses.

Walking toward the visitor center, we encountered two women who asked, "Could we take your picture?" Before we could answer, they pulled out their cameras and snapped our photos! I always thought I would be famous one day. Lonnie, on the other hand, wasn't very happy, saying it made him feel like some kind of side-show attraction. The snarky comment he'd wanted to say to these pushy women, was, "Sure, you can take our picture, if you give us a ride into Lincoln."

A while later, he happened to see a young man carrying a daypack across the parking lot headed to his car. Catching up to the young man, Lonnie asked if he could give us a ride.

The young man, Yoni, a university student from Israel who was visiting his brother in Boston during his summer vacation, not only gave Luncher, Lonnie and me a ride, but took us to the post office, waited as we picked up our mail drop, then drove us around until we found a motel; another wonderful trail angel! He told us that since he was a little boy, he had always wanted to hike the A.T. Ironic how us meeting, and him hearing our stories, had connected with a childhood dream of his own; and would maybe fuel his own enthusiasm around hiking the trail.

That evening we headed to a Chinese buffet restaurant, where we ran into Matt, the camp caretaker from the Garfield Ridge Campsite. He recognized us as well.

"So Matt," Lonnie said, "How did you get down here?"

It was a fair question, after all, since we never saw him on the trail, and he had beat us into Lincoln. Matt gave us a devilish grin, and said, "There are shortcuts down off the mountain." I could tell by the look on Lonnie's face that he wished Matt would have told us about the shortcuts in advance.

Matt was eating with some friends, and told the owner of the restaurant, "Take good care of those guys! They just came down off the mountain." To our delight, we were given a great discount. Many of the restaurants do give discounts for thru-hikers, but it was nice being treated extra special. We chatted for a while with Matt, sitting at the table next to him and his buddies, and told him how the clouds lifted just as we went over Lafayette. He told us how many times he had to perform rescues on that mountain when bad weather rolled in.

17

THE REDSTONE ROCKET

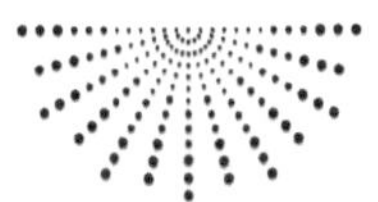

Refreshed from our night in town, Luncher, Lonnie and I tackled the Kinsman North and South Mountains, which were mostly in foliage with few notable views. But it wasn't until we hit the 2000 foot ups and downs that Luncher and I struggled to keep up with Lonnie, who seemed to be unfazed by this crazy, roller coaster trail. By evening, we were all tired, even though we hiked less than ten miles.

We left the Eliza Brook Shelter the next morning, convinced the day would be easier. But it wasn't. Somehow the notes misled us; instead of the unchallenging tread we expected to find, we had to endure an arduous, gnarly plunge into Kinsman Notch. With the day turning bitter and rainy by the time we reached the Lost River Road parking area, we opted to head back into Lincoln when a day hiker offered us a ride. This time we stayed at the hostel owned by Chet West.

Chet had been an avid hiker and guide until 2001 when, checking his camp stove, it exploded, engulfing him in flames, leaving him blind and in a wheelchair. Experiencing near-death moments, and numerous extended hospital stays, he chose to view his life as a trail angel, making his home a safe haven for thru-hikers. Though he now was able to feel tingling in his toes, and was regaining some of his ability to see, he was still considered legally blind. We felt blessed to have met this extraordinary, special young man.

At Chet's hostel that evening, we met another hiker, Canoe, around our age, who headed out with us the next morning. It was Friday, September 18th, when the four of us, Lonnie, myself, Luncher and Canoe left Chet's place early. After a huge breakfast at McDonald's, we got a ride with a guy in the parking lot, who drove all of us back to the trail.

On this blustery morning, the four of us began our climb up the last section of the White Mountains. Along the Beaver Brook Cascades, a huge waterfall flowed into the Kinsman Notch. We traversed steep rock slabs, climbed up wooden ladders and steadied ourselves on temporary railings.

By noon we crested Moosilauke Mountain, at 4800 feet, and were met by fifty mph winds, rough, rocky tread and freezing fog. The plants, bushes and scrub grass were encased in a thin shell of ice, creating an otherworldly beauty, everything glistening like glass. After hiking across the long, flat crown of Moosilauke, we began our descent toward Glencliff, the air still cool, the sun trying to push through the thick clouds.

It wasn't long before we came upon a stranger wearing a large backpack and standing a few feet off the trail. His name was Bill, from the Boston area, who asked if one of us was Canoe. Evidently, Bill had been following Canoe on his online trail journal. Canoe had started the A.T. at Springer Mountain in Georgia the previous January. Unfortunately, he ran into difficulty, becoming sick, not eating enough for the cold weather, and had to postpone his hike. Later in the summer, Canoe started in Maine and headed south, just seeing how far he could go. Upon learning from the journal that Canoe would be climbing Moosilauke today, Bill, this ambitious and affable young man, drove to the trailhead and planned on surprising him with trail magic. Since they had never met in person before, it was quite a surprise for Canoe.

Bill brought sandwiches, cold root beer in bottles (that he carried nearly to the top of the mountain in his backpack), baked goods and fruit. It was quite unexpected, and what a treat, not only for Canoe, but for Lonnie, Luncher and me, as well. It was a pleasant bonus in our day, just eating, drinking and chatting about the trail, standing in the cold amidst stunted pines. Bill, hoping to hike the trail in the near future, was soaking up as much hiking information as possible.

Heading down Moosilauke with us, Bill talked with Canoe along the way, Luncher, Lonnie and I following behind. (As an aside, a number of years later we would meet Bill again when he and his wife hiked the trail, and Lonnie and I were trail angels for them.) The farther down we went, the day grew warmer, with us eventually passing northbound day hikers heading to the top wearing T-shirts and shorts.

Later that afternoon, we arrived in the small village of Glencliff at the Hikers Welcome Hostel, with the post office across the street. Phat Buddy, the owner of the hostel greeted us, then led us to a huge tent for hikers in his backyard where Luncher settled in. Lonnie and I elected to camp in our own tent, with Canoe deciding to avoid the hiker quarters as well. He hung his netting-covered hammock between two trees near us.

After we were settled in, Phat Buddy drove us to a convenience store in Warren. I restocked my supply of Ripple potato chips, a great source of sodium—which tends to deplete during strenuous activity— and chocolate-coated cookies, a great source of contentment. For Lonnie, it was Snickers candy bars. Things we never eat at home had become staples out on the trail. However, my chips and cookies would become a source of friction later on.

After the convenience store, Phat Buddy drove us to see this little community's main attraction: an actual missile, the *Redstone*, sitting behind the buildings, poised and *seemingly* ready to launch into outer space. The Redstone rocket was installed in honor of Alan B. Shepherd who was born in Derry, New Hampshire, a neighboring town.

Shepherd was the first of the Original Seven astronauts to fly into space. The other six included Scott Carpenter, Gordon Cooper, John Glenn, Gus Grissom, Wally Schirra, and Deke Slayton. On Friday,

May 5, 1961, the Redstone rocket, carrying the Freedom 7 Mercury capsule with Shepard aboard, hurtled sixty-three miles into space at a velocity of 5,180 mph. This altitude is known as the Kármán line, where space begins. Fifteen minutes and twenty-two seconds later, it parachuted into the Atlantic Ocean.

Many years earlier, watching all of this on television, I dreamed of becoming an astronaut. That night at Phat Buddy's hostel, as I looked up at the stars, I thought back to the trip I made years earlier to the Smithsonian National Air and Space Museum in Washington D.C. to retrieve moon rocks encased in glass, for my third-grade students to study. Borrowing these, required permission from NASA, since they are considered a national treasure. I never did reach the sixty-three-mile marker above the earth, but I was climbing to the tops of many high mountains.

The next morning Canoe said, "I had a little visitor this morning."

I said, "Really?"

"The sky was just getting light," Canoe said. "I heard a noise under my hammock, where my pack was sitting. I peeked over the side, and spotted a big, black bushy tail sticking out of the pack. Then I saw the white streak on its back!"

Just the thought of being sprayed brought to mind when my dog tangled with a skunk one evening and had to sleep in the abandoned chicken coop.

Canoe continued, "I laid there, not moving, realizing that the sun was almost up. But still, I didn't wanna get sprayed. So I waited and waited, wondering what he could be after? Then it dawned on me; I didn't take my trash out of the pack! The little guy finally gave up." Canoe added, "But it was weird! I didn't have any food left in that trash bag!" Obviously, the skunk had been attracted to the residual smell. Given how close we had been camped to Canoe, I was glad we didn't all end up smelling like skunk.

18

TOO EERIE AND OTHERWORLDLY

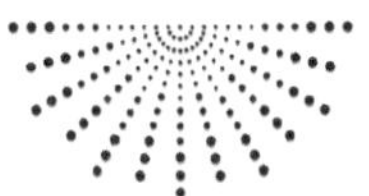

Several days later, I climbed the fire tower on Smarts Mountain while Lonnie chose to stay below and powder his feet. Two days later we stealth camped near the Velvet Rocks Shelter, a few short miles from Hanover, New Hampshire. The next morning, we ran into Luncher. We hadn't seen him for several days after we left the hostel in Glencliff. The trail went through Hanover with our first stop, a restaurant for pancakes and eggs. Afterward, Lonnie, Luncher and I rode a bus to the Sunset Motor Inn to spend the night.

Before doing laundry, getting resupply and cleaning our water filter, we chose to relax in the room. On the trail, every day is about hiking lots of miles, then more the next day. From our huge picture window, I gazed out at the Connecticut River, thinking how streams and rivers were impediments to deal with on our hike. In this moment though, watching the ripples and swirls meander past, I was struck by how the river is constantly flowing, day and night, always trusting its journey toward the ocean. Just then the water became a natural balm, filling me with a sense of peace I hoped would stay with me on our trek, reminding me to enjoy the moment, with no absolute goal.

As a young girl, with her church group in Shaker Heights, Ohio, Molly went on numerous Outward Bound backpacking adventures in New England and the Southwest, discovering how rewarding spending time in nature could be. After college, Molly learned of outreach groups who took struggling teens into the outdoors to offer them a new perspective, and help them toward over-coming their difficulties. She found a position working on a wagon train in Arizona for two years that took Los Angeles gang members into the forests, showing them a different path. She told her dad she'd be working as a teacher, that the kids she'd be working with had been given one last chance. "And, guess what, I'm going to be helping them!"

After this two-year experience, she began working for another group based in Kansas that took small groups of middle school kids into the wilderness to help them find an alternative way of viewing their experiences and decisions. There she met Geoff, both of them sharing a desire to help troubled youth. When that job ended, they decided to hike the trail, both still wanting to help troubled kids. The plan was, after they finished their hike at Springer Mountain in Georgia, they would attend graduate school in Cincinnati to get the education needed to formulate their own program for assisting and supporting disadvantaged youth. But their dream would never happen.

After a while, though, it was time to get things done. We were headed to the grocery store when we ran into Luncher. He had started his laundry at the motel, and was wearing his rain pants until his hiking clothes were done. While waiting for his laundry to finish, he felt a beer and food run was in order, and was headed back to the motel carrying a six-pack, along with a dozen doughnuts and a grocery sack full of food when we passed him. Juggling the beer, groceries and doughnuts, he was unable to deal with his droopy rain pants, which were starting to fall down. In his raspy voice, he said dead serious, "Lonnie, can you pull my pants up?" Lonnie hesitated a moment, giving Luncher a curious look. "Just this once, Luncher.

Never again!" We were both laughing, but Luncher failed to see the humor.

With shopping, laundry and everything done, we hung out in our room, which was so pleasant, we decided to spend an extra day just to have more time to relax. A zero day—just sitting around, eating, watching television, and not hiking.

The following morning, we bid the motel farewell and walked several miles of trail that followed the streets of Hanover, realizing later we could have taken a bus. But walking enabled us to make one last stop for the important stuff: ice cream and other goodies.

Walking across the bridge over the Connecticut River, we entered our third state, Vermont. Blazes led up a steep road to the trailhead, finally moving into the woods. Later that afternoon, I was running on fumes. I couldn't keep up with Lonnie's pace. My pack was heavy with food from our resupply box and what we'd bought. Maybe I overestimated how much I could carry. When I caught up to Lonnie at a viewpoint, I complained about his fast pace. This led to his oft repeated rebuttal. "You buy all these cookies and chips," he said. "That extra food makes your pack too heavy!"

I came back with, "Well, you're eating those chips and cookies, too!"

"I don't need to eat them, though. I only eat them because you're always carrying them. All that extra food is dragging you down!"

"My gait is shorter than yours, so I have to take more steps. That's why I can't keep up!"

"Oh, brother!"

This went on a bit longer, till we saw someone coming, then stopped yelling at each other. After dropping this recurring argument, continuing to hike on, it appeared we were okay. The situation hadn't resolved itself then and there, but maybe helped us look at it differently. Despite his hiking ahead of me, I did enjoy the freedom of hiking by myself. Often, he was a hundred yards or more ahead, and usually waited at the top of the mountains until I caught up.

This part of Vermont was thick with trees, with limited views only at road crossings where we could see sky. This had dampened

Lonnie's mood. Although always being in trees didn't bother me, I understood his feeling of being closed in. When we came to a field, a particularly beautiful spot with limitless sky, we ate lunch, where I witnessed a change in his demeanor. He seemed much more relaxed. We even considered staying there for the night. But it was only eleven in the morning, way too early to camp, so we moved on, with the intention of finding another special spot.

And we did! Coming upon this vast open field, we both decided this was the perfect place to camp, even though it was just a little after three in the afternoon. It was such a gorgeous area, surrounded by lush green forests dotted with vibrant fall colors. Vermont received its nickname, the *Green Mountain State,* named by the French, *Vert Mont.*

By early evening, the sky had vanished behind thick gray clouds. This was Vermont after all; if there was lots of snow for skiing, then it held that the rest of the year, there must be lots of rain. For us, this was the start of rain, and more rain, and much more rain.

During the night, raindrops started pelting the tent. By morning, rain sizzled across our tent fly. Once again, we packed up under the protection of the fly, perfecting our technique for taking down the tent and stowing our gear during heavy rainfall. It worked quite well, keeping us and our packs relatively dry, as well as the tent. The day remained gloomy, the cold rain steady, the trail pocked with muddy puddles.

Just before the Stony Brook Shelter, we climbed a fairly steep hill in a chilling mist. Nearing the top, a sheer rock face, about ten feet high, stood in our way. This was the trail—up the wall! And the way to do that—a simple household aluminum ladder, leaned against the rock, fastened with ropes to keep it secure. We had encountered many makeshift devices for traversing difficult spots on the trail, but this one, so far, topped the list.

The next morning, we headed for the Long Trail Inn located near Killington, excited to dry out our gear. Even with best practices, it's nearly impossible to keep everything dry during persistent rainy spells; the moisture manages to get into everything.

With ten miles to go we passed the spectacular Thundering Brook

Falls, a magnificent cascade dropping one hundred and forty feet. About a mile later, the trail brought us to a dock at Kent Pond, a hundred-acre lake with largemouth bass and perch. Lonnie wished he'd had his fishing rod to test drive this charming little lake. Instead, we ate tuna sandwiches on the dock, a muted, gray sky overhead, the sun peeking out intermittently.

Two miles later we came to the Sherburne Pass Trail, the original Appalachian Trail, which we realized would have taken us directly to the Long Trail Inn two miles sooner.

The Long Trail Inn was named for the footpath that travels through Vermont from the Massachusetts border to Canada. It's the oldest long-distance trail in the United States, constructed between 1910 and 1930. The A.T. and the Long Trail are the same trail for one hundred miles, before they part company once again to go their separate ways.

Arriving at the Long Trail Inn, we settled in our room, then enjoyed Monday night football on a big screen television and ate great food at the downstairs Irish pub.

The next day, after checking out, we caught a bus to the Killington post office and nearby grocery store. We picked up our food mail drop, bought other supplies, then packed everything outside the grocery store, getting rid of unneeded packaging in their trash cans. Thirty minutes later, we caught the bus that took us back to the trailhead. It was the first time that our mail drop food really worked well.

We had been supplementing our freeze-dried meals with buns, cheese, cereal, and peanut butter. And of course, candy bars, trail mix, and smaller packages of chips and cookies; buying small bags of chips and cookies from convenience stores helped solve the problem of too much weight. Plus, the variety was a bonus, with several flavors and brands to choose from.

With the sky clouded over, we started up the trail in misty rain, arriving at the Cooper Lodge Shelter in thick fog, everything dank and dreary. Adding to the already gloomy day was the shelter itself, a dismal place built in 1939—dirt floor, window-sized openings on either side, making it drafty and cold. We pitched our tent on a platform behind the shelter.

By morning, nothing had changed, the weather as dreary, foggy and miserable as the night before. With visibility crippled, it was pointless to climb the two-tenths of a mile side trail to the top of Killington Mountain, which boasted an impressive 360-degree view of *Vert Mont*.

It was the last day of September, the sky perpetually overcast, but luckily, no rain. Even as bleak as it was, the fall colors were ablaze as we crossed over one hill and then another.

Descending to Route 103, we scrambled down the treacherous remains of a boulder avalanche, reminding us of Maine. Lonnie, in stride, traversed one huge rock after another. I followed, until I came to the five-foot drop he had just maneuvered easily, not knowing how to get down this. With my legs not long enough to extend to the next boulder, I resorted to a technique I used often in Maine when confronted with steep drops. I handed my pack down to Lonnie, then turned around, facing the boulder, and slid down the rock on my belly, grasping onto anything I could to keep from falling too suddenly.

A short distance later, a speck of sun shone through the clouds, reflecting off flashy, eerie sparks of silver preceding us down the trail; a hiker with scraps and patches of shiny, silvery material covering several parts of his body, looking like something from outer space. This young man had cut apart his silver and orange thermal blanket, then used duct tape to attach sections at his arms and torso, and around the tops of his shoes, in order, we guessed, to keep himself dry from all the rain. When he stopped to let us pass, we spoke briefly. He told us he was headed to the Whistle Stop Corner Restaurant. We told him we'd probably see him there, planning to walk the half-mile down the highway to grab lunch.

Reaching the highway, we stopped to check the notes to be sure we went the right direction. The young hiker with the foil patches caught up to us and told us he was headed to the Whistle Stop to find temporary work so he could continue his journey. According to the notes, there were other places along the trail where cash-strapped hikers could find work. We were going to wait for him, but he told us to go on, that he had to change out of his *suit* and become more presentable for hire. We laughed and told him we'd see him there.

The Whistle Stop had great food and rich, chocolate milk shakes. We had finished eating, but were still lingering, looking at train prints on the walls. After using the restroom, we decided the hike wasn't going to hike itself, so we headed out. With no food in front of him, the young hiker was seated outside at one of the tables, telling us he'd found work, that the guy would be by soon to take him to the job site. We were happy for him, but felt terrible he hadn't had money for lunch. Yet, we understood; this was his way of hiking the trail—H.Y.O.H. *Hike Your Own Hike*, the motto repeated by hikers from Georgia to Maine.

Back on the trail, we were excited to cross the *swinging*, walking suspension bridge that spanned the Clarendon Gorge, a breathtaking, granite-walled canyon with stellar views of the cascading white-water rapids of the Mill River. Built in 1974, the bridge was dedicated to the memory of Robert Brugmann, a seventeen-year-old youth, and a budding environmentalist, who was attempting a southbound thru-hike of the A.T.

On July 4, 1973, during a flood, Brugmann was crossing an older version of the bridge when he was swept away by the raging waters and drowned. The year after Brugmann's fatal accident, the A.T. Green Mountain Club rebuilt the bridge to make it safe for generations to come.

When the first woman to solo thru-hike the entire A.T., Grandma Emma Gatewood arrived at this crossing in 1955, there was no bridge at all. Two hurricanes had come up the coast and created a roiling, dangerous river. She could not cross on her own, so she waited for help. Six hours later two young Navy guys, out for a ten-day hike, came to her rescue. They attached a rope around their waists with her in the middle, but Grandma didn't tell them she couldn't swim. They were more fortunate than Brugmann and luckily made it across. One of the Navy guys never forgot the fear he felt crossing that river. On this sunny, calm day, I was thankful we had the suspension bridge.

It was after five when we left Clarendon Gorge, needing to go two and a half miles to the Minerva Hinchey Shelter. It was dark when we settled in our sleeping bags, deciding to pitch the tent in the shelter on this freezing night, figuring no one would be showing up this late. But we were wrong. A young German woman arrived. We chatted through the tent fabric as she ate her meal. She had saved her money, quit her job, got rid of her flat, put her furniture in storage, and set out to backpack around the world, fulfilling a bucket list of places she wanted to see. The mountains of Vermont were on her list, so she figured hiking the Appalachian Trail was the best way to accomplish it. Her journey had already taken her to Japan for the cherry blossoms, Moscow and Siberia, national parks in the U.S. and Canada, and now, after exploring New England, she was headed to Argentina.

The next day we left before our German traveler, and were climbing up to White Rocks Cliff, when we found a kind of magical spot. In the middle of the shady forest were white rocks of various sizes strewn everywhere. On both sides of the trail, previous hikers had stacked them to form shapes, creatures, and other oddities of nature. It felt like a museum, sacred, yet a bit strange, and at the same time, extraordinary. I gathered together a few rocks to create a small statue of my own to contribute to this enchanting site. There are places along the trail that are so special, and at times so hard to leave, never knowing if we'll ever return.

By the time we reached Danby Road we were tired and decided to camp. Finding a nice spot near the dirt road along a stream, we set up our tent, made dinner, and crawled into our sleeping bags.

Crossing rocky ledges the next day, we were treated to a serene patchwork of farmlands far below us, with majestic views of the Green Mountains. Along with all the greenery, Vermont has three official state rocks—marble, granite and slate—which have been used for buildings and monuments all over the country. We scrabbled over some of this sharp-edged stone, then traversed two more peaks before we started our climb up Bromley Mountain late that afternoon.

Near the top of Bromley at dusk, a dome, looking like a space ship, appeared at the edge of the verge. Upon reaching the open summit, it was quickly apparent that the *dome* was the roof of the chair lift located at the juncture of several ski slopes. About fifty feet to the right of the lift was a small building with numerous windows and a ground level deck and railing, with an observation tower next to it.

Lonnie had already started up the tower when I took off my pack to join him. Fall had exploded with color, but off to the west was a slow-moving fleet of portentous, steely-gray clouds headed our way. We climbed back down to check out the building with all the windows.

By the door was a sign that read, *Shelter*. We walked across the deck, and to our surprise, found the building unlocked. We stepped inside, onto a metal grid for stomping snow off ski boots, realizing this was a refuge for chilled skiers. Checking around the interior, which was quite spacious, I suggested to Lonnie, "Hey it looks like rain, why don't we set the tent up in here." It seemed like the perfect place to sleep for the night; roomy, with a bench on one side, some countertops, and several large windows across the front; the perfect cover if those clouds developed into a storm. There was even a phone on the wall. I lifted the receiver, amazed to find a dial tone. "The phone works!" I told Lonnie. I thought he might suggest ordering pizza, as a joke, instead, he said, with a concerned tone, "What if somebody comes up here?"

"Oh, you've got such an imagination," I said. "Who's going to come up this mountain? And anyhow, how would they get up here?"

After some discussion, we settled on pitching the tent inside the shelter. For me, the tent was our *trail home,* but for Lonnie, the tent provided one more line of defense against mice who might have taken up permanent residence.

After eating supper, we climbed into our sleeping bags, Lonnie having difficulty getting to sleep, readjusting himself constantly, likely still thinking about unwanted visitors. At some point in the night, still half-asleep, I saw light outside the windows, suggesting it might be morning. Since it was Saturday, it seemed possible that the ski resort was bringing people up to see the fall colors, until I came fully awake and realized it was still night. That's when I heard voices and whispered to Lonnie, "Somebody's coming…"

We both sat up, bright orange lights illuminating the fog outside the windows, like a UFO landing in a Spielberg movie, right by the chair lift dome I thought earlier was the top of a spaceship! Everything was far too bright, too eerie and otherworldly for this mountain top. We felt around for our headlamps, slipping them on, looking out the tent screening toward the lights burning through the drifting, misty fog. It was then four beings clomped onto the front deck, the figures silhouetted by the diffused, brilliant light.

One of them said, "Hey, there's hikers in there. I'm goin' back to the truck." The other three, wearing no backpacks, padded across the deck, opened the door and came inside. By this time, Lonnie and I were standing outside the tent, me on my side and Lonnie on his. When our headlamps fell on our visitors' faces, we could see they were teenagers.

"Hey, we didn't mean to wake you up," one of the young men said. "We were just out cruising, nothing to do, Friday night and all, thought we'd come up here. I've lived down at the bottom of the mountain all my life, never been up here."

"Want a beer?" another said. All three of these guys had beer cans stuffed in their pants pockets, their jeans dragging down off their hips. "Nah, we're good," Lonnie said to them. I kept quiet. Then Lonnie asked, "How did you get up here?"

"We got a Ford F-150 four-wheel drive. It'll go anywhere," one of the boys said, almost like a commercial.

"We took the service road. Comes right up," another added.

"Hey, do you guys blaze?" the one in front asked.

"Blaze?" Lonnie said.

The only blazes I knew were the white rectangular ones on trees, posts, and rock faces that we'd been following since Maine.

"You know, Highway 420," the young man continued, rambling off a bunch of other monikers for pot that were meaningless to me. "No," Lonnie said, and I shook my head as well. The guy who'd gone back to the truck started blowing the horn. The white and orange lights, along the front and back of the cab roof, were still glaring in both directions through the misty rain. "Well, we better get going," the kid said. "Sorry 'bout waking you up and all."

They walked back to their truck. The two of us were still standing back from the windows, watching. The truck just sat there a long time, the lights burning through the mist, the engine grumbling. This group had seemed harmless enough, but now, neither of us were very comfortable with our original assessment.

I said to Lonnie, "What do you think they're doing?"

He just looked at me. "Highway 420?" Then I understood —marijuana.

After several more minutes, the lights moved, the truck backing up, and for another moment, seemed undecided about which way to go. Just then, the truck veered directly toward the shelter, Lonnie and I taking a step back. Then the truck cut a sharp turn left, disappearing over the edge of the mountain, down what I was convinced was a ski slope. I recalled seeing it earlier in the day, when we were atop the tower.

Finally, they were gone, the darkness at the top of the mountain restored, but not before leaving a residue of doubt and fear. We climbed into our sleeping bags, both staring straight up at the ceiling of the tent, eyes wide open. After some time, Lonnie said, "Nance, are you asleep?"

"No," I said.

"What do you want to do?" he asked.

"What is there to do?"

In that moment, I remembered the phone on the wall, but what good would that be; we didn't need help. At least we didn't think so. However, several days earlier we had passed a shelter, I couldn't recall which one, with a note to hikers: "We don't advise staying at the next shelter. A road goes right to it, and locals have been harassing hikers." Though we had passed that shelter, and it was nowhere near this place, that ominous warning flashed inside my head like an alarm.

"Well, we could leave and head down the mountain," Lonnie suggested.

"In the dark?" I said, turning my head toward him.

"Yeah, I know those guys seemed harmless, but what if they tell someone we're up here?"

"You're thinking about the note on that shelter, aren't you?" I said.

When he didn't answer, I said, "Yeah, let's do it."

By that time, it was one-thirty in the morning, the wind blowing, a dense, wet fog drifting across the mountain. We pulled down the tent, packed our gear, switched on our headlamps and headed out the door to find the trail.

The light from our headlamps was nearly useless in the thick fog, making it difficult to find the next blazed post. After a several-minute search, we found it, realizing the trail followed another ski slope down the mountain. Mostly wet grass and some ruts, the slope wasn't as steep as we thought it could be. After about a hundred yards, the blazes led us back into the woods. We hiked for several more miles until we came to a stream, and a good, flat place to make camp. At that point, it was probably close to three in the morning, the foggy-night hike more slow-going than we had imagined. We pitched the tent.

The next morning, we slept in. When I woke, I saw the wonderful little stream trickling by about ten feet away. Our campsite was more heavenly than I imagined, with lots of ferns and low green plants. It felt good splashing the fresh cold water on my face. I headed back to the tent to find Lonnie stirring.

After our night trek down Bromley Mountain, we had two miles left to hike to the highway that led into Manchester Center, where Eric, Lonnie's son, was picking us up the next day. From there we'd drive to a family wedding in North Carolina. Most of that morning was gray but dry, with rain starting to fall when we arrived at the highway. As good fortune would have it, someone stopped and gave us a ride down the mountain into town, dropping us at the Avalanche Motel. Being Saturday, the motel was pretty full, but the clerk somehow managed to find us a room.

~

The outdoor wedding, nestled near a waterfall, was wonderful, and after eating lots of town food while visiting with friends and family, we returned to Vermont. My brother Dick, and his wife Bonnie, brought us back to the trailhead with Lonnie excited to break in his new Vasque hiking boots, both of us anxious to be back in the woods. It was a dreary Tuesday, October 13th, the trail wet with lots of mud and fallen leaves. A week off did not change the weather pattern of Vermont, but we didn't care, at least for the first day.

It was cloudy, and by the time we climbed Spruce Peak, there was fog, which soon turned to rain. We set up camp along a stream, and weren't in the tent long before it started sleeting, then turned to snow, our first snowfall of the hike. It was actually rather pretty, neither of us minding the cold, preferring it to hot, muggy days.

Knowing we were headed into colder weather, Lonnie had bought a down sleeping bag for extra warmth. Which was a good thing, since we woke to a very frosty morning and... frozen boots! Before going to sleep, we'd been leaving our boots outside the sleeping bags, yet inside the tent. On this frigid morning, they froze. Our feet battled the cold leather of our boots, our toes numb, our feet gradually warming as we hiked. Unfortunately, the higher we climbed, the colder it became, and the more difficult to keep them warm.

It seemed too early in the year for this much snow and freezing temperatures. At the peak of Stratton Mountain, 3,936 feet, we encountered as much as several inches in some places. At the spruce tree-covered summit, we were surprised to see eight people milling about. Two of the people were US Forest Rangers tasked with the job of taking down the solar panels from the cabin. Two of the people helping the rangers were from the Green Mountain Club, and had served as caretakers living in the mountain cabin through the spring and summer until fall. There were also two SOBO's, plus a couple hiking the Long Trail. Climbing the fire tower gave us gorgeous views of pines and spruce newly christened with snow, but with the cold wind whipping past, we didn't stay long.

At the summit of Glastenbury Mountain the next day, there was another fire tower, this one abandoned. We sat at the top, boiled water, added chocolate powder, then sipped our drinks, looking down at the inspiring Berkshires and Taconic Mountain ranges in the distance. Even though the day was blustery, the stunning views and hot chocolate were worth a little discomfort.

Trekking over Harmon Hill was sunny and beautiful, a welcome change to the previous days' weather. That evening, both of us tired, we camped by a stream just before Roaring Branch. The next morning, we hiked out of Vermont just as we had entered the state, with lots of sun.

19

SOMEBODY'S COMING

*L*eaving the Green Mountains of Vermont, Lonnie and I entered Massachusetts and were soon in mountain laurel, vegetation we had not seen so far on this hike. At Sherman Brook, a sparkling river of cascading falls, the trail hugged the shoreline, the churning water strewn with glistening boulders, some exposed boulder tops covered with orange, yellow and red fallen leaves. Brightly colored trees reflected like fire from the water's surface, the stream guiding us right into the town of North Adams.

Leaving this tranquil brook, we followed the trail through the town. We came upon a Chinese buffet, unlimited food sounding very good. We kept going back for more, then topped off dinner with ice cream sundaes at Friendly's. Even with all this high-caloric eating, we'd both lost weight on the journey, Lonnie more than me. Hiking increased our metabolism, which made it impossible to consume enough calories to keep up with the demand. So our bodies relied upon muscle mass and fat to offset the deficit in calories, the result: weight and muscle loss.

Another fascinating and silly thing was our butts had turned to mush, not sure why. After resting a bit, we left town, the trail rising 1700 feet to the first peak of Greylock Mountain. The tread was fairly smooth, gravel and dirt, though long and steep, making it difficult at times. At the top was a scenic camping spot overlooking neighboring towns in the valley, and being almost dusk, a great place to stop for the night.

~

8/7/90 After about 3 miles we reached the beginning/end of the Long Trail and the Vermont/Mass. Border. A few more downhill miles and we arrived in North Adams, MA where we enjoyed the "family nite special" at Pizza Hut. With the leftover pizza strapped to the top of my pack we started our ascent of Mt. Greylock. We arrived at a beautiful overlook just as the sun was setting and made camp not far from there. ½ more of Greylock to climb tomorrow. ML & GH

~

The lights of Williamstown and Williams College were nestled in the valleys and fields far below, the towns rimmed by distant mountains. Lonnie yearned to camp on top of a mountain, and with clear skies, I agreed it was a great idea. Remembering what happened at Bromley Mountain in Vermont, though, Lonnie was concerned about late night visitors. "Do you think anyone will come up here? We're right on the trail." He waited for my bit of sarcasm, but I said nothing, thinking no one would attempt that tough, strenuous trek, especially in the dark.

We pitched our tent to the side of the trail, then took some snacks out to sit on the amazing ledge and enjoy the view. Ready for bed, we tucked into our sleeping bags, and it wasn't long before we fell asleep. Sometime later I woke to lights bouncing off the sides of the tent. I whispered, "Somebody's coming."

Lonnie, still half asleep, mumbled, "What?" We laid very still, lights moving closer, approaching the tent. Then we heard voices. "See it wasn't so bad," a man said. "Hey, there's a tent up here," another man said.

Hearing four male voices, we watched through the mesh as these guys went to the rock ledge where we'd sat a few hours earlier. The young men started talking about the stars. "Hey, there's the Big Dipper." "Where, I don't see it." "I never saw it before." The discussion went from the cosmos to some friendly debate of an existential nature, then to other topics that brought laughter, until finally, about thirty minutes later, one of them said, "Well, let's get going."

After they left, Lonnie said, "Do you believe this! They climbed that mountain in the dark!" We couldn't figure it out, especially when one of them said the trail wasn't too bad.

I woke an hour later. "Lonnie, somebody's coming…"

"Not again!" he said.

After the second group left, Lonnie said, "That's it! We're moving!" We found a side trail, packed up our gear, then Lonnie picked up the entire tent and carried it, with sleeping bags and pads still in it, to the new spot. It took me a while to get to sleep since we were on a slight hill, but later, I heard voices again; it was becoming obvious this was going to be an all-night phenomenon.

In the morning, we discovered Pattison Road with a parking lot, six-tenths of a mile on a fairly flat, easy trail from our campsite. Our intuition was right; they hadn't come up that grueling climb after all. From then on, I took a good look at the trail notes before we made camp.

Clouds moved in, the day growing windy, the sky graying, the air turning chillier. By ten that morning it was snowing. We couldn't help but wonder if this was a harbinger of frigid, blustery weather ahead for the rest of our hike.

With snow still coming down, we started up the main peak of Greylock Mountain, the highest in Massachusetts at 3,491 feet. In the 1850s, Herman Melville lived in a village called Pittsfield at the base of this mountain. Viewing Greylock from the window above his writing desk, Melville was fascinated by the contour of the mountain, which reminded him of a whale breaching the surface of the ocean, serving as his inspiration for Moby Dick. Melville's seventh book,

Pierre: or, The Ambiguities, was dedicated to Mt. Greylock, possibly the only book ever to be dedicated to a mountain.[1]

On this snowy day, we neared the top surrounded by the drone of machinery: weed eaters! Two guys were working in this snowstorm clearing out a section of mountainside for a ski event in February. I asked if the lodge at the top was open, and they believed it was. Reaching the summit, we found not only a restaurant, but cars, and throngs of sightseers at the Bascom Lodge.

The snow was a few inches deep by then. Inside the lodge, we warmed ourselves with a bowl of hot soup, then finished with ice cream. Chatting with the caretaker, Brad, we learned that people enjoyed driving up the mountain for dinner.

As new arrivals walked in, Brad reminded them that if the weather turned worse, they'd close the road. Three to four inches was expected, but his concern was ice-glazed macadam. That wouldn't affect us, so after a pleasant respite from the wintry weather, we headed out, walking past the immense stone tower at the peak of this mountain, a memorial to soldiers from Massachusetts who had died in war.

Quiet snow fell around us, the descent down Greylock a pleasant walk. At the lower elevation, the once serene and bewitching snow higher up had now turned to fog. Day hikers slogging up toward Greylock through misty rain and mud, were surprised to hear we had hiked down through snow.

At the base of Greylock was a convenience store and the Cheshire Post Office. Not much else. After our wet and chilly thirteen-mile day, we decided to find a ride to Dalton and get a motel. We had a resupply box at the post office, and since it was Sunday, we'd have to wait until Monday to pick it up. But being Sunday, there was no bus service to Dalton. A clerk at the convenience store was kind enough to call a taxi for us. The taxi would cost $35.00. Dalton was only ten miles, and

---

1. Herman Melville, "Dedication to a Mountain", *The Book of the Mountains*, 1955, A.C. Spectorsky, Ed.

because it seemed pricey, we were hemming and hawing, but with no other choice, we agreed.

The clerk was finalizing details on the phone with our taxi ride driver when a customer standing in line to buy lottery tickets said, "$35.00! That's outrageous!" Before we knew it, we were riding to Dalton in George's van; he'd offered to take us for twenty. So that's how we met George, who was full of stories, telling us how he'd go up on the ski slopes after the snow melted, looking for all sorts of treasures, stuff that fell out of pockets on the ski lift, or was lost when people fell. One year, George found $1300 in change, plus ski equipment, and loads of watches.

The first town we came to with George was Coltsville, a few miles before Dalton, teeming with restaurants, a grocery store, and a shopping center near a Motor Lodge. Staying in Coltsville made more sense than going on to Dalton. We gave George his twenty bucks, which he planned to use on more lottery tickets. In the convenience store in Cheshire, we saw a photo of a guy who had recently won a million dollars there; we hoped George would be next.

To our delight, down the road from our motel was a Starbucks. It seemed we had a sixth sense when it came to our favorite coffee shop, even while on the trail. Lonnie said, "Some people can divine water. I divine Starbucks; an important skill set when in the wilderness." Not really coffee drinkers, we were mad for Frappuccinos, our Achilles heel, especially the green tea variety.

The next morning, we left most of our gear in the motel room, then jumped on the bus back to Cheshire and picked up our food box, stowing our new supplies in our nearly empty packs. We left Cheshire, hiking the trail back to Dalton, where we'd grab a bus to take us to our motel in Coltsville. A mile out of Cheshire, we crossed over The Cobbles, a solid marble rock formation, which overlooked the Hoosic River Valley.

Unfortunately, Lonnie could hardly walk. The *tops* of his feet felt inflamed, causing pain with every step. This seemed odd to both of us, since it's usually blisters on the toes or heels, or soreness along the bottoms of the feet that create issues. I was experiencing the toe-blister problem, but there was nothing to be done about any of our foot maladies, so we pressed on.

Several hours later, the trail dropped down into Dalton, where we caught the bus back to Coltsville. It stopped at the Walmart, with our motel and Starbucks close by. Sitting down with a frosty green tea Frappuccino, Lonnie kicked off his boots to give his throbbing feet a much-needed timeout. He removed the insoles from his boots to air them out, and discovered that without the insoles, he could walk around the coffee shop nearly pain-free. He had bought the insoles separately from his boots, a specialized brand which had come highly recommended by the outfitter. The problem was, the *arches* on the expensive high-tech insoles were much more pronounced, and did not match Lonnie's arches, causing undo pressure on the bones along the tops of his feet. He bought generic insoles at Walmart, which seemed to alleviate the pain, and the problem, at least for a while, and he was ready to hike again.

20

LIKE A MIRACLE

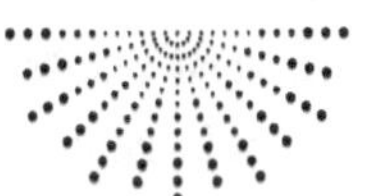

We left the motel in Coltsville and boarded the bus to Dalton to resume our hike. Both of us hoped Lonnie's new insoles would eliminate the pain he'd been experiencing. But they didn't. We had only gone a few miles when the tops of his feet hurt with every step, but Lonnie plodded forward. According to the trail notes, Great Barrington, over thirty trail-miles away, was the first place with stores to replace his boots.

Two days later, a Thursday afternoon, we discussed possible ways to get to Great Barrington, to hopefully find an outfitter to purchase new footwear. The pain on the tops of his feet was overwhelming at this point. After climbing The Ledges, a pretty spot with slab rock overlooking a forested valley, it was nearing four-thirty as we came down the mountain looking for Benedict Pond, where we planned to have an early meal. I caught up to Lonnie just before the pond, where he was discussing with a couple, Luke and Shawna, on how we could get to an outfitter. "Well, the easiest way," Luke said, "is for you to head to our car with us, and we'll take you to one!"

"Are you serious?" Lonnie said.

"Yeah, our car is down the side trail just ahead. You'll have to hold your packs since our trunk is full, but we'll get you into Lenox. I think there's an outfitter there within an easy drive to Great Barrington." They were headed to Lenox to shoot photos. We walked by Benedict Pond, then to the parking lot where we got into their car. It was like a miracle. Barely an hour before, we were wondering how we could get to a nearby town, and now, here we were pulling into the parking lot of an outfitter. To further the miracle, the only night this outdoor gear store was open late was *Thursday!* We were awestruck by our good fortune.

Lonnie tried on shoes instead of boots, and ended up buying a pair of Salomon trail runners that felt really great right out of the box. While waiting for Luke and Shawna to return, we sat at the outfitter's small café having a muffin. After a short while, Lonnie started to question our good luck, wondering if our trail angel couple was going to come back for us. I assured him they would, but it was apparent he didn't have as much faith as I did. Just then, Luke and Shawna pulled into the gravel parking lot.

By now it was dark outside, and we needed lodging. Luke was upbeat, and said he knew a place. When we pulled into the Days Inn in Great Barrington, Luke told us to wait in the car while he went into the motel to haggle a deal for the night. We were just hoping they had a room, but Luke came out a short while later and said, "You're all set!" He'd secured a great price for our room; all we had to do was go in and pay and get our key. We said our goodbyes to our wonderful trail angels, who were headed back to Boston, still pinching ourselves over this stunning serendipity. We should have been used to this kind of magic on the trail by now, but it never ceased to astonish us.

Dumping off our packs in the room, we headed to Bubba Louie's for pizza, then ice cream at the SOCO shop, Lonnie loving his new Salomons on the short walk from the motel.

In the morning, we mailed Lonnie's boots to Kent, CT, (we had a resupply box waiting at Kent) just in case he had difficulties. We hadn't even started hitchhiking when a car pulled over to the shoulder. The driver, called out, "You guys need a ride somewhere?" Slim, who had hiked the trail in '05, shared memories of his trek as he drove us to the trailhead.

Two hiking miles after he dropped us off, we were peering down the Ice Gulch, a daunting, yet wondrous rocky chasm. This narrow, deep gorge with one-hundred-foot cliffs runs more than a half-mile down the mountainside. Even in summer you can look down between boulders to see snow or ice. Luckily, it wasn't part of the A.T.

The trail from that point turned to slab rock, overlooking the valley far below, often weaving close to the edge. At the Housatonic River and Route 7, the sky was gloomy and dark with threatening rain clouds. Another decision—keep hiking and possibly get soaked to the bone, or hitch a ride back into Great Barrington, with dry accommodations at the Days Inn. Tough choice. When we arrived, the clerk said, "I thought you guys cleared out!" "Well, we did, but now we're checking back in!"

It rained on and off all the next day, so our zero in the motel room was a good idea. We did our laundry, ate out and ate in, snacks scattered across the bed, soda and ice cream in the little fridge, a college football game on the television. Lonnie, helping himself to plenty of town food, said we could have hiked on, feeling guilty over us being such lightweight slackers.

"You just wanted to watch Penn State football," he said, munching on chips. Since I used to live in Happy Valley, home of Penn State, and took classes there, he may have been right. The next morning, we left Great Barrington with pleasant skies and fall temperatures, easily finding a ride.

A few miles down the trail, we came to a road, with a marker indicating that the field beside us was the site of the last fight of Shays' Rebellion, named for Daniel Shays, a farmhand who had fought in the American Revolution. He, along with four thousand of his compatriots, began the uprising in the fall of 1786 over Massachusetts taxing people's trades.

Daniel Shays and his countrymen forced the Supreme Court in Springfield, the capital of the state, to adjourn. They were angry over farmers being jailed because they were unable to pay their taxes. Shays' coalition eventually liberated the imprisoned debtors. In February, 1787, Shays and his men were defeated in the very field where I was standing. Nevertheless, the rebellion was considered successful. Their efforts helped lead to the formation of the Constitutional Convention, which began just three months later on May 14, 1787, in Philadelphia. That famous convention determined how America was going to be governed between the states and the federal government, which ironically is still being fought over today.

Interesting to note, twenty years before Shays' Rebellion over taxes, citizens of nearby Boston had fought a similar battle, rejecting taxes the British Parliament had placed on glass, paper, paint and especially, tea. That rebellion ended with the Boston Tea Party, and eventually the American Revolution. As I looked across this field, soft with rustling grasses, the trees shedding their leaves, I contemplated this last fight, and its impact on the history of our country.

The colors of fall—oranges, reds, and yellows—were all around us, bright fallen leaves wet and pasted to slippery boulders as we climbed the peaks of Mt. Everett. Crossing several rocky outcroppings, we eventually came to Guilder Pond, where I heard a cell phone chime. Looking around I spotted a guy sitting on a rock nearby, talking to someone. I didn't own a cell phone during this hike, and Lonnie left his Tracfone at home. The jarring interruption was a reminder of why we had not brought phones on our wilderness journey.

Race Mountain, with its fantastic views and stone slabs, soon dropped into the narrow gorge of the impressive Sages Ravine, with its massive boulders and frothy, rushing cascades. We wore our crocs to cross the shallow stream where it flattened out; the water cold, but refreshing. This marked the boundary between Massachusetts and Connecticut.

Numerous hikers became trail mates with Molly and Geoff during the thousand miles they were on the trail. Paul Nussbaum wrote that a hiker who had lunch with them in Massachusetts said, "They were such good people— they'd share everything they had with anybody... Even when I met them, they

had reached the point you get to on the trail, where you would trust a rattlesnake."[1]

They hiked through Massachusetts in August, when they could not always enjoy the scenery since the trees were leafed out. At one of the shelters, they wrote in the journal, "We had the best view we've had in a long time. We could see for hundreds of miles. The view was like a gift, given for our efforts of hiking." This was most likely after Race Brook Falls, where the trail opens up to broad views across the Housatonic Valley and many miles east across Massachusetts, just before the Bear Rock Stream and waterfall.

On May 25th, 1991 the Appalachian Trail Conference spokesman, Brian King, announced the ATC will use donations to buy ninety acres of surrounding gorge with a three-hundred-foot cascading waterfall (Bear Rock?) along the trail in southwestern Massachusetts as a permanent "celebration of the dreams and vision of Molly Ann LaRue and Geoffrey Logan Hood."[2]

1. Paul Nussbaum, *"For two hikers, the Appalachian Trail led to death"*, Philadelphia Inquirer, September 20, 1990.
2. Mike Feeley, *"Crews gets death sentence"*, Sunday Patriot News, May 26. 1991.

21

GHOSTLY TORRENTS

After entering Connecticut, our fifth state, we climbed Bear Mountain, the highest in the state, 2,316 feet, which was challenging with its extensive rock climbing and steep bouldering. All the work paid off when we arrived at a huge mound of rocks, marking the highest point of Connecticut. There had once been a tower built atop this huge hummock of large stones in 1885 by a local mason, Owen Travis, who was hired by Robbins Battell to prove that Bear Mountain was the highest peak in Connecticut.

When we came to Lions Head Mountain, with its yellow and brown grasses, it reminded me of a lion's mane. From a distance, photos revealed that the mountain resembles a lion prone, with its head up.

Descending from the top, we realized Salisbury was only four-tenths of a mile down Route 44. It was five in the afternoon, so we decided to hike into town for dinner and maybe even stay for Monday night football.

First, we strolled into a bistro for salads and chocolate cake. Then off to the grocery store for resupply, shoving our backpacks into carts. It was still early. With such a pleasant evening, we sat on a bench outside, near the store entrance, and waited until it was closer to game time. People stared as they walked past, giving us guarded looks, maybe wondering if we were homeless, or maybe they'd never seen thru-hikers before and were shocked by our shabby clothes, worn shoes and tatty backpacks.

Later that evening, at the White Hart Inn, we sat at the bar, guzzled soda, ate pizza and French fries, and watched football. Danielle, the bartender, made sure our glasses were never empty, and our plates were always full, and seemed to enjoy our visit. Other patrons welcomed us too, or maybe just thought we were a harmless oddity, like the couple who sat at the table near the bar. The man said, "This is such a special gift you are giving yourselves." The woman added, "Are you taking lots of photos to remember your journey?"

"Oh yes, we are," I said. Later, reflecting on the evening, we realized how often people we met along the way shared *gifts* with us, when they weren't even aware that they had. Just a few days before a guy who gave us a ride said, "*Go slow.*"

Around ten o'clock, we decided to leave since it was halftime, and neither of us could eat or drink anything else. It was so pleasant heading up the mountain, the night air fresh and cool; what a joy returning to our journey after such a fun evening. Hiking into towns is so special, knowing that your visit is merely a brief intermission, that your adventure always lies ahead, out in the woods. We hadn't gone more than a half-hour from the bar when we came to a flat area partway up the mountain, just right for our tent.

The next day offered up more magnificence, burning bushes ablaze with brilliant crimsons and golds lining the trail. Sunlight illuminated the thin skin of the leaves, making the colors glow, electrified. Not long after, we were met by the deafening roar of the Housatonic River, its timeless waters plummeting fifty feet, spilling over ancient rocks and boulders, culminating in clear eddies and boiling cascades winding through the community of Falls Village. *The Great Falls,* so aptly named.

At an overlook hang gliders use as a jumping-off point, four older guys were sitting on the ground drinking beer, their mountain bikes lying along the trail. Bikes are not normally allowed on the A.T., but who were we to make a fuss? With all the rocky ups and downs in this section, it was hard to believe they were able to navigate the unfriendly terrain. When we asked if the going was tough, one of them said, "Well, we do a lot of carrying the bikes, too."

At the Pine Swamp Brook Lean-to that evening, we tented not far from the shelter, the rain falling off and on throughout the night. By morning the rain had stopped, but the sky was still hung with thick, dreary clouds. Within a few hours, the day grew darker, the rain coming in sputters at first, then slashing at the trail in ghostly torrents over the next four miles. We still had six miles until the next shelter, so we slogged on. This was the hardest rain we had experienced yet.

Arriving at Route 4, we had a decision to make. We could push on through the deluge to the next shelter, or trek a short distance, maybe a half-mile, down the macadam toward a little out-of-the-way deli, with the Hitching Post Country Motel nearby. A few other hikers we had camped with the night before were congregated at this road crossing with a similar idea, to get out of the rain and eat deli food. One was a southbounder named, Strong Back.

After a quick walk down the road, we all piled into the deli and shed our drenched rain clothes. Warm, dry and well-fed, Lonnie and I weren't wild about heading back out into the cold rain, so we checked out the motel. Strong Back was low on funds, so with his partially dried clothes, he headed back to the trail. Lonnie and I felt fortunate to be able to avoid the crappy weather when needed, but it begged the question—how would we ever finish our hike if we kept stopping?

The next day, with no rain, we checked out of our room, our gear dry, our minds ready to tackle the A.T. again. The trail gods must have approved of our cowardly move, treating us to a pleasant gravel road along the Housatonic River, a nice, flat, five-mile stroll. Or maybe they just felt sorry for us.

We headed up St. John's Ledges, a straight-up climb over boulders. My legs were wobbly by the time I arrived at the top, but Lonnie scrambled right up.

By late afternoon, we headed into Kent to pick up our food box. With scores of private schools in Kent, there were students everywhere. We stopped to have ice cream cones, then retrieved our food box and Lonnie's boots, which he didn't want anymore. His new shoes were comfortable and cushy. We left Kent toward evening when Dan, the local outfitter, gave us a ride back to the trailhead. He took Lonnie's boots for his hiker box; maybe another hiker's arches wouldn't be so squeamish. With the sky fading quickly, we hiked the darkening trail to Thayer Brook and made camp.

HALLOWEEN & THE BIG APPLE

After hiking fifteen miles over fairly easy trail, we entered New York, our sixth state. I didn't realize until later that it was October 30th, the day before Halloween. When Lonnie and I decided to thru-hike the trail southbound, August through January, we knew we'd be hiking during holidays; friends and acquaintances would be eating turkey, playing games with family, or socializing with others, while we'd be sitting in our tent, eating a granola bar. But we were okay with that.

After dark, I sat in the tent tucked in my sleeping bag using my headlamp to read the trail notes for the next day. We already had our foot rubs, Lonnie almost asleep, but I didn't care—I wanted him to hear what I just read. "Lonnie, listen to this. It says four miles from here, the trail crosses train tracks and there's a train station right there on the A.T. that takes you into New York City for $11.50 one-way. But here's the best part: it stops on Saturday at two forty-one pm. And guess what? It's Friday night. Plus, right on the highway we cross before the train stop is Pete's Landscaping, who is hiker-friendly. We could do this!"

He simply answered, "OK," and rolled over back to sleep. I pondered how this could work because there was one hitch in the plan: having to spend the night in the city. The train would take us in on Saturday, but no return trip until Sunday morning, departing Manhattan at nine-fifty am. I presumed we could hang out and sleep on a bench at Grand Central Station until morning. Apparently, my hiker mentality of, *I can sleep anywhere* led me to this unsavory conclusion. Finally, I managed to fall asleep.

When I turned over in the morning, Lonnie was awake. I asked him if he heard my plan the night before. He said, "Yeah, is this something you want to do?"

I said, "It sounds exciting." I hadn't been in the city since my daughter was eight, when I had driven her and my parents to see the Christmas show at Rockefeller Center. That was over twenty years before. But he was more concerned and asked, "When does the train bring us back?" I reluctantly told him that it wouldn't be until Sunday morning. He did not like that, so we decided to…*just see.*

After hiking several miles, I heard traffic and knew we were close to the highway, and the railway crossing. The possibility of this excursion propelled me down the trail. Somehow, I had to convince Lonnie it would be a fun trip.

Pete's Landscaping store was on the other side of Route 22. We crossed the two-lane road and walked to the door, realizing his business wasn't open yet. It was a little before ten, so we went to check out the train stop. Behind his place the A.T. crossed the train tracks which paralleled the highway. Nearby was a simple wooden open-air platform, big enough for several people to stand, with five steps leading up to it. A sign read, *2:41 pm Saturday train to Grand Central Station,* and *Sunday, 9:37 am return trip.*

We walked back to Pete's store, which was now open. Pete saw we were hikers, so he invited us to use the shower. It was good to wash the grunge off. We told him we were considering taking the train into the city. "We aren't open on Sunday," he said. "But you can leave your backpacks in the shed over there." He pointed to a small building at one end of the parking lot, about fifty feet back from the highway. "I can leave it unlocked for you. They'll be safe until you return tomorrow."

It was obvious Pete had helped other hikers on their crazy New York City larks. He directed us to a deli less than half-mile away where we could get lunch.

Spending the night at Grand Central Station weighed heavily on both of us, as we sat eating our food. With common sense prevailing, we both knew that was not a good idea. Then I thought of a story-telling acquaintance of mine, Rennie, who lived in New York City.

When we returned to the landscape store, I asked Pete if I could use his computer. He said, "Sure." I emailed Rennie, and asked if she was going to be around, that we were coming into the city. She was home and emailed right back. Rennie suggested we meet up, then directed us on how to get to her apartment from the station.

But she added, "Are you sure you want to come to the city. I live in Greenwich Village, and it's Halloween. There will be a 100,000 people here for the parade." Being on the trail we had lost track of what the date was, only that it was Saturday.

"Hey Lonnie, it's Halloween, and there's this huge parade with 100,000 people in Greenwich Village tonight. Are you still good to go?" In Pete's office, Lonnie was attempting to coax Pete's pet cockatoo to talk, while I sat at the computer typing.

"Halloween?" He put his hands up and said, "Yeah, why not." The idea of having someone to meet up with made our decision much easier. I sent the reply and the plan was set; meet at her apartment, then head out for dinner together. But we still didn't know where we'd spend the night.

After stuffing necessary things in our pouches, we secured our main packs in the shed, trusting Pete's nearly nonexistent security. Arriving at the platform twenty minutes early, we still could not believe we'd soon be on the train headed into the largest city in America; *on Halloween!* Three other hikers materialized and were soon standing with us on the platform.

I stared at Lonnie and he had the same stunned look on his face—where did they come from? When we heard the whistle, we weren't even sure the train would stop. But within minutes we were in our seats zipping down the tracks, chatting with one of the guys who boarded with us. He told us he was getting off the trail, heading home to meet up with his girlfriend. No hiker liked to say, "I'm quitting. I've had enough." But the look on his face told the story. Lonnie and I sat in silence—always sad to hear of someone getting off the trail—wondering if we would ever reach that point.

From Grand Central Station we followed Rennie's directions, the subway trains taking us to Greenwich Village. After a few moments of catching up with Rennie, we decided to continue our conversation over dinner. She suggested a nice restaurant within walking distance, near the New York University campus. By the time we left the restaurant, huge crowds had already gathered to watch the parade, all in wild, colorful costumes.

When it started to rain, Rennie recommended we watch the parade from her kitchen window, telling us that the procession went right past her apartment building. The rain came harder as the three of us crowded around the window. Just then, a cacophony of yells and screams rippled through the crowd when the sky opened, drenching everyone on the street.

A while later Rennie asked where we were staying for the night. Lonnie and I looked at each other. I was about to say, "Grand Central Station," when she said, "Why don't you stay here? I have the extra bedroom. It's my son's room, but he isn't around right now."

With that gracious offer, we put our pouches in the room. By the time the parade ended the rain had stopped. Rennie was tired, so she gave us her key and we headed out to the streets. There were hundreds of police, on foot and with motorcycles, and thousands of partiers in crazy, glittery costumes, shouting, dancing, having fun. And there we were, dressed up as thru-hikers, one of the few times we visited a city and fit in. I even had my picture taken with the Ghostbusters, and a Chinese dragon. We had actual New York bagels, then followed up with huge hot pretzels and fruit smoothies. Trail hunger was no match for New York City, with all its dining opportunities.

Around two am, we headed back to Rennie's place and had a nice comfortable sleep. In the morning, we woke early, said goodbye to Rennie, and told her she had given us the most wonderful trail magic.

She mused, saying, "Just think, a trail angel, right here in New York City!"

The sounds and sites of the previous evening reverberated in our heads as we walked down several streets. It was early Sunday morning; a few cars went by, but the city was still asleep, everyone recovering from the Halloween festivities. We had a great breakfast in a little side street diner, then headed to the station. On the kiosk, in the largest train station in the world, according to area occupied and number of platforms, the schedule read, *Appalachian Trail* as one of the stops.

At promptly nine thirty-seven am, the train headed north from the station. Within a short time, the extravagant vibration of Manhattan started to fade, our bodies lulled by the swaying of the train. Our memories brimmed with exotic aromas, splashes of color and laughter, the taste of authentic NY bagels still on our tongues.

Urban fervor gave way to solemn suburbs—cookie-cutter houses, malls, myriad roads. Green foliage grew plentiful on surrounding hills dotted with homes, the railway slipping through valleys, past verdant expanses of rich vegetation and trees, the world transforming outside our window.

After picking up our packs from Pete's shed—where they had remained safe, just as he promised—we were back on the trail by noon. We hiked six and a half miles, not speaking, wrapped in the silence of our own thoughts. That evening, while setting up camp, I said, "Did these two days really happen?"

We looked at each other, still in a strange space, quietly reflecting. Later that night, in the unrealistic solitude of our tent, Lonnie said, "Can you believe we were in New York City this morning?" I just shook my head, chuckling to myself; it seemed impossible.

23

HIKER POWDERING UP

An interesting phenomenon occurred that next morning—the inside of our tent was soaked, even though it never rained. The moisture had apparently developed, maybe relating to the dew point? But more disturbing, a theory I wasn't about to share with Lonnie, not just yet anyway, was that the weird dampness was the result of passing Nuclear Lake a tenth of a mile before we camped. My supposition was probably wacko, but...

In 1972, an experimental nuclear research facility sat on the shore of Nuclear Lake. One day, an unexplained explosion blew out two of the windows in the lab. It was reported that an unspecified amount of bomb-grade plutonium shot out across the lake and the surrounding woods. After the Park Service acquired the land for the A.T., the buildings were razed, followed by an extensive cleansing process, hoping to dispel any fears of contamination. Nevertheless, the so-called cleanup notwithstanding, I still wondered why our tent was so wet.

Five miles later, at the Morgan Stewart Shelter, we met a trail maintainer preparing to clean the latrine. We thanked her for her diligence, Lonnie *especially* understanding her disagreeable task. Back in Maine, when we stayed in such comfort at Honey and Bear's hostel,

Bear made one request of Lonnie as we departed from his kindness at the trail crossing of Grafton Notch. He asked if Lonnie would take a stick, go into the privy at the next shelter, and get rid of the *cone* that develops over time from excessive use of the outhouse.

At first, Lonnie thought Bear was kidding, but then realized, he wasn't. When we stopped at the Speck Pond Campsite, Lonnie grudgingly accomplished this job. Afterward, he felt good that he had carried out this necessary aspect of trail maintenance.

The next morning, we had an unexpected surprise—a brand-new convenience store by two intersecting roads and the trail. This treat haven included numerous breakfast choices: even a pancake egg sandwich. We tried all of them, spending about an hour continuing to go back for something else. Hikers walking the thirty trail-miles of New York have called it Deli Alley, where loads of convenience stores and delis are within walking distance of the trail. Many hikers don't carry much food through New York, relying on these high-calorie sanctuaries.

It's good we had plenty to eat though, because we soon needed it climbing Shenandoah Mountain, which was only 1,282 feet. Despite its relatively tame elevation, it was a tough climb. At the top, we sat on slab rock, the stone surface adorned with a painting of an American flag, a tribute to those who died during 911. It was Wednesday, November 4th, an exciting day because we would cross the Hudson River on the Bear Mountain bridge, known for its spectacular vistas of the Hudson River Highlands.

In 1868, the prospect of building this bridge had entered the planning stage. However, the structure never came to be until the 1920s. The state legislature authorized the private Bear Mountain Hudson River Bridge Company to complete the project, its board member financiers, E. Roland Harriman and George W. Perkins. The BMHRBC charter guaranteed that ownership of the bridge would eventually revert to New York State, which occurred in 1940.

When the bridge opened on November 27, 1924, it was the longest suspension bridge in the world with an overall length of 2,255 feet, at a cost of four and a half million dollars; the first of its type to have a concrete deck. Its construction methods influenced other longer bridges, including the George Washington between New York City and New Jersey, and the Golden Gate in California.

Walking across this amazing, multifunctional bridge, we watched boats moving under it along the Hudson River, a train rumbling past one level below us, and cars passing beside us on Route 202 along the pedestrian walkway. On the western side, we entered the 5000-acre Bear Mountain Park, immediately walking through a small zoo. Then passing a lake with picnic groves.

At the top of Bear Mountain sunny skies prevailed, and we could see the incredible skyline of Manhattan, where we had been only three short days before. We saw a professional photographer who took photos of a young, well-dressed couple, perhaps engaged or just married, with the city skyline in the background.

Our water supply was low, but we managed to wheedle some from unsuspecting tourists visiting the park. That night we found a campsite two miles down the mountain, a short distance before Seven Lakes Drive.

Our next hurdle was a tight, vertical rock crevice known on the A.T. as the Lemon Squeezer, which we *squeezed* through quite easily. By evening, the clouds had moved in and rain came down. At Route 17, there was a phone booth right beside the trail. Taped to the pay phone was a card with the number for a taxi service. We both crammed under the small awning to escape the storm while making the call. When the driver arrived, we asked to go to Southfields where we had a resupply box. "You don't want to go to Southfields," the driver said. "There's nothing there. You'd be better off in Harriman. Lots of motels, stores and restaurants."

That night we slept in a warm, dry bed in Harriman. The next morning we went across the highway to the Target store and shared a Starbucks frappe before calling the taxi. The driver first took us to Southfield to pick up our food drop-box at the post office. Lonnie and I hurriedly divided the new supplies into our packs while the driver waited. Then back to the trailhead.

There we encountered the Agony Grind, a steep, tough climb, but that was only the first of one rocky ridge after another; we experienced *agony grinds* all day.

On Mombasha Point, the Manhattan skyline showed itself one more time. Later, after descending, we walked past the remains of a coal mine, a desolate blackened area piled with discarded coal debris. I felt for all the men and boys who had worked there over the years; the area was demoralizing. That night, we made camp at an old village site with crumbling stone foundations. The next day, we gazed on Fitzgerald Falls, then scrambled up the Pinnacles. Seven miles later, stepping across bedrock painted with NY/NJ, we entered New Jersey.

Bouldering down another escarpment, we hiked through twilight into darkness, unable to find a campsite. Wearing our headlamps, we finally found a clear, flat place with an overlook. To keep bears from getting our food, we hung our meals at night in a waterproof Sea to Summit bag from a high tree limb using a lightweight rope. While I set up the tent, fixing our gear inside, Lonnie trudged around in the dark looking for a tree with a sturdy limb about twelve feet from the ground to sling the bag over.

With our tasks completed, we sat on Luther's Rock eating our Pasta Primavera Mountain House meal. Below us sat a seamless black abyss, pinpricked with tiny lights sparkling across the valley. Sometime in the night, I woke, unable to sleep. Lonnie stirred, too.

"Are you awake?" I said.

He rolled over. "Yeah. Can't get back to sleep."

"Me either. What time is it?" I was ready for breakfast.

He looked at his watch, mine had stopped working. "Three."

"I'm hungry."

"So am I," he said.

"Should we get the food bag down and have some cereal?"

"Yeah." With headlamps on, we crawled out onto a landscape lit by the moon. After finding the tree, we lowered the bag—leaving the rope over the limb—then walked back to the tent. Within minutes, tucked in our sleeping bags, we were both crunching on Fruit Loops and Cheerios. After our late-night raid on the *refrigerator,* we rehung the food bag, then climbed back in our tent and quickly fell asleep.

The next day, the trail skirted one corner of the Wallkill River National Wildlife Refuge for two miles. With more than 5100 acres of land, the refuge was managed primarily for wetland conservation. Various birds populated the lake and marshes, though the only one we recognized was a lone heron standing knee-deep in the water looking for minnows. After eating lunch on a bench near the lake, taking in this peaceful scenery, we headed back into the woods.

In this area, the trail was in New Jersey for about eleven miles, then moved back into New York for a short distance, sideswiping a small community called Unionville, with a hostel run by the Mayor. Bill, the hostel owner, actually had been the mayor of Unionville for twelve years, but after retiring, he opened his house to hikers. The problem was, we didn't know how to find his place when we entered the small community. Spotting a pizza shop, we went in and sat down. After Cokes and NY pie, we walked out to find several SOBO's across the street who were headed to the Mayor's.

Bill lived on the main floor, leaving the lower level reserved for hikers. The downstairs had two rooms, one on each side of the stair-well, and a bathroom. Bill and his helpers had built numerous bunkbeds into the two spacious rooms, which could accommodate plenty of hikers.

The Mayor had a list of rules, the main one being: every hiker new to the hostel had to watch his video. The short film expressed the importance of being positive, friendly, and respectful while at the Mayor's. It did get a little preachy, but we were okay with it, since it was such a nice arrangement, and free.

In the morning, we heard the Mayor talking with his two helpers, Butch and Petey. Petey and the Mayor lived in the hostel. Butch had a home nearby, but came over to help with meals and slack-packing hikers. Petey, the cook, was a skinny, old cranky guy.

We headed up to the main floor for breakfast, our three hosts bantering back and forth, keeping us hikers in stitches. Petey and the Mayor's antics were like a comedy routine with Don Rickles and Rodney Dangerfield. Despite their droll complaining about each other, they certainly seemed to be having fun, and Petey, like a salty old sailor, could really cook. They put out a delicious breakfast and dinner for hikers at no charge, and encouraged everyone to eat up. They did have a donation box on the wall in the kitchen, but donations weren't mandatory.

After breakfast, Butch drove us to Deckertown Pike where we would slack-pack north for fourteen miles, ending up later that afternoon back at the Mayor's. Being southbounders, this would be the first time we hiked north. The trail from Deckertown Pike took us through High Point State Park, but didn't go to the summit. Since we still had eight miles to go, and were both tired, we blew off the arduous climb. Just like Greylock in Massachusetts, High Point also had a tower at the summit, 220 feet high with 291 steps, honoring New Jersey war veterans, the highest point in New Jersey at 1,803 feet.

8/28/90: Day 86 of our journey on the A.T. We started our hike and the clouds started to rain. It was a short hard rain. So far New Jersey is a considerably lower state. Most of what we hike through is swamp land. The rain has brought on more mosquitoes causing me (Geoff) to write of them as "Moreskitoes" in a shelter register...we decided to roadwalk to avoid the woods. On the last part...a guy pulled over to offer some bug dope. He ended up giving us a ride the last mile, as we were already off trail and miserable we said yes. It turned out that he was a N.Y.C.P.O. That night there was a terrifically strong thunderstorm—it shook the shelter we were in! An exciting end to our worst day. ML & GH

Molly and Geoff had now hiked 800 miles. But the next day, the last entry in this journal, they wrote: *8/29/90: We were pleasantly surprised w/how well today went after such a miserable day yesterday. There were some mosquitoes as we broke camp...but not too bad and the sky was blue! We picked up our mail in*

Unionville...we followed old blazes up to High Point State Park. There was a good view from there. We then had a very nice mosquito free ridge walk in the state park. We stopped by the visitor center but decided against a campground so we hiked a couple more miles on the trail until we found a nice spot on the ridge. A good day—reminding us how neat the trail can be. ML & GH

Arriving back in Unionville after a long day, Lonnie and I were happy to be back in the graces of the Mayor's hospitality. That evening, with hikers gathering around the dinner table, a young guy came up from downstairs, scooting each foot forward a few inches at a time. After he sat, he stared at the table, his face grim. After a moment, speaking to no one in particular, he said in a low, strained voice, "My feet hurt so bad."

Lonnie and I just chuckled to ourselves, not making fun, but because we understood.

Lonnie said, "Big miles?"

"Yeah, too many miles, I guess."

Lonnie told him our trail names and he introduced himself, Dry Mouth. He said he had done twenty miles the day before. He told us that in high school he competed as a triathlete—running, biking, and swimming—but hiking was so much harder. We were shocked. Never did we expect that to be the case.

After dinner that night, Butch, who was the youngest of the Mayor's *family,* shared this story. He told us one night when the Mayor returned after dark, that he, Butch, was sitting at the community table in the dining room, and said, "You've got to go downstairs and see what we have down there." The Mayor asked, "What is it?" "Just go down, and see." He headed down the steps, detecting a peculiar odor, unlike the usual *hiker smell.* Reaching the bottom step, he saw a creature looking up at him. A goat! Its master asleep on the bunk next to it. The Mayor hurried back up the stairs and looked at Butch. "Okay, so that's a new one. Are we gonna have goat crap all over the place? Is it gonna chew everything up?" "No, the hiker said the goat is *house-trained*, and would be no problem."

Butch went on to tell us that the hiker did run into some problems later on. Apparently, a forest warden waited for the hiker at a road crossing and fined him for having a goat on the trail, citing the, *No hooved animals on the A.T. rule*. Butch theorized that the rule was to keep horses off the trail, then ended his story by simply saying, "We just never know what may come through our door."

Later though, Butch did add one sad note. "Once we had a hiker steal money from the donation box. We like offering services to the hikers, and love hearing their stories, and meeting so many friendly people, but I guess you have to have one sour grape in every bunch. That's when the Mayor started requiring all hikers to watch the video in order to stay."

After leaving a donation in the box, and saying good-bye to Petey and the Mayor, it was time to leave this first-class haven, and start tromping south again. Butch drove us back to Deckertown Turnpike and gave us a warm send off.

It was Tuesday, November 10th, an unusually hot and humid day with no wind. Lonnie reached the Culver Fire Tower before I did. When I arrived, there he stood with his pants dropped. Lonnie referred to himself as a *poly-hydrator*, which meant he sweats a lot. He was using the Gold Bond Powder, but not for his feet (like we usually did when taking rests during the day), but to "cool off" the nether regions.

There was a picnic table, which on the trail was a luxury. I placed my backpack on the bench, then walked over to the tower. We passed lots of old lookout towers, and even met a hiker who spent the night in one. While Lonnie aired out, I hoped to catch a view at the top. Off to the side of the tower, was a trail that led down the mountain, not part of the A.T. probably for day hikers. "You know, there's a trail over here," I said, wanting Lonnie to know he may not be alone for long.

"Yeah, I checked, nobody's around," he said, continuing his *chill* session, his shorts down around his ankles. A sign at the base of the tower read: *USFS requires permission to climb tower*. With nothing to see,

I headed back to the picnic table for a snack. Lonnie's maintenance was still going on when we both heard a very familiar sound.

At first, I shrugged it off. But Lonnie was on full alert, glancing over at me, then letting his eyes scan the surrounding woods for the source of the sound. When the phone rang again, we both looked up. Neither of us thought it was possible, until we heard a voice say, "Hello." Up there, in what we thought had been just another abandoned fire tower, was a man, probably a forest ranger, who had been working there the entire time. I never saw Lonnie pull his pants up so fast, get his gear together, his backpack on, and start down that mountain. Ten seconds tops! Maybe a trail record. I laughed the whole way, following behind. When we arrived at the bottom, I said, "Well, I suppose your photo is now on the home page of the US Forest Service with the caption, *Hiker Powdering Up*."

The section of trail we'd been on for several days, basically since we'd entered New Jersey, was called Kittatinny Ridge. This name came from a Lenni Lenape Native American word meaning *endless hill* or *great mountain*. The ridge spanned the northwest corner of New Jersey all the way into Pennsylvania, leading us through a forest of oaks, birches and maples, with smatterings of softwoods, like hemlock and white pine.

Throughout our nineteen-mile hike the next day, we crossed bedrock along the edge of a ridge with scenic views of the New Jersey valley—small fish ponds, a patchwork of farms, and shimmering macadam roads. We rested on a log eating peanut butter and jelly sandwiches, the valley stretching out to a blue haze that eventually touched the sky.

Lonnie looked back to the trail where we had just come from and said, "There goes a bear." Sure enough, a bear ambled across the trail, then down the mountain. Three months on the trail and the first bear we see is in New Jersey! Lonnie couldn't help but chortle at the irony in that. However, I learned later, other than the Smokies, New Jersey has a high density of bears, especially in the Appalachian Trail area, with no natural predators and an ample supply of food.

Late in the day, nearing the Delaware Water Gap, we followed the shoreline of Sunfish Pond, the southernmost glacial pond on the A.T., remnant of the Wisconsin Glacier which receded during the last ice age, 75,000 – 11,000 years ago. Sunfish Pond was declared a National Natural Landmark in January, 1970. Due to the acidic quality of the water, only a couple species of fish can survive—sunfish and perch.

It was nearing dusk when we navigated chair-sized boulders at the water's edge. Just past the pond, we entered the woods with our headlamps on, searching for a place to camp. The trail widened, pointing down the mountain. Signs along the trail said no camping allowed, while the notes indicated a backpacker campsite nearby.

We never intended going all the way to the Delaware Water Gap that day, but finding no campsites, we had little choice. Ahead of us, two people moved slowly through the enveloping darkness, with no lights at all. They stopped to let us go by. Lonnie said, "Do you want us to guide you down the mountain with our headlamps?"

The young man looked frustrated as he helped the older woman. "Yes, that would be good. This is my mom, and for her seventy-ninth birthday she wanted to hike to this pond. But it has taken us much longer than we thought."

Lonnie and I slowed to match their pace, our headlamps shining the way. I asked, "Did you come up from the highway?"

"Yes, but we went up the side trail, around Sunfish Pond, then joined the A.T.," he said. His mother took short steps, her eyes focused on the ground. I wondered how she had maneuvered over those boulders around Sunfish Pond that had given Lonnie and me so much difficulty.

"Thanks so much," the birthday mother said, shuffling down the old forest road, her son supporting her by the arm.

"We certainly had underestimated how long it would take us to hike this," the son added, following beside her.

We led them down the four miles to the parking lot beside Route 80, which left us with no camping options. The situation quickly resolved itself when her son offered to drive us to a hotel on the other side.

Driving over the Delaware River, I wondered with all the travelers crossing this bridge, how many realized it was also the Appalachian Trail. We entered Pennsylvania, our eighth state, and my home state. The young man took us to the Pocono Inn. This time *we* had been the trail angels. And our treat for that, a wonderful pie place down the road in the little town of Delaware Water Gap. And it was still open!

Geoff and Molly also visited a pie place, maybe it too was at Delaware Water Gap, where Geoff suggested Molly choose the pie. They had her favorite: strawberry rhubarb.

24

THE TAJ MAHAL

The trail climbed a thousand feet from Delaware Water Gap to the Pennsylvania portion of the Kittatinny Ridge. We stopped at several outcrops overlooking the river, its fast waters streaming through the gap. Struggling with the steep climb, I lagged behind. When I finally reached the ridgeline, there was Lonnie, standing atop a concrete footer that at one time supported a corner of a fire tower. He was posed like a statue, body leaned forward, looking outward toward the river. All I could do was laugh. I had no idea what his goofy antics represented, but after that tiring climb, the comic relief was exactly what I needed. After moving across the ridge for several miles, we came to Route 191.

Referring to the next seven miles, the notes simply said, *Wolf Rocks*. Wolf Rocks began as a rocky ridge with boulders the size of small cars, where we had to move carefully and slowly, trees and shrubs growing between and around them. If the hiking continued to be this rough for seven miles, it would take at least ten hours to traverse. By then it would be nearing midnight, and we would still need to make camp. We had passed the Kirkridge Shelter just before Route 191, but it was too early to stop then. The trail eventually led off the boulder-tossed ridge, which eased my mind, but now had turned to a spate of smaller rocks, bowling ball sized, the going still precarious. As a matter of fact, the entire mountain ridge was one huge field of rocks and boulders, left behind from north-receding glaciers thousands of years earlier.

Leaving the ridge, we proceeded down toward the town of Wind Gap, still navigating rock-cluttered tread. Nearing dusk, with my headlamp on, I tripped, stumbling forward, the weight of my pack driving my right shoulder into the ground. Lonnie, who was ahead, heard me yell. By the time he reached me, I had rolled over, sat up, undid my pack, and slid out of it, finding a little blood on my hand from scraping the rocks. "Are you okay?" he said.

"Yeah, I think so," I said, twisting my arm back and forth, recalling breaking my right shoulder ice skating as a teenager. But it was all right. "Let's just get down off this mountain."

The traffic noise from Route 33 meant we were close to Wind Gap, a narrow passage between two mountains, its geological nature giving it its designation as a gap, and is considered the gateway to the Pocono Mountains. Traveling with my family through this gap as a young girl, I always imagined extreme wind had created it. Now I understand that was not the case at all. Eons ago, water ran through this area, wearing away the rock. Unlike the Delaware Water Gap, where water still flows, Wind Gap lost its flow due to *stream capture*, the water eventually diverted along a more viable route, leaving a dry bed between the mountains.

Wind Gap's namesake, however, had nothing whatsoever to do with wind. An early Dutch settler, with the last name Windt, settled in the gap area a few centuries earlier. German settlers who came after referred to it as Windt's Gap. Over time it was shortened to *Wind Gap*.

Normally when gaps are formed, they have gently inclined sides, but tonight, picking my way down the steep mountain into Wind Gap, the incline didn't feel so gentle!

After crossing the highway, we found the Gateway Motel just fifty yards from the trail, tucked into a flat area at the base of the next mountain. That evening, glad to be off the trail for the night, we ordered food from an Italian restaurant a mile away in the town of

Wind Gap. Waiting for dinner to arrive, I cleaned the cuts on my hand, ready to slump back against the headboard and watch the tube.

Most of the trail in Pennsylvania, if only to hikers, is infamous for its rocks. This section of the Kittatinny Ridge, known as Blue Mountain, lived up to its gnarly reputation. Blue Mountain extends for one hundred and fifty miles, beginning at the Delaware Water Gap, then continues on to Big Gap in south-central Pennsylvania.

After fifteen miles the next day, we arrived at a fairly level ridgeline to find a freaky, bizarre situation; no trees to hang our food bag. We felt we had arrived on some unknown planet, a barren, surreal place. Surprisingly, the tread was rock-free, with scattered huge stone piles beside and near the trail, and tufts of tall tan grasses. We followed a desolate dirt road several miles with no change in the stark terrain. I'd like to say it had a certain, indescribable beauty about it, but felt more as if it had been abandoned, forgotten by time.

The small community of Palmerton sat at the base of this section of Blue Mountain. For almost a century, from 1898 until 1980, the New Jersey Zinc Company had a smelting operation in the town, extracting zinc from anthracite coal they mined north of Palmerton. By the 1980s, the business shut down due to a poor market, but also, because of new environmental regulations. By that time, over 3000 acres of Blue Mountain had been destroyed by air and soil contamination. Toxic heavy metals from the zinc smelting contaminated the top six to eight inches of topsoil, rendering it sterile, while also polluting the groundwater and local streams, including the Aquishicola.

The Aquishicola Stream (meaning *where we fish with the bushnet*, named by the Lenni Lenape tribe), at the base of the mountain, meandered through Palmerton, then flowed into the Lehigh River. Blue mountain, the Aquishicola, the Lehigh River, Palmerton, and the entire valley were the first of the largest Environmental Protection Agency's Superfund clean-up sites east of the Mississippi River beginning in the late 1980s. The clean-up process, often contentious, has continued for the past forty years.

We trusted we were safe walking across this reclaimed area, though the notes did warn that the trail down to the Lehigh River required extreme care, not from contamination, but due to a steep, hazardous descent. Not wanting to succumb to superstition, and all the potential dire outcomes of climbing down this perilous route in the dark, I tried to push away the fact that it was *Friday the 13th!* The descent, according to the notes, had no clear pathway, the trail routed indeterminately over and around horse-sized boulders, with the occasional white blaze painted on a rock. But there was a less difficult blue-blazed trail.

It turned dark while crossing the ridgeline. When we finally arrived at the end of the dirt road, we still had not seen the blue-blazed trail. Panic set in, feeling we had missed it. The idea of going down the sketchy boulder trail in the dark did not appeal to either of us. But we kept moving forward, coming to the less treacherous blue-blazed path a short distance later.

Starting down this alternate route, our headlamps guiding us, we were still hoping to find a place to camp. Even in the dark, the area was dismal, as we switchbacked down a steep, treeless slope, the tread mostly easy, yet following a narrow ledge. After traversing several long switchbacks, we came to a pathway, more like a grassy road, though still not at the bottom of the mountain.

Cars raced past below us, headlights and taillights burning along the dark highway. Even though the trail was flat and wide enough for a tent, we were both weary from the long day and chose to move on, neither of us wishing to contend with the taxing thrum of traffic noise all night. After crossing the bridge over the Lehigh River, glad to leave behind the frenetic motorists whooshing by, we started up the next mountain, exhausted, with throbbing feet, having already hiked twenty miles.

At a spring beside the trail, two guys with headlamps were getting water. We knew we weren't far from the George W. Outerbridge Shelter, and asked about camping. They told us there was a campsite just above the shelter. I asked if they had a cell phone, wanting to call my sister, whom we planned to meet at Bake Oven Knob eight trail-miles away. They gladly offered their phone.

When I told my sister where we were, and that we would probably reach Bake Oven Knob shortly after noon, one o'clock at the latest, she said, "Nancy, it shouldn't take you more than a half hour to get there. It isn't that far!" I laughed to myself, reminding her it was eight miles, and that we were *walking*. To non-hikers—people accustomed to covering miles in minutes in their cars—the concept of *hiking ETAs* was a bit foreign.

Our plan was set; my sister, Sandra would meet us the next day. That night it stormed; driving rain, with gusty winds constantly rocking the tent. We were so glad to be camped among trees, much less exposed than we'd have been on that barren mountain.

Through mist and fog the next morning, we headed across another section of Blue Mountain where the Pennsylvania turnpike tunnels through the mountain, via the Lehigh Tunnel. From my vantage point on the A.T., roughly a thousand feet above the tunnel, I had hoped to see cars entering the Lehigh, but it was impossible with the limited visibility.

The Lehigh Tunnel opened to traffic in 1957. My family drove our old Hudson through it many times to vacation in the Pocono Mountains. As a young girl, I would often picture myself on top of the mountain above the tunnel, able to see tiny cars entering on the narrow two-lane highway below. Of course, back then, I didn't even know the Appalachian Trail crossed that ridge!

Though I couldn't see the cars as we hiked above the tunnel, at least I heard them. In 1991 an additional tunnel was added near the first, allowing two lanes of traffic in each direction. Lehigh is the only highway tunnel that runs under the Appalachian Trail.

A little before noon we negotiated Bake Oven Knob, a boulder-muddled mountaintop named for a strange dugout area in the shape of a bowl at its base, reminding early settlers of an old-fashioned bake oven. With its multitude of huge boulders, the knob demanded care, making us cautious of every step. Forty-five minutes later we arrived at the parking lot where Sandra waited. That evening at her apartment, she and I prepared veggie burgers, salad and other side dishes. My brother, Dick and his wife, Bonnie joined us for dinner where we all had a great time visiting and laughing. Lonnie kept us going with stories of our trail antics; though he is an introvert, in small groups he is quite the storyteller.

The next day, borrowing my sister's car, Lonnie and I drove to New Jersey to visit my daughter, Caryn and her husband Josh, and their seven-month-old son, Caleb. When we returned to Sandra's apartment, we found her standing by her closet door, camping equipment scattered across the entire floor. She looked up at us, "Did you have fun with your new grandson?"

I told her we had a great visit, then said, "What are you doing?"

"I've been trying to figure out how I could meet up with you so we could camp out together."

"Oh, wow," I said. "It looks like you have plenty of equipment for it." It appeared she was bringing everything but the kitchen sink. Oh, wait a minute, she had that, too! A blow-up version for camping.

"Did you figure out how we could camp together?" I asked. By now she had stopped pulling things out of the closet and looked serious.

"Yes. Blue Rocks Campground is about forty-five minutes from here, *driving time*, that is," she said, smiling, "which is still open. I've camped there before, but I'm not sure how far it is for you to hike. There is a side trail to the campground from the A.T." We studied the notes, and discovered to make it work Lonnie and I would skip the five-mile section from Bake Oven Knob to Route 309, which would have been too many miles to hike in one day. (I did hike that section by myself several years later.)

The next morning, she drove us to the road crossing. "See you in about seventeen miles!" I said, as we hugged and hoped this would work. She had a lot to do, getting her camping gear in order, then setting up her tent at the campground.

"I'll have dinner cooking." she said. "Just follow the smell of food. See you later!"

I adjusted my pack, which now had only the things we needed for the day; water, a bit of food, maps, and other essentials. The rest of our gear was loaded in her car so we'd be able to resume our hike from the campground the following morning. As she was pulling from the parking lot, Lonnie said to me, "Do you feel this is going to work out okay?"

I understood his concern, and felt a bit of dread watching our gear heading down the highway. Even though my sister said there was a side trail to the campground, that didn't mean it would be marked, or that there'd be a sign or any way of knowing where it led, or if it would even be there. Lonnie and I passed numerous side trails all the time that had no designation. Since we didn't have cell phones, we had to trust. Hopefully, we would be able to find her and the campsite, or we'd be spending the night huddled together in our coats.

Walking atop the ridge, we passed the road that led to the Hawk Mountain Sanctuary. The A.T. skirts this world-famous site dedicated to the conservation of birds of prey. The HMS maintains this area as a model observation, research and education facility. Watching for hawks on these mountain tops was quite popular. Unfortunately, we could not take time to walk up the mountain to it.

Two weeks earlier in New Jersey, we came across two guys on a rocky ledge using a plastic owl atop a post as an incentive for hawks and other birds of prey to approach. The men searched the sky with binoculars. One of them had told us, "Once we saw a peregrine falcon fly across the valley and dive for an owl."

After leaving the Hawk Mountain Road, we began the five-mile climb to the Pinnacle overlook which was down a side trail. Nearing dark, with nearly a half-mile to the campground side trail (according to the notes), we chose to skip the overlook.

Darkness was closing in when we found the side trail. Trudging down this rutted-out trail over rocks and exposed roots demanded extra caution. Lonnie took a nasty spill on one of the roots, dropping him down on his tailbone. Luckily his backpack took the brunt of the impact. When the trail flattened out at the bottom of the slope, I scanned the campground, and saw a light to our right. "Somebody's over there," I said. "Do you see that light?"

"Yeah, I see it now. Let's hope it's your sister."

When I saw her car, I called out, "Hey, Girl!"

Sandra yelled back, "You made it!"

Lanterns hung from posts jammed into the soft dirt, illuminating the chairs and her humungous tent, which looked like it could easily accommodate ten people. Her intention had been to use it with groups for hiking adventures, but she had yet to do that. After having a tour of all her equipment and her massive tent, which Lonnie quickly nicknamed *The Taj Mahal*, we sat around like car campers, ate salmon, broccoli and salads, told stories, and enjoyed the second campfire of our hike. That night Lonnie and I slept side by side, but this time there was another person ten feet away.

The next morning, while Lonnie and I lounged around on camp chairs, Sandra treated us to a breakfast of eggs, pancakes, and toast browned between two mesh holders over the open fire; a nice change from cereal in a metal cup. After breakfast we planned to climb the three-mile trail from the campground to an overlook on the Appalachian Trail. Since Lonnie and I figured to head out from there, we carried our full packs.

Leaving the Blue Rocks Campground, the three of us, my sister carrying a small daypack, crossed fields of large blue rocks. When the glaciers melted, the boulders left behind were an amazing shade of cerulean blue, resembling a sea made of rocks. The precarious span of boulders took a long time to cross, especially for my sister, who heeded each step, cautiously moving forward, careful not to trip and fall. The rocks were tricky. I gave her one of my hiking poles to steady herself; she hadn't experienced the seven miles of Wolf Rocks Lonnie and I did a few days earlier, or the thousand miles of hiking over the past few months.

Our reward for this intense climb was a scenic vista of Pennsylvania farmland. Past the fall colors of nearby trees, we saw patches of brown fields mingled with green 1500 feet below us, the valley spotted with houses and barns. All around us on the flat overlook were weathered stumps of natural sandstone, the area called Pulpit Rocks, so named because the individual formations resembled a preacher's pulpit.

Beginning 390 million years ago, this area had been covered by an inland sea where these pillars formed from multiple layers of sandstone separated by thick layers of limestone laid down over the centuries. We sat on several chair-sized structures, remnants of the pillars, enjoying the tranquility of the moment, Lonnie and I debating what to do. Already three pm, it seemed too late to resume our hike. Without too much hesitation he and I looked at each other, and headed back down with my sister to spend one more night as *car campers*. We drove to nearby Hamburg and the Kings Supermarket, where we bought more food, then returned to the campsite for another fun evening eating and enjoying the campfire.

The next morning after breakfast, it *really* was time to move on, though it was sad to leave. We helped my sister take down the *Taj*, then gathered up all her camping equipment and packed it in her car. After hugs and sad goodbyes, she wished us a great rest of our journey.

Later that day we headed into Port Clinton, a short walk from the trail, to pick up our resupply box. Rain was forecasted, so after eating dinner at the Port Clinton hotel, we decided to stay, our first night in an old trail hotel. We had a wall-papered room with a small television, a simple brown dresser, the bed and two wooden chairs, the bathroom down the hall. There was an old-world feeling to the place, especially since we kind of felt like *pioneers* hiking the trail. Though at this point, it seemed we were doing more lodging and lounging than hiking!

The Port Clinton hotel began in the early 1800s as a stagecoach stop between Philadelphia and Sunbury, a hundred and fifty miles apart. It became a great social center, with patrons signing the hotel register, then adding any news they thought might be of common interest. How ironic; that's what A.T. hikers do when they stay in trail towns and sign the hiker books found in hotels, motels, and gear stores, often leaving their names and notes for other hikers. News and information traveled up and down the trail through these logbooks, just as it had with the travelers two hundred years ago!

When we left the next morning, after spending so much *easy* time over the past few days, we decided to push more miles; Springer was still a long way off. I suggested that fatigue might be mitigated during the long days if we rested and ate something every five miles or so, maybe even taking our shoes off to rub our feet for a few minutes. These rests made the day go faster, leaving us refreshed and ready to move on.

We arrived at the Hertlein Campsite near dusk—an eighteen-mile day. Two older, local guys were cooking steaks on a makeshift grill over a campfire. They asked numerous questions about our journey. While they ate their steaks, we satisfied their curiosity, sharing our stories. I supposed if we were meat-eaters our mouths would have been watering, but we were more concerned about bears coming around, hoping the guys cleaned up well. When we woke to sunshine, with our food bag still hanging safe and secure, all was good.

At the end of the next day, darkness fell quickly as the trail led down into Swatara Gap. After going under Route 81, the highway running from Tennessee to New York, we crossed the walking bridge over Swatara Creek thinking we might camp on the other side, but the bank sloped too steeply to the creek for a tent. Houses sat nearby along the road, with no places to camp. The notes never mentioned Swatara Creek as a water source, though it could have been polluted. Nevertheless, we filtered enough to cook dinner and for use overnight. We ate our meal by headlamp sitting on the edge of the walking bridge, then headed up the mountain to search for a flat place for the night.

After finding a spot, we set up, and in the morning, were surprised to find the trail around the tent site overgrown with weeds. Very odd for the A.T. to be weed-choked with all the foot traffic. Nevertheless, after packing up, we followed the weed strewn trail down a slope, arriving at another trail which went in two directions. That made no sense to us, especially with no visible white blazes either way.

A guy happened by and told us it was definitely the Appalachian Trail. We turned the way that felt right, hiking for about fifteen minutes, when I saw a bridge up ahead, though, according to the notes, there shouldn't have been. It looked a lot like the one we'd eaten dinner on the night before, but now in the daylight, I wasn't sure. About the same time, Lonnie and I both realized it *was* the Swatara walking bridge! It took a few minutes to figure out that we were headed north instead of south, unable to process how we had gone in a circle.

Retracing our steps, we came to the tree we had seen the night before, with a faded blaze, that now in the daylight revealed a rough pathway that turned to the left, swallowed by knee-high weeds. Obviously, in the dark, we mistook this abandoned trail for the actual one, following the old Appalachian Trail up the mountain. Not realizing it at the time, we got ourselves straightened out by following a spur trail back down the mountain that had rejoined the current Appalachian Trail. After our little snafu, we were finally heading in the right direction, moving south once again.

Later in the day the trail dissected a coal mining area called Rausch Gap, that thrived from 1830 until 1910. At the height of Rausch Gaps' coal production, over a thousand people toiled to carve out a living in the various communities dotting the area, all connected to working with the mines or the railroad, which by 1854 was a fifty-one-mile railway. By 1872, the rail headquarters had left the area, which marked the beginning of the community's decline. By 1900 the area was basically deserted.

Near the Rausch Gap Shelter I thought about all those who struggled to live and work there. It's rumored that Rausch Gap is haunted, that when the railroad left, and the community fell apart, some who died there, may never *have* left—remaining as *ghosts*. Where the trail crossed Rausch Creek there's a side trail to a small cemetery from the 1850s; I was glad it was still daylight. Along this stretch of trail for almost seven miles, we followed a nice flat path, most likely the railroad bed, since the tracks had been removed in 1945.

That evening we crossed over Stony Mountain, easily finding a place to camp by a stream on the way down.

25

REALLY NICE KIDS

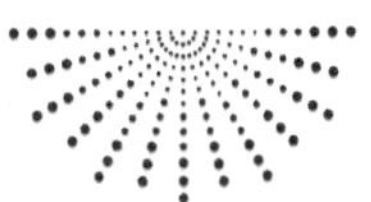

After Stony, the trail led up six hundred feet to the ridgeline known as Peters Mountain, where we traversed fifteen miles across, spotting the Susquehanna River through the foliage, the longest river in eastern United States. Approaching Duncannon, I thought of Molly and Geoff, knowing this was their last trail town.

"Are you ready for a snack?" I said.

Lonnie turned around. "I thought we were out of food."

"I have a surprise."

He stopped at a fallen log. I sat down and took out a tuna pack. Using our plastic sporks, quite an ingenious little tool—a spoon and fork in one—we enjoyed that tuna right from the pack.

"I never thought a plain old packet of tuna would taste so good," Lonnie said.

I agreed. But now that late afternoon sugar craving needed gratification. I didn't tell him I had one Rollo left in my pocket. I sucked on them as I hiked which made them last longer, while he chewed his up. So, I opted not to share, figuring what he didn't know wouldn't hurt him. Besides, in my defense, I knew of the restaurant at the bottom of the mountain, where the trail crossed the highway and the Susquehanna River, then led into Duncannon.

The descent had numerous pockets of boulders, made all the more difficult by our throbbing feet from the long day. Dark clouds were gathering over the mountain. We had just started down a series of switchbacks when the rain came, light at first, quickly turning into a torrent. We hurried to put on rain jackets and pack covers, even though in a downpour like this, everything would still get wet; some peculiar mechanics of the trail.

My mind had been on Molly and Geoff all day. Descending this same mountain nineteen years earlier, they had not known this would begin the last two days of their hike... and their lives. I wondered what kind of day it was for them as they came down the mountain, and if they were looking forward to town food as much as we were.

With their memory filling my thoughts, I noticed a white moth, then another, and another, which seemed odd for this time of year, a few days before Thanksgiving. Hundreds of white moths fluttered near where Lonnie and I were hiking.

I looked back to him and said, "Do you see these?"

Quietly he answered, "Yeah, I see them."

We both stood watching, the white moths like snowflakes filling the sky around us. Apparently seeing a white moth is a harbinger of good news, indicating positivity, hope and peace.

As we proceeded down the mountain, it was difficult to say where they went, if they had just flown away, or blended into the overcast sky and disappeared, but their presence impacted both of us. They were not to be the last unusual phenomenon as we descended toward Duncannon.

Just as we started across the highway, thousands of starlings coalesced into an undulating fabric against the gray sky, moving in sync, rolling and swaying as one entity. Neither of us spoke. This marvel, known as a murmuration, is a natural phenomenon that still remains a mystery to scientists. We had seen things like this before, but this time it was special, watching in awe as the birds moved in one direction, then in unison another, hovering over the river as we found our way across the Clarks Ferry bridge, cars and trucks carrying workers, heading home from Harrisburg. Wrapped in a cacophony of traffic, we moved in silence, both of us under a spell.

By the time we reached the truck stop, the rain had eased to a drizzle. Leaving our packs outside the restaurant, we hobbled to a table, our feet still throbbing and burning. I looked at the menu and wanted everything. I was so hungry. It took about ten minutes to get our order in.

After the waitress left, I got up to use the restroom and wash my hands, and found I could barely move my feet, the pain so bad. I tried shuffling away several inches at a time, Lonnie fighting back laughter at how ridiculous I must have looked. After hiking eighteen miles, then sitting down to rest, the stiffness set in. It was a common occurrence, but we still found it funny and ironic, that we could hike all day, then sit for just a few moments and were practically unable to move.

Finishing our scrumptious meal, we needed to find a place to stay for the night. George, the manager of a nearby motel, said he had a room, and even picked us up.

Cars rushed by on the rain-soaked highway outside our room, noises we were not accustomed to sleeping in the tent. Lying in bed, dry and warm, I thought about our hike, and what tomorrow would bring. How would I feel climbing out of Duncannon, up the mountain, nearing the very place where Molly and Geoff were murdered? I remembered those white moths we had seen earlier that afternoon. People say that sometimes butterflies come to those who are remembering someone who passed. Our visitors weren't butterflies, but they were beautiful and awe-inspiring.

George from the motel graciously drove us into Duncannon the next morning. We ate breakfast at Goodie's, a small restaurant on the main street. With rain still falling, Dry Mouth showed up. He had recognized our packs outside the restaurant, and decided to join us for breakfast. Since there weren't many hikers heading south, our packs stood out for him. Dry Mouth had stayed an extra day at The Mayor's in New York, and we hadn't seen him since we left. Him showing up at our table was a welcome surprise. He had come into town the night before and stayed at the Doyle Hotel across the street.

Eating breakfast, we joked about how we couldn't move our feet the evening before, just the way his feet were at the Mayor's. Waiting out the rain, and caught up in conversation, we sat so long it was time for lunch. Dry Mouth suggested we go across the street to the Doyle.

While we sat at the bar, Vicki, one of the owners, took our pictures for her hotel scrap book of hikers, which she'd been doing for several years. I asked her if she was there when Molly and Geoff were killed. "No, but I heard about it."

She changed the subject and asked, "Now, do you two have orange to wear up on that mountain?" She looked right at Lonnie and me. Apparently, Dry Mouth had already heard the lecture.

"Yes, we have orange hats," I said.

She seemed to ignore my response. "Now let me tell you why you want to be wearing orange." Vicki went to the sliding glass door of the cooler and pulled out a six-pack of beer, clomping it down on the bar in front of us. "This is why you need to have orange. And the more orange the better."

Being from Pennsylvania, I knew it was almost deer season. Young boys couldn't wait to be old enough to go out with their dads and shoot their first deer. Where I had lived and taught, the entire school district would shut down for the first day of buck hunting season, the Monday after Thanksgiving. (It was widely known the school super-intendent was a deer enthusiast.)

Many hunters would play cards and drink beer until the early hours, then be out in the woods before dawn. All in the name of hunting and getting their buck. "You just never know what those hunters have been doing before they enter the woods," Vicki added, putting the beer back in the cooler. We understood and assured her we would be careful.

After signing Vicki's thru-hiker registration book, we noticed the rain had almost stopped. We looked at Dry Mouth and he looked at us and we all said together, "Time to hit the trail."

It was late afternoon when we headed up the mountain. An interesting thing happens when you leave town. As soon as you place your foot on the trail, your connection to society is severed, as if you've entered a different universe. You're on the trail, not in town anymore. Whatever you're carrying will have to be enough until you arrive in the next town, which can be many miles away. We climbed the steep slope, the afternoon turning to a misty, cold blackness by the time we reached the ridge.

I wondered what Molly's and Geoff's thoughts were as they got back on the trail, not realizing they were heading up the last slope they would ever climb. The night before their death they stayed at the Doyle Hotel. Paul Nussbaum wrote in the Philadelphia Inquirer, "Tim Yeoman who was the bartender at that time, pulled down the traditional book that all thru-hikers sign from where he kept it on top of the beer cooler. When the pair saw the last entry that indicated it may be by the last southbounder, they had to reply: 'Hey Greenhorn, you most certainly are not the last entry of the season. As you can't read this, we'll tell you when we catch you! As we hear it, we're about mid-slip of the south bounders moving down. Oops. Getting food on the book. Good food, too, time to go.' Clevis and Nalgene." Tim Yeoman also said, according to Nussbaum, "They were really nice kids. They talked a lot about working with delinquent kids --- they liked helping people."[1]

Molly and Geoff were by themselves as they proceeded over the rock ridge toward the Thelma Marks Shelter. Had Molly developed a rhythm as she maneuvered over the rocks, finding it easy to proceed, each foot bouncing, or balancing, from one rock to the next? I learned years later, according to her dad, that at this point in their hike, their boots were falling apart. Their families were planning on meeting them in about a week at Harpers Ferry. "Don't forget to bring me new boots!" Molly had requested when she talked with her parents the day before. I suppose she was not able to bounce along on the rocks. Geoff had hinted to his mother when he called from Duncannon

---

1. Paul Nussbaum, *"For two hikers, the Appalachian Trail led to death,"* Philadelphia Inquirer, September 20, 1990.

on September 11th, that if he couldn't find boots there, maybe she could get a pair for him in Harpers Ferry, maybe an early birthday present. He even added, "Bring a bucket and scrub brushes so we can clean our sleeping bags, and if you can, a pumpkin pie, too."

Molly and Geoff in Kent, Connecticut. (Photo: another hiker)

Molly's great aunt, who lived a short distance from Duncannon, came to have lunch with them the day before. While listening to their stories, her Aunt Kay said later, "I had never seen Molly so radiant." During their stay, Geoff took time to send his sister a birthday gift, who was turning twenty-two on September 13th. It was a button with a portrait of Gandhi on one side, *and on the other, the words, "Practice Nonviolence." His sister, later, wore it each day at the trial.[2] On September 13th 1990, around five o'clock in the afternoon, a couple of hikers, a man and his wife, found them at the Thelma Marks Shelter. According to authorities, they had been killed sometime early that morning.*

In the following months, many messages were left in the Thelma Marks shelter journal for the pair. David DeKok wrote, "one message dated October 18th, 1990, included: 'Sad to realize (that) horrible things can happen to people who are in the process of enjoying such peace and solitude while wandering through the woods.'"[3]

DeKok added that someone had placed a small plaque on an oak tree with Molly's and Geoff's names and birthdates. "At the base of the (oak) tree, in a circle of stones, are two pine seedlings. No one... knows who placed them there."[4]

Ten years later, as reported by Tim Craig in the Baltimore Sun, in 2000, the Thelma Marks Shelter was burned down. The ashes were spread over the grounds of the new structure, not far away from where the Thelma Marks stood. Forty-six volunteers from the Maryland Mountain Club, which maintains thirty miles of the A.T. in Pennsylvania and eight miles in Maryland, spent 4,000 hours building the shelter, which is made out of recycled timber from a nearby barn. Their parents did not want the shelter named after them. There had been a memorial ceremony at the new shelter in the fall of 2000. Jim LaRue said, "This is a memorial to life, not death. We don't want people remembering the death. This is about affirming life."[5]

It was pitch black when we arrived at the side trail to the shelter. Lonnie looked at me and asked, "Do you want to go down?" I knew a new shelter had been built, though I did wonder if there was some-

---

2. Paul Nussbaum, *"Trail killer sentenced to death"*, Philadelphia Inquirer, Sunday, May 26, 1991.
3. David DeKok, *"The trail leads to W. Virginia"*, Patriot News, March 11, 1991.
4. David DeKok, *"The trail leads to W. Virginia"*, Patriot News, March 11, 1991.
5. Tim Craig, *Parents' grief leads to comfort*, The Baltimore Sun, October 23, 2000.

thing there in their memory. I simply answered, "No, let's go on." They were constantly on my mind. Fascinating how things go; Lonnie and Dry Mouth were busy in conversation in the lead, which gave me time to be alone with my thoughts. When we still had several miles to the next shelter, I stopped and yelled ahead to them, "Hey, I have to go to the bathroom." The night air had gotten very cold and it was still drizzly. At least it wasn't snowing. But later my hands were freezing. I hadn't realized I had left both of my gloves lying on the ground after my potty break.

From Duncannon, we had hiked twelve miles, arriving at the Darlington Shelter. That night Dry Mouth stayed in the shelter. There was such dense fog, that once Lonnie and I found a tent site, we had to talk each other back to it when we went to the bathroom. Even our headlamps couldn't guide us; the fog was so thick.

We were impressed with Dry Mouth's backwoods ingenuity. He was determined to start a fire to get enough heat to boil water for his dinner. When we left, he had smoke going in the fire pit, but with the damp wood, the flames were hard to rouse. Lonnie and I fired up our Jet Boil and had no problem getting dinner ready. With the meal cooked, and us tucked in our sleeping bags, we shared our dinner in silence, both of us unable to escape thoughts of the tragedy that had occurred only a few miles from where we were camped.

AN EXPLOSION OF SWEAR WORDS

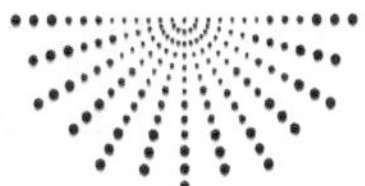

*E*d, a friend, planned to pick us up in Boiling Springs for Thanksgiving, fourteen trail-miles away, so we packed up early. Dry Mouth, still in his sleeping bag at the shelter, saw us, and said, "Bye." He woke up enough to add, "Hey, I did get enough fire to boil my noodles!"

"Yay for you, Dry Mouth! You earned the *Boy Scout Fire Starter When Everything Is Wet* badge!" Lonnie said, as all of us laughed.

Through fog, not as intense as the evening before, we wandered up the trail to a more populated area, past rows of field corn waiting to be harvested for animal stock, frequent wooded areas and several road crossings. A few hours later we heard footsteps behind us, Dry Mouth catching up. It was nice to see him again. He and Lonnie seemed to pick up their conversation from the previous evening, and I followed behind.

At one point I yelled, "Hold up. I've got to stop and take off my boots." Between the tall weeds, wet grass, and muddy areas, my socks now squished like a sponge. I plopped down on the ground, slipped off my left, wet, stinky sock, and couldn't believe what I saw.

"My little toenail's gone!" I said, but the guys didn't care. At least they stopped to wait for me, continuing their conversation. I was shocked, not by Lonnie and Dry Mouth, but wondering if a new one would grow back.

Since that day I've learned that shedding toe nails is a common thing on the often-wet Appalachian Trail. My toe didn't hurt, just felt weird. I decided to wait until I arrived at Boiling Springs to change my socks, since I didn't want to have another pair drenched and smelly. This section of trail led us across more farmland, the bridge over Route 81, the Pennsylvania turnpike, dumping us out in a matrix of roads in forested neighborhoods. In the middle of a mowed field was a single tree, very zen, barren of leaves, all alone.

We eventually walked along another road for a short distance, the white blazes leading us into the small community of Boiling Springs, named for its natural artesian wells. On the corner, across from the Appalachian Trail Conference's Mid-Atlantic Regional Office, sat a pizza place. (Now this office is located in the nearby town of Carlisle.)

The timing worked out nicely since Ed picked us up right after we finished eating. It was sad to leave Dry Mouth all alone, and I wondered if we would see him again. (We did run into him much later. He told us that on Thanksgiving morning he came across a day hiker, an older woman, who invited him to her place for dinner, so he wasn't alone out in the woods eating a granola bar for the holiday.)

Ed and his girlfriend drove us to his home near Philadelphia. What a delightful zero day we had, celebrating Thanksgiving, and eating enormous amounts of food.

On Friday afternoon, he returned us to the trail. We reached Dogwood Run Creek just before dark, and found a clearing with a flat spot for the campsite. As I set up the tent and our gear, Lonnie scouted for the best tree branch for our bear bag, a fairly large Sea to Summit sack containing all our food, trash items, as well as Chap-Stick, cough drops, toothpaste, toothbrushes—anything with a smell. We would hang it from a branch about twelve feet high and at least four to six feet out from the tree trunk. For the thousand miles of our hike, it had been working well. (Now we use a bear vault canister which we secure between logs, tree trunks, or roots as well as a bear resistant bag we securely tie around a tree. Each year new equipment is available to make hiking easier.)

Once Lonnie found the perfect limb for our food bag, he'd find a rock, place it in a six-inch by four-inch canvas pouch attached with a clip to a lightweight rope and swing it up over the limb. Then he'd tie it off on a nearby tree until we were done eating and ready to stow all our smelly items away from nosey bears. The last step involved pulling the food bag up about twelve feet above the ground, then tying the rope back on the tree to secure our food out of reach for the night.

Pennsylvania is well-known for its rocks, but in this particular campsite, not even in the creek, were there any rocks to weight our canvas bag for the initial toss. Lonnie thought, "What do I have in my pack that will work?" He found the perfect size bag, his small blue Sea to Summit containing enough stuff to give it a good weight for throwing. He tied the bag to the rope and swung it back and forth to get the height for the limb. Meanwhile, I organized our things in the tent.

All of a sudden, I heard an explosion of swear words! I looked over and saw his blue bag up on the limb, stuck on some small tree stubble… I knew exactly what was in that bag that was now stuck in the tree. On the trail it had been important for Lonnie to know where all his things were located so he had different colored bags for the various items. In that particular bag was his toilet paper and hand sanitizer, now about fourteen feet above the ground with no town for the next several days. Lonnie always felt good when he found that perfect limb to hang our food, but he did not expect this. With the work of both of us tugging on the rope, and a long stick to poke at it, his toilet paper finally came free, and with the rope nicely strung over the limb.

Through the night, the cold wind howled in the trees and blew all the next day, as if winter were closing fast. It was almost dark, a steady, dreary rain and frosty chill in the air, when we arrived at the Pine Grove Furnace State Park, opened year-round. By the late 1800s, the trees on this mountain and the ones to our south had all been cleared. The wood was burned in furnaces to smelt iron—the Caledonia and Michaux Furnaces south of here, and this one, the Pine Grove Furnace, now the name for the state park.

Built in 1764, it was used to forge iron into ten-plate stoves, iron kettles, fireplace backs, and munitions during the Revolutionary War. In 1864, Pine Grove Furnace became the South Mountain Iron Company. John Birkinbine, in 1877, became the furnace's engineer who realized the forests were dwindling, and determined that the furnace could still run on coal and coke.

By the 1890s there was a restoration program beginning around the country to bring back the lost wilderness. Birkinbine became a founding member of the Pennsylvania Forestry Association. When the Pennsylvania government wanted to buy these lands, the iron companies complied, since there were no more trees to cut down to run their mills.

The Pine Grove furnace remains are still visible along the trail. When we reached the Pine Grove Furnace State Park parking lot, day hikers were milling about. I found one who had a phone and borrowed it to call a friend from college who lived nearby. I had hoped to visit her while on our journey, but there was no answer. With the temperature now below freezing, and nightfall an hour or so away, we waited until everyone left the park, then set up our tent on a grassy area near the restrooms.

We had discovered that not only were the restrooms open, but they were *heated!* Inside the women's room there was even a bench to sit on. We cooked our dinner outside, then ate it sitting on that bench, which on this wintry night was a welcome refuge. We lingered there until dark, then ran to the tent, crawled inside our sleeping bags, and placed our down coats around our heads to keep our ears and necks warm.

Outside, a wintry, frigid wind screamed through the trees, but our ten-degree bags kept us warm. In the morning, with the park deserted, we ate our cereal sitting on that bench in the warm bathroom.

The next evening, nearing dark, we descended to the Caledonia State Park after hiking almost twenty miles, mostly up and down on the ridge line. It was Sunday, November 29th. Deer season would begin the next day. We still had Michaux Mountain to cross, with only eighteen miles to go before entering Maryland. Following trail signs through the state park, we came to Route 30.

The notes indicated Taormina's pizza and ice cream shop three-tenths of a mile down the highway, and was supposed to be open till ten, so we hoped that was still true. When we spotted lights, and cars in the parking lot, we were thrilled. We hoped to eat and then figure out what to do. As soon as we sat down and ordered, the waitress asked, "Are you hiking the trail?"

"Yes, we're headed south."

"You don't want to be up there on Michaux Mountain tomorrow. It's the first day of deer season, and during the whole deer season, it's never good to be up there."

We stared at one another; now what? When she came with our food, she added, "There's too many guys up there who can't see straight, and would easily mistake you for a deer. No sir, I would not want to be up there hiking across."

A group of older guys sat in the booth adjacent to ours and added, "No, you don't want to be up there for the next two weeks."

Numerous people we saw along the trail warned us that many hunters, especially around the Michaux State Forest area, may very well be under the influence of Jack Daniels as they hunted. We trusted everyone's judgement, so when I saw in the guide book the Rite Spot Motel was down the road three and a half miles, and another customer offered to give us a ride, our decision was made. I was bummed we didn't get out of Pennsylvania before the season started. Just one day too late! But maybe this was the actual *right spot* for us after all.

27

EYES IN THE NIGHT

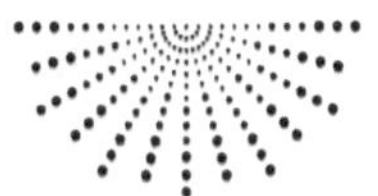

In the morning, I called my friend, Avis. She was excited to pick us up, but couldn't come until the following day. We bed-blazed and relaxed the rest of the day at the motel. Early the next morning, Lonnie and I visited with her over breakfast in Chambersburg sharing lots of stories from our hike. Then after a quick stop at Starbucks to have our favorite Frappuccino, Avis drove us to the trailhead on Route 16. As she pulled away, Lonnie and I looked back across the road to the trail heading north up Michaux Mountain, sad to miss that section in Pennsylvania, but felt it was the safest thing to do.

We entered Maryland, our ninth state, just before the Pen Mar County Park. In the late 1800s and early 1900s a trolley took fun-seekers to the park from Baltimore. Known as the *Coney Island* of the Blue Ridge, there was a roller coaster, merry-go-round, fun house, and a miniature railroad. A three-story hotel housed four hundred guests. Those things are gone, but today on summer weekends in the last remaining pavilion, bands perform and a small museum opens to entertain guests with the park's rousing history.

Three miles later, we climbed to High Rock, surprised to see lots of people, but then discovered a parking lot a short walk later. This is the highest mountain in Maryland on the A.T., at 1,950 feet. The summit consisted of a series of boulders culminating with a flat slab rock which also served as the perfect departure point for hang-gliders. Far below, a gridwork of fields and woods dissected the countryside against the backdrop of Blue Mountain in the distance. But even with all this beauty, I found myself distracted by the plethora of graffiti desecrating the overlook; garish colors, spray-painted names, symbols and glyphs, destroying the natural summit of boulders and exposed rock. I suppose some people relish these adornments.

After a day of rain, the sun and blue skies returned as we arrived at the Washington Monument, not the one in Washington D.C, but, the original monument built to honor our first president. Damp, with no windows, the stone tower felt dungeon-like as we climbed twenty or so steps to the top. A plaque explained that the people of Boonsboro in Washington County of Maryland built this tower and dedicated it to the memory of George Washington.

Boonsboro had had a slow start with just a few families when it was founded in 1792. By 1803 there were twenty-four families. But when the National Road was built, their little town grew. Early on the morning of July 4th, 1827, Boonsboro citizens gathered at 7:30 am to climb South Mountain above their village, with one townsperson leading the group carrying the Stars and Stripes. They started building the tower that day, and by nightfall, it was fifteen feet high. They returned to Boonsboro to finish celebrating their first Independence Day. In September, town volunteers returned and completed the forty-foot tower.

During the Civil War, the Union Army used the tower as a signal station. Fighting during this phase of the war up and down and across South Mountain became known as the South Mountain Battle. By 1922, the Washington County Historical Society owned the tower and the land around it. During the 1930s, the Conservation Corps restored it to its original condition. By 1934, it was donated to Maryland for a state park. Today the entire forty-mile ridge from the Pennsylvania border to the Potomac River is considered the South Mountain State Park.

At the tower, we took the opportunity to dry our tent, soaked from several days of rain. We draped the tent fly over a short piece of nylon rope between two trees, holding it with a few plastic clothespins. There was no American flag flying on the mountain that day, but we did have our orange tent fly flapping in the breeze.

Eventually we headed down to Gathland State Park, our last few miles in Maryland. When we walked out of the woods, the trail opened up onto a field with picnic tables. I thought about camping there, but we needed water.

Fifty yards later, we crossed the two-lane Gathland Road which came up from one side of the ridge, then over the narrow crest and down the other side. Beside us stood an enormous archway. We were taken aback by the impressive style and size of this stone monument, dedicated to war correspondents of the Civil War. It was fifty feet tall and forty feet wide, decorated with parapets, and three arched openings representing, Depiction, Description, and Photography's Light, aspects of the war correspondent's pursuits.

George Alfred Townsend, 1841-1914, purchased this land and designed the arch and buildings for his home and estate. He was a war correspondent during the Civil War, writing under the pen name, *Gath*: his greatest achievement, the majestic Memorial Arch. It is the first memorial in the world dedicated to journalists killed in combat; today considered a National Historic Monument.

The trail followed a park road that led to the two remaining structures of Gapland, Townsend's name for his estate. Gapland Hall, which was his eleven-room home, is now a visitors' center and the second structure is a museum of Townsends' work. Since it was early December, both of these buildings were closed, along with the public restrooms. The drinking fountain outside the restrooms was also shut off.

With no way to replenish our depleted water supply, we were debating what to do when an official SUV pulled into the nearby parking lot. Two uniformed officers, a man and woman, the local sheriff and a deputy marshal, stepped toward us carrying a piece of paper with a man's photo on it. They didn't even ask if we were thru-hikers; they could tell just by looking at us.

The woman held up the wanted poster and asked, "Have you seen this man?" We studied the poster of the blonde-haired man with piercing blue eyes. I shook my head.

Lonnie said, "No, we haven't seen him. What's he wanted for?"

"He fled after being indicted for drug trafficking," said the deputy marshal. "We believe he's hiding on the trail. We combed the area south of here yesterday, but we believe he's somewhere on the A.T., we just don't know where."

Lonnie said, "Is he dangerous?"

"We don't think so, probably not to civilians, but we don't know."

"Does he have a gun?"

"We don't know."

They left, with us just standing there dumbfounded, attempting to figure what this could mean for our hike. We still needed water and would have to go to the next shelter, the Ed Garvey, named for the 1970 A.T. thru-hiker and past president of the Potomac Appalachian Trail Club. Climbing up to the ridge, Lonnie in the lead, me following, I continually looked behind us as we moved across the crest. We stayed close together for the four miles until we stopped at the side trail that led to the shelter.

"What do you think we should do?" Lonnie asked. "I don't feel so good staying at that shelter tonight."

After looking at the notes, I said, "Water is a half-mile down a steep side trail past the shelter."

"You know we have everything on our backs this man needs," Lonnie said with concern.

I thought of Molly and Geoff; they hadn't even known a killer was on the trail.

By this time, it was past dusk, and without hesitation, we decided to hike to the next town, Harpers Ferry, which meant adding more miles to our already very long eighteen-mile day. Even though it would have been nice to be settling down in our tent, our feet already hurting, neither of us wanted to spend the night in the woods.

I read the notes, then said to Lonnie, "We have just a little way to finish this ridge before we start down. Once off the mountain, it looks like we're hiking along a highway. Maybe there'll be a motel nearby."

We put on our headlamps, hiked across the now dark ridge to the end of the mountain and started down seventeen switchbacks. Near some car-sized boulders uphill from the trail, we heard a clicking noise. We both stopped, looked behind us, then up at the large rocks, but didn't see anything. When we heard it a second time, my feet were so close to Lonnie's you would have thought we were one person. We moved on, never looking back.

Nearing the bottom of the mountain, Lonnie stopped and whispered, "Stay close, there's someone up ahead without a headlamp." I visualized the wanted man from the poster. Looking past Lonnie, my headlamp illuminated two eyes shining back at me, but they were low to the ground. It turned out to be two guys with day packs and a dog. We offered our light to help them get down off the mountain, but they declined, so we scooted around them.

At the bottom, we found a desolate road and small parking area, and kept moving, hoping to come to water or lodging. The trail turned weedy, cutting through thick, dark woods. When I heard water flowing below us, I was hopeful, but the area was overgrown with dense weeds and brush, the stream sounding a significant distance down the hill and most likely unreachable. I took a sip of water from my nearly empty bottle.

A short while later, hearing traffic, I thought we might be coming to the highway, and hopefully, a motel. The trail continued descending, but the highway didn't, and we soon found ourselves walking beneath an underpass, a major highway above us, the trail taking us through a dark tangle of trees and brush.

"I have to stop and eat something," I said, suddenly hungry. As I munched on a bar, I looked at the notes again. "We have to cross some railroad tracks, then walk the towpath of the canal for—" I stopped reading, unable to believe my eyes, then blurted, "We have to go another two and a half miles!" At this point I wasn't even sure I could go another two and a half feet.

The towpath, a pathway for mules pulling barges, was part of the Chesapeake and Ohio Canal system, that extends from the Georgetown section of Washington D.C. to Cumberland, Md., a length of 184.5 miles. Interestingly, construction of the canal began on July 4th, 1828, one year after the Boonsboro citizens began building their Washington monument, but this major undertaking would not be completed until 1850.

Mules walked this towpath pulling mostly coal barges east. By 1924, railroads became the major method of moving coal and other products east. In 1961, President Eisenhower established the towpath as a national monument. Today, bicyclists and walkers enjoy the scenic atmosphere of this historical pathway. I guess I should have felt differently hiking on this portion of history, but there was nothing fun about this dismal stretch of trail on this black night.

The eerie darkness wrapped around the narrow cones of our headlamps, the only light in our world. After crossing the tracks, we were finally on the towpath. Woods and tall cattails rose on our left, with the canal on the right. I noticed a smell, and assumed any water in the canal had to be stagnant.

Lonnie, who was in front of me, stopped and looked to his left, his headlamp shining toward the woods. In one motion, he lifted his trekking poles, pointing them at the woods as if to protect himself. I looked over to my left in the same direction, where I saw what had led him to his defensive posture—five sets of glowing eyes, illuminated by my headlamp, staring back from the edge of absolute blackness!

He whispered, "Let's get out of here." Wolves or wild dogs? Ready to pounce? But we didn't wait around to find out. Lonnie had thought the same thing, but didn't mention anything until we had put some distance between the eyes and ourselves. He had looked back one more time before we scooted out of there, and saw one set of eyes lift and instantly knew what they were.

"Deer," he told me when we were a hundred yards down the tow path. "Probably feeding." I think he told me that as much to reassure himself as to comfort me. Another hundred yards or so I yelled to him. "I'm stopping to rest." Just as I started to sit on the towpath, something ran up beside me on my right from the dry, wooded canal area. I yelled out, "I'm okay. I can keep going!"

Could that have been one of those deer? I never found out.

A little later I saw a circulating light up above the canal. In the instant of wondering what it could be, I heard it—a train with a rotating light coming up the tracks far above the tow path. Looking up, watching the train go by, I saw a passenger wearing a long-sleeve white dress shirt, protected behind metal and glass. I wanted to be up there with him. A commuter train, its passengers heading home from work. When it vanished, we were in darkness again, leaving me unsure where the train had gone. What a weird night this was.

Moonbeams rippled across the water fifteen feet from us, the Potomac flowing now beside the towpath on our left. I felt safer with the moon now guiding our way. "I'm going to turn my headlamp off," I said. Lonnie did the same. "This is so amazing. If only my feet weren't pounding."

"Do you want to take a break?" Lonnie said.

"No, I'm okay. I can make it."

Gentle waves swept over the rocks, the river making its way quietly toward the ocean, moonlight reflecting the beauty and tranquility of the night. Another train approached; I watched it go by, then disappear, like the one earlier. It was strange, Twilight Zone stuff, until we arrived at the railroad bridge that crossed the Potomac leading into Harpers Ferry, where I finally realized the trains had entered a tunnel through the mountain, then emerged just before the bridge.

We crossed the Potomac River on the Goodloe E. Byron Memorial Pedestrian Walkway, part of the Winchester and Potomac Railroad Bridge. Once on the other side of the Potomac, we entered the historic section of Harpers Ferry and West Virginia, our tenth state. At this time of night, Old Town Harpers Ferry appeared abandoned, the buildings shuttered, the street empty.

The road followed a bend heading away from the river, with buildings on one side, and a parking area on the other for daytime visitors to Old Town. The houses were dark, some with electric candles flickering in the windows.

While we were debating which way to go, a policeman drove by. "Can I help you?" the officer said, stopping next to us on this darkened road.

"Do you know where the Comfort Inn is?" I said, recalling it from the notes.

"Not far up this road."

We continued on, still questioning if it was the right way; there seemed to be nothing up ahead except more darkness. We flagged down another driver who told us the same thing.

"Not far, just up this road."

For some reason I didn't trust these people, not even the policeman; their directions didn't comport with my reading of the notes. It wasn't until later that I discovered I had read the map incorrectly, getting myself turned around backwards. The trail traveled over two different bridges, the one we just crossed, and the other over the Shenandoah River, the bridge heading south, the one we'd cross when we left Harpers Ferry.

Turning the corner, leaving the darkened Old Town, we saw the lights of the Comfort Inn. Lying on that comfy bed in the room, having soaked my feet in a hot bath, with pizza and salad on the way, I was grateful we never came in contact with the wanted man.

When the couple who found Molly and Geoff at the Thelma Marks Shelter arrived at the Duncannon Police Station, the police separated the couple and questioned the man privately, as if maybe he had committed the murder. After a rigorous interrogation, the police finally decided the man was innocent and began their search for the real killer. News of the tragic event spread quickly among hikers. Searching the crime scene, police discovered that Geoff's green Gregory backpack and his boots were missing from the shelter. They also found no sign of the gun or knife used in the murders. It was conceivable that the killer had these things with him. Hikers throughout the

trail had to make a decision to continue their hike or get off the trail. Many chose to end their journey.

Witnesses came forward describing a man they had seen in the section of the various roads and fields before Boiling Springs; some had even given the stranger a ride. Their reports said the man seemed out of place, without the usual gear of a hiker. Soon descriptions of the man led to a composite sketch. A manhunt began, for the missing backpack, boots, weapons, and hopefully, the killer.

One of several hikers who stayed on the trail to help find this man was walking near Harpers Ferry when he came upon a guy who matched the sketch. He had a green Gregory backpack, and was wearing Hi-tech boots, the same kind Geoff wore. The hiker notified the National Park Service that the man was headed toward Harpers Ferry.[1] Two Park Rangers waited for this possible suspect to cross the bridge into Harpers Ferry on Friday, September 21st. It was just after eight pm, eight days after the murders, when this killer ambled across the metal bridge wearing the pack on his back, and the Hi-tech boots. The man was arrested, still in possession of the gun and knife used to kill Molly and Geoff.

One of the first things the couple did when they arrived in any trail town was to phone their parents. Their families were looking forward to greeting the hiking pair in Harpers Ferry. It was to be a joyous time, celebrating their completion of over half the trail. The true halfway point is in Pennsylvania near Boiling Springs, but often hikers and families gather at Harpers Ferry, the location of the Appalachian Trail Conservancy's main office. There the hikers sign the book, making their hike official. Molly and Geoff had planned to volunteer at the center for a few hours as well. The day the suspect was taken into custody was the day the families were to gather with Molly and Geoff and celebrate the first half of their journey.

---

1. Mike Feeley, "Trail hiker tells of day he spent seeking suspect", The Patriot News, Sat. May 18, 1991.

28

A LONG, MISERABLE DAY

Thru-hikers looked forward to signing the hiker book in the ATC's Harpers Ferry office, their hike added to the records. We too enjoyed this recognition of our efforts as they took our photo beside the building. (When we visited Harpers Ferry a few years later, during a road trip, we checked the hikers' logbooks just for fun and found that we were the last 2009 southbound thru-hikers to sign it.)

A gear store in Asheville had mailed my new boots to the Harpers Ferry post office, but unfortunately, when we picked them up, they were too small. Apparently, my feet had flattened out from all the miles, and now I needed a larger size.

The staff at the Asheville store were so helpful, agreeing to send a new pair to Whitebeard Otter's home, the section-hiker we met in Maine months earlier. Whitebeard lived south of Harpers Ferry, and we had made a plan to meet him in a few days. The boots I had started with at Katahdin were ripping at the seams, but they had to last a few more miles.

We ate a late lunch at a restaurant near the post office, then knew it was time to start hiking. People were forecasting snow. The day was overcast and not very cold, making such weather hard to imagine. Lonnie and I crossed the Route 340 bridge over the Shenandoah

River, then headed up the mountain. After a few miles, we found a good campsite and settled in for the night.

It was a cloudy, cold day with flurries beginning to fall as we broke camp. An hour later the white, wet flakes were coming even harder; already covering the dried leaves. We entered our eleventh state, Virginia, in this snowstorm. At Keys Gap there was a mini-mart, three-tenths of a mile from the trail—a good place for us to get a few snacks, but mainly, to warm up. Looking out the window of the store, with snow still swirling, we watched a cinder truck drive by, wondering if it meant lots more on the way.

Hiking in this wet, slick snow proved to be troublesome, with both of us falling often. Six miles later, the Blackburn Trail Center side trail tempted us with the promise of warm shelter and maybe even something hot to drink. Whitebeard had forewarned us not to bother going down there. However, when I saw the trailhead for the private center, I couldn't help myself.

Being wet, cold, exhausted and hungry, I needed a break. Even if we couldn't get a snack, or possibly some hot chocolate, maybe we could get indoors for a short spell to warm up. Steep and slippery with fresh snow, the hike down to the facility was making me rethink my decision; we would have to climb back up this when it was time to leave. Both Lonnie's and my shoes were already soaked and our toes numb.

When we reached the center, there was much commotion, some kind of youth activity happening inside. Some kids stood on the porch, whom we asked if we could warm up for a bit inside. A man came out and explained he couldn't let anyone enter, except members of the group who had rented the facility. He directed us to a free bunkhouse just down a path where we could take shelter. It was a dilapidated shack that felt colder than being outside, so we hurriedly munched down peanut butter sandwiches, wishing we had heeded Whitebeard's warning. Battling the elements and our own frustration, we climbed the steep, snowy trek to the A.T., knowing this had been a bad decision.

The tread had turned dicey, causing more than a few slips and falls, mostly while heading downhill, but the snow did help to cushion our feet over the rocky terrain. We weren't officially to the section known as the *Roller Coaster*, a thirteen-mile corridor of climbing and descending countless steep, rough, rocky ridges and hollows, but it felt like it. After a long, miserable day, we arrived at Snicker's Gap in darkness. The notes mentioned the Horseshoe Curve Restaurant, just three-tenths of a mile down the road. This warm refuge could possibly turn things around and salvage this crappy day of hiking.

Being the only guests on this cold evening, we were thankful they were open. We treated ourselves to a hot meal, which was good, but sitting there in our wet clothes, we never warmed up; the chill had already driven deep into our bones.

The owner assured us a half-mile up the next mountain was a hostel, the Bear's Den, which was open. I couldn't help but doubt the man who owned the restaurant, thinking the hostel had most likely closed for the season. Plus, being turned away a few miles back still lingered in my mind. With snow blowing through the night sky, and drifts growing deeper, we charged back into the snowstorm, still chilled, hoping and praying the Bear's Den was *open*. We crossed the highway and started up the steep, rocky trail. All we could see was light bouncing off the snowflakes from our headlamps against a seamless black night.

It took half an hour to navigate the mountain when we came to the partially snow-covered sign indicating the side trail to the Bear's Den. The trail was dark and I knew both of us were thinking: this could be yet another frigid, fruitless misadventure.

A short distance later, we came upon the most heartening sight imaginable on this dismal night—*lights!* We walked around to find the door, then headed up the stone steps onto the porch. More lights! — and a door that opened with a smiling, friendly face; no one turning us away.

The caretaker greeted us and welcomed us to the Bear's Den. He guided us through this amazing old building, reminiscent of an old ski lodge, and familiarized us with all the hiker amenities. Basking in this outpouring of love, we forgot about the opposite experience only a few hours earlier.

The caretaker took us to the lower-level bunkhouse. Lonnie and I each picked a bed, were given towels for hot showers, and shown the computer and television. He invited us back upstairs where ice cream and pizza were available for purchase. The most treasured device he pointed out, which amazed me, as I had never seen one before, were *dryers* for our soppy hiking shoes.

We showered, watched some television, ate Ben and Jerry's and sat around relaxing. "We're in heaven, We're in heaven..." On this night, it did feel that way.

The Bear's Den is open all year for guests as well as hikers. There is a long road up the mountain to the den which makes it hazardous for those driving during ice and snowstorms, but we didn't think about that.

The next morning in the house kitchen we made pancakes, then sat in the dining room enjoying them. A few guests having breakfast at the communal table learned that we were hiking the A.T. and were interested in hearing about our adventure. The stay at the hostel had been the proverbial port in the storm for us, but alas, it was time to leave this phenomenal sanctuary and begin the recalcitrant *Roller Coaster.*

Mostly we clomped through thick snow, which made climbing difficult, while going down felt like skiing. Yet the day was glorious, the sunshine chasing the billowy, winter clouds away, leaving behind a deep and perfectly blue sky. Being rested, well-fed and warm, made the hiking wonderful, even though we soon tired of going up and down hills. After arriving at the Rod Hollow Shelter for a rest, a few miles from the end of the *Roller Coaster,* we decided to spend the night.

Early the next morning, we broke camp and started hiking with a lot of miles to cover to meet up with our friend, Whitebeard Otter. After a mile or so we ran into a deer hunter. He didn't look as crazy as what we had heard about those Pennsylvania hunters. This hunter told us he hadn't seen snow like this so early in the season for many years.

Just our luck!

In Sky Meadows State Park, we came to a popular spot for hawk and raptor watching, though it was vacant today. Similar to New Jersey, there was a pole in this open field for enthusiasts to place a fake owl to entice predators.

In the distance, gunshots echoed through the valley, a constant reminder of hunting season. We wore our orange sock hats for an added level of visibility. Heading down the mountain, we saw White-beard Otter coming up the trail to meet us. What a happy reunion as we followed him down to his car, then headed to the Washington D.C. area for a few zero days.

2 9

SITTING ON SANTA'S LAP

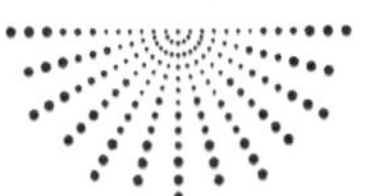

During our hike we traveled to New York City for Halloween, visited near Philadelphia during Thanksgiving, and now were headed to Washington D.C. for the beginning of the Christmas holiday. Whitebeard Otter was a gracious host, taking us to shop for needed supplies, including new insoles for our shoes. My boots had arrived from the Asheville store, and Lonnie bought a new pair of trail runners.

On the next evening, even though it was drizzly, Whitebeard drove us to the Ellipse, the grassy area south of the White House, to view the colorful, lighted *National Christmas Tree*. This tradition began in 1923, when President Calvin Coolidge on Christmas Eve *lit* the first tree. Coolidge stood at the foot of the tree and touched a button that brought the lights to life, a rare occurrence since not many people at that time had electricity in their homes. The Electric League of Washington had donated 2500 electric bulbs in red, white and green, to illuminate the nation's first Christmas tree.

Whitebeard told us when President Obama lit the tree, thousands of people had been there to watch. On the night we were there, despite the rain, it was quite pleasant, with no crowds whatsoever. There were Lionel trains coursing around numerous platforms, and huge yule logs burning in a pit. Decorated trees from each state, including five territories, as well as the District of Columbia, were added to this holiday tradition in 1954 with a pathway that led visitors around each one. This event has become known as, *The National Christmas Tree and Pathway of Peace.*

We also visited Santa's Workshop, a new attraction, added the year before. The three of us entered at the far end of a long corridor, with Santa on a chair at the opposite end of the smallish enclosed trailer. Feeling a little frisky, and with no children present to have their picture taken with Santa, I suggested, "Maybe I should sit on Santa's lap and get my picture taken... and tell him what I want for Christmas."

Santa's eyebrows shot up; obviously the jolly old elf was a little shocked. I didn't sit on Santa's lap, but I really surprised Whitebeard, and even Lonnie, since I'm usually pretty reserved.

Walking away from Santa's realm, I observed the Washington Monument in the distance, remembering it was just a week ago we explored the monument to our first president at Boonsboro.

This Washington Monument was built in three stages, due to financial difficulties and the Civil War. The cornerstone was laid on July 4th, 1848, with over 20,000 people in attendance including President James K. Polk. All construction at that time was supported by private funding. In 1854, the second section was completed with public money, but by 1857 the project stalled.

Sadly, it sat unfinished for twenty years, until July 5, 1876, when Congress provided funds to finish the project. On December 6, 1884, a windy day, the 3,300-pound capstone was brought out through a window, heaved up to the scaffolding at the dizzying tip of the monument, and was miraculously set in place, to the shouts of all the onlookers. Setting the capstone marked the completion of the Washington Monument, some fifty-seven years after Boonsboro's tower had been built with no funding at all.

Finally, it was time for hiking. Whitebeard took us back to the trail to do the next section just before the Shenandoah's. He dropped us at Route 55, where we had met him a few days before, and we slack-packed to Front Royal. After finishing this eight-mile section, we stayed at a motel in town. The next morning, he drove us to the trailhead to begin our trek through the Shenandoah National Park. The plan was that he would meet us in a few days where Route 33 crossed the Shenandoah's, sixty-two trail-miles away.

30

A SNOWSTORM COMING

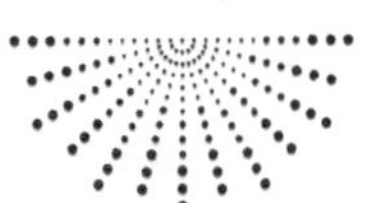

On the morning of Friday, December 11th, we said good-bye to Whitebeard and entered the Shenandoah's, planning to meet up in four days. We hoped this would work, since we had no way to contact him. The snow was crusty which made walking difficult.

Heading over Compton Peak, we glimpsed the multitude of mountains around us which were quite impressive. We had not seen this many since New England. However, coming upon a set of huge bear tracks in the snow did make us wonder if we'd be seeing more than just beautiful peaks.

Two days later, climbing out of Thornton Gap with sunshine and frosted snow, we trekked along the edge of a mountain with views to the south and east. With numerous icy patches, the incline required dedicated attention to our steps, while patches of dirt and grass, though scarce, helped greatly with footing. That night we stayed at the Byrd's Nest #3 Hut, a wooden three-sided open-air shelter at 3,290 feet. Gusty winds scoured the mountain top, making for a frigid night.

The next day the air felt a bit warmer, though the ice-crusted snow still played havoc with our feet. Summiting Little Stony Mountain to our south, the profile of Stony Man's face was visible on the nearby mountain. Arriving at a bed of slab rock that overlooked the valley, we stopped for lunch, and I was convinced I heard a baby crying. After heading back to the trail, we heard voices. Just past some boulders was a family with several children and a baby, all having lunch, too. The father said to us as we passed by, "Nice weekend for a little backpacking." We nodded and smiled, thinking about our five-month backpacking adventure and chuckling to ourselves.

Just before dark, at David Spring, a sizable buck, most likely injured, stood very near the trail, unfazed by our presence, as if asking for help. But there was nothing for us to do except feel bad when we hiked on.

Reaching the Big Meadows Campground after dark, we knew it would be closed, but hoped to find a pavilion to set up our tent. Using our headlamps, we did not find any protected place. It seemed like it could rain, possibly even snow, so we kept looking, the temperature dropping. Eventually we found a piece of pavement beneath a roof overhang at the juncture of two buildings. Not giving much thought to the ice-covered ground at the edge of the sidewalk, we set up our tent.

To our surprise, there were two phone booths by the locked showers, both with dial tones. We took this opportunity to call Whitebeard, since we knew we would never make it to Route 33 the next day. There was no answer, so we left a message. That night, the wind howled, shaking the tent, which wasn't quite as protected tucked into the corner as we'd thought. Rain hammered against the nylon fly, powered by gale force wind. It was a rough night, our sleep interrupted constantly with the roaring wind and rain.

Curiously, the temperature warmed up overnight, melting the ice, and by morning the interior of our tent was soaked. But it wasn't ice melt that caused a problem, but the convergence of leaky roof gutters above our tent directing the deluge down on us. Upon further scrutiny, we discovered that our backpacks, which we kept near our heads tucked in one end of the tent, and much of our gear, had also succumbed to the flooding. We moved our wet gear to a drier spot in front of the building while we sopped out the tent. Fatigue aside, I couldn't wait to be off this mountain.

We packed up, drying our gear as best we could. I tried Whitebeard one last time, but still no answer. I left a message—we were headed to the Bearfence Mountain Hut—wondering if the parkway was closed. If so, our plans with Whitebeard would be nixed.

As soon as we were off the mountain, the wind died down, though probably still blowing where we had camped. Hiking in a misty fog, we stayed relatively dry. To lift our spirits, we started singing Christmas songs, like, *These Are a Few of My Favorite Things*. Lonnie knew the lyrics and was teaching me. I had never even heard the song before. The scent of New England pines would have added a nice touch to our manufactured holiday spirit. They always made us think of the holiday.

After climbing Hazeltop Mountain, we began our descent passing Bootens Gap. I kept looking for the shelter, knowing it was near. Meeting up with Whitebeard at this point seemed questionable, especially since we had not been able to reach him. Where the trail leveled out, we came to a parking area with one car. It looked like Whitebeard's SUV. I was ahead of Lonnie, and as soon as I saw the license plate, with its A.T. theme, I hollered, "Lonnie, he found us! I see Whitebeard's car!" Whitebeard wasn't there, so we decided since Lonnie's feet were hurting, I would go to the Bearfence Mountain Shelter that was close by, and see if I could find him. A short distance ahead I looked up and saw his red jacket—a welcome sight.

Whitebeard told us only the central section of the *Skyline Drive* was open, the section we were in. Apparently, there must have been more ice in the northern and the southern sections. He never did get our phone messages, just decided to look here, and while waiting, decided to check the nearby shelter and clear any debris. Luck, synchronicity, or more marvelous trail magic; regardless, we were thankful. Since we could not get to the cabin he had rented, (it was in the southern section), we left the *Skyline Drive*, and found a motel on Route 33.

With an early start in the morning, Whitebeard drove to where he had found us, then went to set things up at the cabin. Fortunately, the parkway was now open in the southern section. We planned to meet him at Powell Gap, umpteen hiking trail-miles away, where the trail crossed the parkway.

Throughout the Shenandoah National Park, the A.T. intersects the *Skyline Drive* thirty-two times. When I was nine years old, my father drove my mom, my brother and me on the *Skyline Drive* during a vacation. I didn't recall much of that trip, only how much my dad loved the woods and mountains. That was 1960, when the road was already thirty years old, having been finished by the Civilian Conservation Corps in the 1930s.

The idea of a national park in the Blue Ridge Mountains was born when President Hoover imagined a *sky-line drive* with views of the valleys and other mountains. Congress provided funding for the project, and by 1931, the *sky-line drive* was financially secured and construction began. It consisted of three sections, with two highways dividing the sections. One section was completed by 1934 with the last by 1939. In 1961, it was incorporated and named the *Skyline Drive*.

That afternoon, we met up with Whitebeard at Powell Gap, and he drove us to the cabin. With the weather still cold, it felt wonderful to be inside with a fire crackling, our fourth one on the trail. He even cooked veggie burgers just for us.

Our first morning at the cabin, we left early with only the things we needed for the day. Whitebeard drove us south to Brown's Gap. We hiked north back toward the cabin, one more instance of heading north instead of south. It was a fun day with some nice views. Rising temperatures had chased most of the snow, making for great hiking. Coming down off one mountain we happened upon Whitebeard doing trail maintenance. As a member of the Potomac A.T. Club, he had taken this opportunity while in the park to clear trail debris.

He said, "Go on, I'll catch up to you soon enough."

There were some steep climbs and descents through this section, so we were pleased to reach the top of the last one. After that, it was all downhill to the cabin and another evening of fun trail talk.

It was so refreshing to go without our full gear for a while, but this was the last day of slack-packing. Whitebeard rendezvoused with us at Turk Gap. He was waiting with the rest of our gear. It was sad to say goodbye, but we had had a good time together. During our three-day visit with him, we asked about his brother, Luncher, who had been hiking with us in Maine, New Hampshire, and part of Vermont. Whitebeard told us he got off the trail sometime in Vermont. We hadn't seen Luncher since, and wondered if we'd ever see Whitebeard again.

Still not fully adjusted to the full weight of our packs, we were exhausted for the last four miles to Calf Mountain Shelter. We hoped to have it to ourselves, and we did for a little bit, but just as we finished setting up the tent, we heard voices.

A young couple came through the woods. We weren't sure how they had gotten there. They were not thru-hikers, and by the way they were dressed, they didn't even look like day hikers. The girl had on tight jeans, a dressy top, and fancy shoes. The guy was more prepared and started building a fire. The sun was setting as we finished filtering water and cooking our meal. On cold nights, we ate in the tent, partially burrowed in our sleeping bags. It was December 17th, so we were surprised to see these kids, but it became obvious that this guy wanted to have a romantic night with his girlfriend. They popped the cork on a bottle of wine, and the aroma of whatever he was cooking over the fire hung in the air.

This was one time we felt like intruders, trespassers to their private party, while at the same time concerned about the heavy food smells attracting night critters. Finished with dinner and snacks, we hung our bear bag and slipped down into our sleeping bags, firelight flickering through the thin material of our tent. The two lovers, by the new silence, were obviously tucked into their sleeping bags stretched out on the deck boards of the open-sided shelter.

When I woke in the morning, the half-empty wine bottle was sitting on the picnic table, with the young couple bundled on the shelter floor. That night the temperature dropped below freezing, making for a brisk morning. We were packed and ready to leave as the guy poked the fire, trying to rouse the embers, only nodding as we left camp. The girl still hadn't stirred. We had seven miles to Rockfish Gap —which marked the end of the Shenandoah National Park, and also the terminus of the Skyline Drive—where Interstate Route 64 cuts across the mountain to the trail town to the west, Waynesboro. The air was chilly, but the sun warm.

We had a good time on top of Bear Den Mountain, inspecting the tower, apparently a radio installation, some say, for state police communications. This tower is visible from Route 64 approaching from the east. There were even old tractor seats to sit on, mounted on posts stuck in the ground. Someone had placed them there, it's believed for elderly berry enthusiasts to rest after gathering blackberries, which grow in abundance on this crest.

The climb down into McCormick Gap was long and steep, followed by more rocky terrain along the ridgeline. At one point we stopped to eat. With a new, steely chill in the air, it didn't take long for our hands to get cold. We hurried lunch, wanting to start hiking again to warm up, but the heat took longer than we had imagined it would. Maybe the temperature was dropping faster than we thought.

The A.T. led down to the Skyline Drive which ended at Rockfish Gap. At this point the scenic mountain road became the Blue Ridge Parkway, which continued south to the Great Smoky Mountains National Park, 469 miles away.

My thesis had finally been accepted, and I was set to graduate, after a month of shipping the laptop forward to finish it. We planned to attend the ceremony at East Tennessee State University on Saturday, December 19th. Lonnie's son, Eric, arranged to pick us up at the Afton Inn located at this gap and take us to Lonnie's daughter's place.

Standing on the road across from the Afton Inn, we could see the trail meandering south following the parkway. Even though we were looking forward to a few days off, it was sad leaving the trail. Except for the family wedding, which was two months earlier, our life had been the trail, just me and Lonnie. Now we would be with family, ETSU graduates, graduate's families and relatives. With a lingering nip in the air, we were somewhat consoled by the fact that we would be hopping back on the trail the following Tuesday.

Maybe it was the "endings" that had us a bit down; saying goodbye to Whitebeard, leaving the amazing Shenandoah's and the Skyline Drive, and now getting off the trail, even if only for a few days—the accumulation of goodbyes producing a palpable letdown, both of us feeling the drag.

But a greater, more pivotal letdown was just ahead, one we could never have imagined. We went inside the inn to get out of the cold, finding an old, rough-looking guy puffing a cigarette behind the counter. Breathing nothing but fresh air for months, we were caught off-guard by the smoke; always lots of adjustments returning to civilization. Fortunately, we only waited a few minutes in the lobby before Eric and his wife, Karen arrived to drive us to Asheville to Lonnie's daughter's place.

We loaded our gear into the car, and headed south on Route 64, then Route 81, enjoying the visit and sharing stories. I began to notice the large, overhead electrical highway signs warning of a weather advisory. "What's that about?" I asked Eric.

"Supposed to be a snowstorm coming," he said.

Sitting in the back seat, I looked at Lonnie and he looked at me. "No way," Lonnie muttered, taking his eyes out the window to the cloud-barren blue sky. When we arrived at Lonnie's daughter's place, north of Asheville, Britt and her husband, Nate welcomed us. But that predicted snowstorm had started in the form of small white flakes. By midnight there was fifteen inches on the ground, and no power.

When we woke in the morning, the expressway, Route 26, which goes over the mountain back to East Tennessee State University was now closed. I would not be going to my graduation. And getting back to the trail by Tuesday seemed questionable, as well. (ETSU scheduled another graduation ceremony for those who were unable to attend during the snowstorm.)

We managed to leave their home after four days, but the snow continued off and on for the next week. We decided to wait until

January when maybe the weather would shift. I tucked Molly's photo away, hoping we'd be able to finish this hike for her, and for us as well.

We visited relatives over the holiday as the snow continued to fall in one storm after another, accompanied by severe, frigid temperatures, the weather pattern continuing into 2010.

With the roads clear between storms, we traveled to my family's homes in Pennsylvania, hoping things might change later in January. We had routinely hiked the A.T. near our home in North Carolina during the winter months and had never encountered weather like this. Most afternoon temperatures reached up into the fifties, even the sixties.

On our way back home, we stopped at Rockfish Gap outside of Waynesboro to check things out, hoping against hope we'd find the trail hospitable to resuming our hike. What we found was bitter, unflinching cold, howling winds, and eighteen-inch packed snow on the trail sheeted now with ice. Beside the trail, the parkway was closed. Everything seemed frozen in time. Not the pleasing conditions we'd left only a few weeks before.

We hadn't given up, though, deciding to hop back on when it was a little warmer with less snow. But snowstorms and below freezing temperatures continued all throughout January and into February.

In so many ways, we felt lost. Not knowing what to do with ourselves, we spent a lot of time wandering around the house, not able to focus on any one thing.

With winter storms and frigid weather unabating, we finally came to the tough decision of finishing our hike the next fall. A sad time for us both because we had been feeling great, both physically and emotionally. We would start in October, 2010.

Earlier in our hike, some stranger we'd met along the trail had chatted us up, then bid us adieu, but not before dropping this ominous warning. "You won't finish the hike!" he had said to Lonnie. Lonnie didn't at all care for his pessimistic prophesy, and had no idea what the man had based his assumption on, but we were now both giving the statement more reflection.

PART III

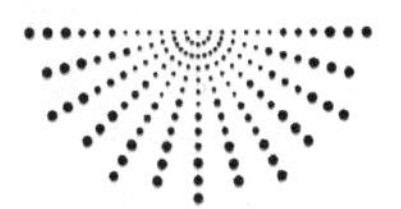

31

10/10/10 AT 10

Ten months later, here we were again, lovers of cooler weather, (though not keen on frigid and snowy), ready to finish walking to Springer Mountain, Georgia. Friends drove us to Rockfish Gap near Waynesboro, the same gap where we ended the previous year.

Sunday, 10/10/10, at 10 am—a glorious day to begin our hike. We arrived at the first shelter traversing fairly easy terrain, had lunch and dipped our feet into the cool stream. The day was warm, but not too hot with just a few annoying gnats. Our goal: to make it to Daleville, one hundred and thirty-three miles away, but that meant carrying twelve days of food—and we felt it.

Just past the trail to the Humpback Rocks overlook, we found a stealth site to camp. After settling in, we retraced our steps back to the side trail to Humpback Rocks and enjoyed the first cooked meal of our new hike, while watching the sun set in the western sky. Wind blowing through the trees was a soothing, welcome sound, connecting us back to the trail.

The next day, the going was slow over rough, rocky terrain. Stopping occasionally to enjoy the view helped ease our heavy loads. That night the tendon beside my right knee throbbed at camp. It started as we headed up a steep, rutted roadbed. Hopefully, Motrin and our evening foot rubs (and knees, too) would take care of it. But it had me worried. "Is my hike over before it's even begun?" It hurt that badly. I took more Motrin in the morning and wrapped my knee, which seemed to help.

At the Hanging Rock vista, there was an incredible view of the Three Ridges. Sitting there, looking across the valley, we were reminded of how much they resembled a ski slope—dipping down, flattening out, then repeating itself, three times—as it plunged to the valley. Twenty minutes later we began our descent down the Three Ridges, the rocky, steep tread often challenging, with several rock-slide areas.

Tye River sat at the base of the threesome where we had planned to camp, but with no clear spots, we hiked on and began our 3,066-foot trek up the massif known as The Priest, the first section of the Blue Ridge Mountains called the Religious Range. The Appalachian Trail however does not cross the other range mountains: The Little Priest, The Friar, The Little Friar, or The Cardinal, all south of the A.T., having been dubbed these names by the earliest settlers in the area.

After ascending the first eight hundred feet, we arrived at Cripple Creek to find no camping spots. We filtered water from the creek and continued climbing. A third of the way up, we were taking a break when a young man came by. "I sure hope I find this dog soon," he said, as if we knew his dog was missing. "You don't know how many times he's made me climb this thing." Meaning the Priest. I had heard a dog barking earlier and wondered if there were hunters in the area. I told him, but what good would that do him now; he still had to climb the mountain.

Soon afterward we found a flat spot to set up the tent. We were both drained. As for my knee—it was great—the brace apparently helping. The discomfort was gone and most of the time I was hiking without thinking about it. The next day we finished the strenuous climb to the top of the Priest, often stopping to catch our breath, and take in the fall colors of the surrounding mountains. After the summit, the trail became less strenuous.

Five miles later a side trail led to a large, fairly flat area that culminated in a huge, boulder-strewn look-out rising above the surrounding field. It was hard to believe that 5,000 Union soldiers camped near this sandstone formation in September, 1861, calling it Spy Rock. At the time General Lee was at Sewel Mountain, which the Northern soldiers could view from this open-topped peak. We climbed the multitude of boulders, imagining all those soldiers, ready to do battle, camped around this natural stone outpost.

Later, at the Seeley-Woodworth Shelter, we cooked a meal. Still early, with the notes indicating water and camping at the North Fork of Piney Creek two miles away, we decided to keep going.

When we arrived, it was pretty ugly with debris—broken branches, weeds and very few places to camp—apparently from storm damage. Scrounging around to find a spot that would work for the night, we finally found one and set up the tent. I washed in the stream as best I could, but washing my hair would have to wait until town. We carried hand sanitizer, so there was an attempt at cleanliness. There is a joke about never shaking hands with a thru-hiker. But it's more fact than funny, considering the number of germs on any hiker's hands at any given time. That's how *the bump* began, hikers bumping fists upon greeting, and in recent years, bumping elbows.

During the night it started to rain and by morning, thunder and lightning. The storm seemed pretty close, yet we felt safe in our tent, which in reality, was not much safer than standing outside. After breakfast we packed up inside the tent, and finished as the rain subsided, leaving behind a ghostly mist.

Four rugged miles of ascending and descending numerous ridges prepared us for climbing Tar Ridge Mountain. With overcast skies, wind mixed with cold rain, we created an ad hoc shelter to eat something before the climb—our emergency space-age lightweight foil blanket held over our heads with clothespins attached to our poles along a fence rail. We'd been using this foil blanket as a ground cloth for our tent. But on this occasion, for keeping off the rain, it worked well as we ate tuna fish sandwiches. About a quarter-mile past our lunch spot we came to an overhanging rock that would have protected us naturally. Who knew!

Then came Cold Mountain at 4,022 feet—which had a bald on top, but no view, mist and fog enveloping the mountain, fueled by a powerful wind. The next summit we came to was Bald Knob. No view there, but the five-mile descent was both long and often steep, dropping us at the Brown Mountain Creek Shelter.

This area along the creek was once the homestead of a community of freed slaves in the late 1800s and early 1900s, until about 1918. Stone remains of buildings still mark the area. On October 7, 1992, David W. Benavitch, from the local Pedlar Ranger District, interviewed Taft Hughes.

Hughes was born in 1909 and lived at this Brown Mountain Creek community during his youth. He told this story during the interview: "My granddaddy told my mother and dad this, because this was before their time… Jess Richardson had a bunch of slaves up here on Brown Mountain Creek. … I reckon that one of these slaves did something that he didn't like, and he almost beat him to death. They said that Richardson was real old, just tottering along, but he could ride a horse. After he beat the slave, he got on his horse and went on down Brown Mountain Creek and went by a rock, I think I still know where the rock is, and something jumped off that rock and grabbed him around the waist, and they tell me the horse started running and went on down and crossed the road and went on home. The next morning, they said that he (Richardson) was dead and the horse was too… After that, they called the rock, Scare Rock."[1]

Knowing there was someone killed here, Lonnie and I hurried past the sign for Scare Rock, neither of us wanting to linger. It seemed these woods are no stranger to tragedy.

Late in the day we arrived at the Punchbowl Shelter and set up our tent. While we ate dinner, an older guy arrived who was out for a

---

1. Oral History Interview with Taft Hughes, David W. Benavitch, Oct. 7, 1992, Pedlar Ranger District, Amherst County, VA.

two-week hike. He baked bread in aluminum foil over the open fire. Even though he offered us some, we declined. He told us a story of how he escaped being attacked by a grizzly bear while hunting in Alaska. "I could see the whites of its eyes, just before I shot it."

Shortly after that, another guy appeared. He lived nearby and had hiked up an old dirt road through the woods from where he had hidden his motorcycle. He planned to spend the weekend at the shelter. After he unpacked crackers, cheese and two six-packs of beer, still cold, three young men showed up, southbounders like us. An impromptu party broke out, the young hikers drinking this guy's beer, sharing stories, and all of us eating cheese and crackers. What a night for the Punchbowl Shelter!

Molly and Geoff loved to take breaks through the day, but their ventures were more heuristic than ours. Earl Swift, who started the trail nine days after them, wrote, "As Molly predicted in one log entry: 'If you're behind us you will pass us." Their glacial pace was no accident. They were stopping to take pictures, to study plants, turtles, and salamanders, to bake bread."[2] Mostly on rainy days or when they were exhausted, they'd try out their bakepacker. With it, they baked bread and often had it for their breakfast.

It sounded like they were having fun hiking, too.

At the top of Bluff Mountain the following morning, I was filled with sadness reading a plaque marking the actual spot where hunters had found the little body of Ottie Cline Powell in 1891.

It had been a dreary Monday for Ottie, with a few inches of snow on the ground. With a chill in the air, and the threat of rain, Ottie didn't let the weather get him down, and only wanted to follow the bigger boys to help gather wood for his teacher, Miss Nannie Gilbert

---

2. Earl Swift, "Murder on the Appalachian Trail", *Outside Magazine*, Sept. 2, 2015

—but he just couldn't keep up. He was only four years old, would have turned five in a few weeks, and was so excited to be going to school, even described as a fast learner. When he did not return that morning, locals formed search parties. Families arrived to help, but he was never found. It wouldn't be until the following spring his body would be discovered. From that day forward, his mother struggled through life, never able to shed her despair.

Standing there, reading the plaque, I questioned if my grief was only for this child, or something more, the loss of Molly and Geoff, and other lives taken in the peaceful wilderness of the trail. The plaque says, *"This is the exact spot little Ottie Cline Powell's body was found April 5, 1891, after straying from Tower Hill School House Nov. 9, a distance of 7 miles. Age 4 years 11 months."* It's even been written in the Punchbowl Shelter logbooks, sometimes hikers see a young boy wandering nearby, then disappears when approached.

We had a long day making many miles, immersed in the brilliant colors of fall, which helped to assuage my gloom. In the morning, we left camp around eight and climbed up out of the James River Basin. The trail traveled the edge of a bowl-shaped valley with rocky bouldering along this gradual climb. The view from the top of Apple Orchard Mountain was a breathtaking 360-degree panorama. Any hope of snacking on apples was soon dashed when we discovered the name for this mountain alludes to the gnarly trees growing there, which only *look* like apple trees. At 4,222 feet, it is the highest point on the Blue Ridge Parkway in Virginia. We hadn't been at this elevation since Mt. Moosilauke in New Hampshire.

That afternoon it was down to the Cornelius Creek Shelter and much needed sleep. Our days revolved around sunlight. Once the sun went down, we hit the sack, which meant we were sleeping longer hours than at home, with our bodies refreshed, at least most of the time, and ready to start hiking again in the morning.

The trail often crossed the Blue Ridge Parkway, sometimes at an overlook. At one such crossing was a man scanning the vast sky for hawks, reminding us of the raptor fans we'd seen in New Jersey. This watcher had counted over five thousand hawks in one day in mid-

September. Quite a migration—I wondered how he kept tally of that many, but failed to ask him.

At the Sharp Top Overlook, we could see Sharp Top Mountain in the distance, which George Washington had used as a base mark for one of his surveys. During the construction of the Washington Monument a huge boulder on Sharp Top was rolled down the mountain, then hauled out by an oxen team to the railroad. Once cut to size, it was used in the construction of the Washington Monument in Washington, D.C.

Leaving Sharp Top Overlook, we still had two days before reaching Daleville. Our packs were much lighter, our clothes and bodies pretty disgusting. The next morning we woke to sunshine, and headed for Bearwallow Gap, then another climb to the next ridge. On our last night before town, rain started again. We donned our rain gear and packed up inside the tent. Not always easy to do, but even so, we made it out of camp by 7:45.

We were pumped—ready for civilization. By the time we arrived at the highway, the rain had stopped, and the familiar orange roof of HOJO's (Howard Johnson's Motel) emerged just beyond the passing traffic.

We had been on the trail for ten days, the longest trail-only time for our entire hike! But none of that mattered, the only question now being; do we shower first, or eat first?

Cleanliness won out at the motel. Refreshed, dressed in a clean set of town clothes (lightweight gym shorts and simple T for me), we crossed the highway to the Pizza Hut for pizza and salads. Then to the grocery store for motel snacks. There we came across three southbounders at the entrance to the grocery store, discarding their unwanted packaging, then stuffing the food they had purchased into plastic bags. Plastic baggies of all sizes are so helpful on the trail. We always put our cereal into a gallon-size one, breakfast powder into a quart-size, usually placing that into another as well, to protect it even more.

Even the plastic grocery sacks were put into service, using them for our trash on the trail. Crazy as it sounds, discovering a trash receptacle at parkway crossings was delightful. Especially since I was carrying the trash, that often amazingly grew quite heavy.

The plastic grocery bags were also useful for wet gear, especially our shoes when it rained. We'd bag our shoes then shove them down into our sleeping bags, nestled next to our legs, letting our body heat dry them overnight. When it was cold, this little trick helped to keep our shoes from freezing, which is something most hikers don't think about. It wasn't always comfortable sleeping with a plastic bag of wet shoes all night, but in the morning, having shoes that were warm and pliable was.

We bid the southbounders farewell, then went inside to do our own shopping, but not for resupply, at least not yet. With a stash of town snacks, we hurried back to the room for a night of TV watching, non-stop munching, and some serious bed sprawling!

THE DRAGON'S TOOTH

The next morning in Daleville was a busy one—buying needed resupply items and mailing some to the next trail town. With chores done, we decided to eat lunch before leaving; huge sandwiches with potato salad and homemade milk shakes at the Mill Mountain Cafe and Coffee shop.

Climbing that afternoon with my belly stuffed, I questioned my decision to eat all that food, still carrying the remainder of my milk shake; I wasn't about to leave that behind. On many occasions I would squirrel away leftover slices of pizza in plastic bags and tuck them in my pack. Lonnie, who doesn't like cold pizza, would just stare at me. But I would not leave them behind.

Under clear skies that evening, we set up camp on a rounded rocky hilltop, witnessing a spectacular sunset, followed later by a stunning full moon. The day had been a short one, only seven miles, which had been just right for me, the slow town rhythm still thrumming in my bones.

The next morning, we headed to Tinker Cliffs, a thousand-foot climb followed by a mile-long cliff walk, with numerous rocky viewpoints overlooking the valley. These cliffs were named for Revolutionary War soldiers who went AWOL during the fighting, hiding and surviving on the safety of this narrow mountaintop. It is rumored that these cliffs got their name from the deserters who *tinkered*, repairing pots, pans and utensils to sell them.

Seven tough miles later was McAfee Knob, an awesome vista offering a sweeping view of Tinker Ridge. A couple of guys from Norfolk were there, day hiking over the weekend. Two young girls arrived at the jutting rock formation, with its outermost point allowing any hiker to dare to stand, looking down 1600 feet into the Catawba Valley. When we were leaving, one of the guys said to the girls, "Will you do me a favor. Go over there with my friend and let me take his picture with you. It's been one of his fantasies." I looked over my shoulder as the two girls, one on each side of his friend, who now had a big grin on his face, all stood right near that scary precipice. McAfee Knob is considered the most photographed scenic viewpoint of the entire Appalachian Trail—even when you didn't know who was in your photograph.

A hazardous, rocky tread made the four miles from the knob to Route 311 difficult. Halfway down we filtered water from a creek, then cooked a meal at the Catawba Mountain Shelter. Nearing evening, we crossed the highway and climbed about a mile before we made camp on top of a spur, off the trail.

Our spot wasn't actually a campsite, but Friday nights, especially this close to a highway, are the strangest times on the trail. We chose this grassy place so that no matter what, we wouldn't be surprised by visitors in the middle of the night.

Even so...around one am, I woke to two headlamps—*Somebody's coming*—all over again. Then a girl's laughter—a girl and a guy out in the night without packs. From about forty yards away, we could see them, or at least their lights. Sitting above them on our dark little ridge, it was virtually impossible for them to see our tent. Eventually they veered to the left of our campsite following the trail, and were soon gone. It had been a good decision to climb farther up the spur, away from the trail to this nice flat area, allowing us to sleep a bit more at ease.

The morning was cool, but pleasant, as we navigated Sawtooth

Ridge, the topography like the teeth of a sawblade. Already bone-tired from the rugged terrain, we walked across several fields, then began the climb to the Dragon's Tooth overlook, a Tuscarora quartzite outcrop projecting almost thirty-five feet upward atop Cove Mountain, reminiscent of a huge tooth. It was named by Tom Campbell, who, in the 1950s, was instrumental in having the trail follow this reroute away from the Blue Ridge Parkway. Being Saturday, there were many day hikers, who were able to reach this popular spot without having to ply the torturous rocky crests we had just crossed.

The trek up to the top of Cove Mountain looked like a hundred feet of a rock face, a very spooky climb. Watching numerous children conquering it with ease, ascending from one rock to the next, I suddenly felt old. But to be fair to myself, they were not carrying a twenty-six-pound pack. In some spots, ladders made the climb a bit easier. At one point, one of my trekking poles slipped out of my hand, but fortunately, I was able to grab it before it fell down the cliff.

The top of this precipice ended with a short side-trail leading to the tooth-like pinnacle. Now on level ground, I stopped to rest my wobbly legs. The two guys from Norfolk (I had taken their picture with the girls on McAfee Knob) had climbed the cliff ahead of us, and were sitting there catching their breath. It was nice chatting for a few minutes. They told us they were taking the side trail to the actual Dragon's Tooth overlook, but with our water supply low, we said goodbye, just wanting to get to camp. A few hours later we stopped for the night at Trout Creek, with numerous tent sites and plenty of water.

On top of Brush Mountain, an old road crossed the crest. Several benches and a large granite memorial sat beside the trail, dedicated to the memory of Audie Murphy, the famous film star and most decorated veteran in WWII. He died on this mountain in 1971 when his plane crashed on a stormy, fog-choked night. We were sitting on one of the benches when a man came by, returning to his truck after placing his deer stand up on the mountain. He offered us water, but we declined, knowing (according to the notes) that we'd find plenty of camping and water up the mountain at Cabin Branch. That made more sense to us than hauling the extra weight during the next climb.

Before reaching Cabin Branch, we came to the Niday Shelter, which showed water seventy-five yards down a hill, but we passed that, too. Soon, though, it became obvious there was no Cabin Branch, leaving us with no water or camping, and only a half-liter in each of our bottles.

The next eleven miles left us hot and sweaty, a grueling 1500-foot climb—over stony ledges and rocky wooded areas—until finally arriving at the Sarver Hollow Shelter. Exhausted and hoping for the best, we headed down a steep side trail of switchbacks to find the shelter, with tent sites, and *water*.

The spring looked like an old well for the Sarver family, who lived on this land from the 1860's until the 1930's. It was not a rushing source like many on the trail, but the water moved just enough to make it possible for filtering. It would have been easy to regret passing on the prior water sources, but unless you're lugging along a crystal ball, you just have to trust your choices.

The next day, strong winds at the aptly-named Wind Rock outcropping put on quite a show. The clouds performed first, their shadows spilling over the distant mountains across the valley. The leaves entered, wheeling round and round like spirited dancers in the open air, immune to gravity. As remarkable as it was, I could no longer watch, suddenly forced to focus on the unforgiving rocky tread below my feet, all too reminiscent of Wolf Rocks in Pennsylvania.

Then, without warning, a tremendous boom, like an explosion, stopped us cold, our eyes scanning the sky. A fighter jet, which for us was actually *below* our eye level, flew through the valley. The pilot performed a maneuver between our ridge and the next, visible for only a few seconds. For a moment I imagined Tom Cruise, *Maverick*, executing an impossible bombing mission on an enemy target. The memory of Audie Murphy crashing on that mountain top, and the fighter jet with its deafening roar, lingered in my thoughts throughout the afternoon.

That evening we came to Pine Swamp Branch Shelter, possibly the worst shelter on the entire trail—beer cans, trash, overgrown weeds. Eventually we found the only visible tent site, and just when we thought our displeasure over this crappy place couldn't get much worse, it began to rain. Later I learned that this shelter, and thirty miles of the trail around it, were maintained by students of the Outdoor Club at Virginia Tech, who were dealing with the aftermath of the murders at the university three and a half years earlier. We then understood the reason for the neglect.

Climbing Peters Mountain the next morning surprised us—an easy switchback ascent. The rain had stopped, the clouds giving us a few teaser glimpses of sunshine. With only a few miles to the next shelter, Lonnie stowed his rain coat. Minutes later, without warning, rain poured from the trickster sky.

At that point the trail followed down beneath a power line, leaving us completely exposed for about a hundred yards. Even running, Lonnie got soaked, and was chilled to the bone from the freezing rain by the time we reached the Rice Field Shelter. After throwing ourselves into the lean-to, Lonnie reached for his jacket. By then, the fickle weather turned back into a sunny, bright day.

The shelter was tucked up the hill at the edge of the woods, providing a beautiful view of the field and surrounding mountains. In a short while Lonnie had warmed up, and since it was only two-thirty, way too early to call it a day, and with Pearisburg only seven miles away, we decided to hike on. How come these awesome shelters don't appear just before nightfall?

The hike down the mountain proved to be rougher than expected, especially for me. By the time we reached Route 460, my feet throbbed. Maybe it was the hard pavement irritating my soles, causing the jaunt along the highway to take forever.

After crossing the Senator Shumate Bridge over the New River, the trail veered back into the woods, appearing to climb another mountain; the downhill route along the road having much more appeal. But this meant my already screaming feet would have to endure more tyrannical asphalt; our decision to head into Pearisburg making this a twenty-mile day.

By the time we came to the motel, my feet would hardly move. Lonnie struggled as well, but he could at least take steps. I recalled laughing at Dry Mouth as he shuffled around at the Mayor's place in New York. Lonnie took care of the room and ordered food. I stumbled around like I had square feet, showered, soaked my whiny tootsies, then plopped on the bed, turned on the television, worked the remote, and said, "Feed me!"

BEYOND BLAND

Two days in Pearisburg. The first day on our town list was lots of relaxation and television time. The second day, checking things off *the town to-do list* in some kind of orderly fashion or our visit could quickly become an overwhelming chore fest.

With my feet doing much better, we ran errands together and by late Thursday afternoon, had completed our list and there was nothing but clear sailing and unhurried motel time. I spent some of mine updating our trail journal on the motel computer.

With our packs heavy with resupply the next morning, we headed up Pearis Mountain, a steep, almost 2,000-foot, slow-going two and a half-mile slope. It exhausted and exasperated me. For the duration of the climb, I never saw Lonnie. He went right up. Nearing the top, I had a meltdown. Lonnie and I differ as hikers—he was the little engine who could and liked to keep chugging away till he reached the top. Whereas I needed to stop and rest along the way. A lot. This time, however, I chose to keep going, trying to keep up with him, my attempt ending in overwhelming frustration. And tears. When I arrived at the summit, where he waited, I hid my tears and my feelings.

For some reason, giving myself permission to go slower and hike these climbs the way I needed to, wasn't an option, at least in my mind. One time back in Vermont, he was so far ahead of me I couldn't even see him. It wasn't that long of a climb, but after becoming upset with myself, maybe more with him, I yelled, "Reeder, Get Moving! What are you doing? Get those feet moving! Move Girl, Move! Get up this Mountain!" like some kind of drill sergeant in my head. Much later in Vermont, I talked with Lonnie. He shared how moving at a steady pace worked for him. Any slower, the ascent bogged him down, draining his energy for the climb.

After reaching the top of Pearis Mountain on this gorgeous morning, we walked to a rock overlook known as *Angels Rest*. Sitting there, I was able to find my calm. About twenty feet away, a hawk sat on a branch. Lonnie saw it first and tapped me on the leg. The hawk took off as we watched it soar out into the open. Perhaps that hawk had been giving me a message. This bird of prey is said to be a symbol of freedom, flight and protection, and can increase your spiritual awareness, leave you feeling more in alignment with your body, mind, and spirit. After telling Lonnie my feelings of frustration and anger during the climb that morning, I felt much better. It didn't change our different styles of climbing, but he heard me, and maybe next time, I would honor the way I hiked, too.

Soon we entered Virginia's *green tunnel,* named by hikers because of its three miles of continuous rhododendron thickets. Traversing the fairly flat walkway, it became apparent the trail might follow the mountain crest as it horseshoed around the valley below us. Later that evening we arrived at the Doc's Knob Shelter and a wonderfully secluded tent spot.

The next day we had lunch at the Wapiti Shelter. "Smoke Week," "Go to Jail," "Do Coke," "Go to Congress," "Do Meth," "Live in a trailor park," "Do all the above," "Be a loser," "Misspell trailer, and you are a burn-out." Just a small sampling of hiker graffiti scrawled across the walls.

After lunch, the trail opened to a spot that gave us a glimpse of the mountain across the valley where we had been the day before. We spotted the *Angels Rest* rock where we'd seen the hawk. At this overlook, another hawk on a nearby limb, startled us as it took flight. A moment later we heard a snorting, huffing sound. It wasn't a deer or a bear, but it was definitely coming from the rocks below the ledge.

Lonnie leaned out and saw two vultures, likely upset by the hawk. We figured the vultures may have had a nest nearby. One of the big birds stepped out, his black wings cloaking his entire body as he swiveled his head one hundred and eighty degrees. The creature appeared to be over two-feet tall. A few seconds later, it soared out into the valley, black with brown along the edges of its wings, apparently content the hawk was gone. Then another vulture flew out. There was more movement below and we soon spotted a smaller vulture fly to a nearby branch. This younger one had his fuzzy, downy head on a swivel, checking in all directions. It flew to another branch, not quite ready to soar out on its own. It seemed to be saying, "I want to, I really do, but I...I..."

Vultures, in mythical symbology, are linked to death, as they are incapable of eating live animals, only dead ones. But they *also are connected to rebirth.* In many cultures, a vulture symbolizes a guardian or messenger between life and death, the physical world, and the spirit world, representing renewal, cleansing and trust. In recalling this day, I couldn't help but think of Molly and Geoff, the idea of a messenger between life and death; had they had any inkling of their impending fate? Most likely not.

~

In 2006, Molly and Geoff's killer was granted life imprisonment over the death penalty, his original sentence. The horrible irony of their tragic event was that this convicted murderer was exactly the type of person they wanted to assist in forging a positive way forward in his life, to help him live free from all the trauma of his past. This man took that away from them, and ostensibly, from all the young people who would never benefit from Molly's and Geoff's influence in their lives.

However, just a few days before their passing, they did reach out to one young man. When the pair arrived in Pennsylvania on September 6th, seven days before their death, they wrote in a shelter journal, "We reached the Allentown shelter for breakfast. There we met Paul, whom we talked with quite a while. He is a 15-year-old who was kicked out of his house. We talked about some different ideas for him to try."[1]

No other kids would ever hear Molly's and Geoff's voices, or be privy to their thoughts, all because of this one senseless night in the Thelma Marks Shelter, where their dreams and aspirations ended.

As we came down from this high perch, we passed a hunter dragging a deer down the trail. Today was the first day of muzzleloader deer season. More hunters appeared at the bottom of the mountain. After we made camp that evening at Dismal Creek, two bow hunters crossed near our tent. It was Saturday night, after all, which meant even more people might show up. Early Sunday morning, still dark, we both woke to two male voices and headlamps glaring in different directions coming up from the woods below the privy—more hunters headed to their favorite spot.

After hiking three miles to Route 606, we discovered Trent's grocery store and deli only a half-mile down the road. Being Sunday, October 31st, Halloween, staying at a motel sounded like a great idea. After ordering breakfast at Trent's, we thought more about our plan. Numerous people, also having breakfast, suggested Bubba, who shuttled hikers. After calling the Big Walker Motel in Bland, we got Bubba's number and he agreed to drive us there.

While we were waiting inside Trent's, a local ambulance driver known as Crowbait, told us a story he heard while traveling in Wyoming. Back in the 1800s a man bought some land without seeing it ahead of time. Tried raising cattle on it—it was too dry. Tried farming—soil too bad. The man decided to sell it. When he attempted to put a For Sale sign on it, the board would not go in the ground. So he got an iron bar to drive the sign in. As he drove it down, it broke

---

1. Earl Swift, *'Murder on the Appalachian Trail'*, Outside Magazine, September 2, 2015

through the crust of earth, and a gusher of oil came out with such force it killed him. His widow was left a millionaire from all that oil. "A hand-dug oil well! Imagine that!" Crowbait had said, smiling.

Bubba picked us up and off to Bland and the Big Walker Motel for a day of rest and football, not quite as adventurous as catching the train into New York City on Halloween the year before. Bland, also the name of the county, wasn't an actual town in the direct sense, as much as an exit off the highway—a country road hosting a gas station across from the motel, and two stores. After the stores, the road devolved into an undefined landscape of nature, bushes and trees. But this little hamlet of services was more than enough for us; a short walk to a Subway for pizza and sandwiches, a Dollar General for a light resupply, and a Dairy Queen across the road at the gas station for massive ice cream consumption.

In the morning, Bubba took us back to the trailhead near Trent's Grocery for a nineteen-mile slack-packing trek which would land us back in Bland. It was a beautiful sunny day as we went over one hill and then another, with only our lunch, snacks, and water. We made good time, as the trail was fairly easy. Bubba picked us up around five at the pre-agreed spot, then back to Big Walker Motel for huge Snicker's Blizzards from the gas station Dairy Queen, and Monday Night Football.

The next day we said a sad good-bye to Bubba when he dropped us at the trailhead. It probably wasn't Bubba we were going to miss, but all that football and food. After several miles with little elevation change, we met up with D-Man who was hiking north. From Massachusetts, he had been section hiking. Lonnie had talked with him at the Bland Motel where he had also stayed. He was heading back to where we started, via Bubba as well. I should add that D-Man was 79 years old, quite the inspiration to us aging hikers.

By the time we arrived at the Jenkins shelter it was 2:30, ensuring us plenty of time to climb Chestnut Ridge. It was a rough climb, but once on top—even rougher—lots of rocks and no place to camp. Arriving at a gap along the ridge, we found a flat place to pitch the tent.

The next day, we stopped at the Chestnut Knob Shelter for a snack, our second time above 4,000 feet since Moosilauke Mountain in New Hampshire. From the shelter there was a view of Burke's Garden. Like a huge volcanic crater, this elongated basin—eight and a half miles long by four miles wide—formed when underground limestone caverns collapsed. The limestone continually nourished the soil within this garden crater.

The Native Americans originally tracked animals in this basin. By 1750, James Patton, a local landowner, had the valley surveyed. One of the surveyors, James Burke, an Irishman, is said to have thrown away potato peelings while working for the group. A year later, when the party returned to the area to complete their work, they found potatoes growing where the peels had been left. It became known as Burke's Garden as something of a joke, because he now had a garden of potatoes. Burke built a cabin and lived on the land for several years. German immigrants arrived in the late 1700s after the French and Indian War, who remained and farmed the land.

There had been no water at the Chestnut Knob Shelter. The nearest water was a spring-fed pond a mile and a half farther on. Though we often had more views of Burke's Garden as the trail curved around this fertile land, our minds were on finding water. Then we arrived at that *pond*. There we stood, staring at this slime-covered, unmoving stagnant pool—but we needed water.

First, we filtered it through my clean handkerchief to remove the thickest gunk, then ran it through our filter twice. With the next water six miles away, we drank only enough to quench our thirst, trusting we'd be fine until we arrived at a better source. One of the motel chores was to clean the filter, having learned this the hard way back in Maine when the filter clogged at Pleasant Pond. Another cleaning would surely be in order at our next motel.

Climbing Lynn Camp Mountain was not fun—a tough climb—but after obtaining great water at the Lynn Camp creek, we were pumped, energized for the final climb up to the Knot Maul Branch Shelter. We set up the tent inside the shelter, since the sky appeared swollen with rain. It poured all night, but inside the shelter, our tent stayed dry.

A soft drizzle lingered at daylight. Later, just past Route 42, we were treated to trail magic—a cooler of sodas, Little Debbie oatmeal pies and honeybuns—left by thru-hiker, Lumberjack '06, according to the sign. Those treats carried us through more rain hiking the eleven miles to the Davis Path Shelter. But there the magic ended. No shelter! It had been torn down. No sense setting up the tent in the rain three miles from where the trail crossed under Route 81 at an exit with a gas station, two restaurants, and a motel. It was Wednesday, November 3rd. With more rain, and snow forecasted, the decision to stay a second night was easy.

Karen, owner of the Exxon station/restaurant, served up a yummy breakfast our second morning. We were saying our goodbyes, ready to head back on the trail, when she told us there was a forty percent chance of snow. Despite a brilliant sun, a bone-chilling cold was our constant companion crossing the crest of Glade Mountain. Snowflakes danced around us as the clouds rolled in. Pushing on without any breaks, we finally reached the Partnership Shelter, with a road nearby. It was huge, two levels, with a working phone, often used to call in pizza according to the notes. Another hiker, Pack Animal, was settled in on the lower level. He had just come out of Marion and was heading north. We were chatting when he shared an adventure he'd had with a mule.

He was working for a farmer who had horses and a mule. One day, when he was headed to town, the farmer said, "Ride the mule over the mountain (a dirt road) to the bar if you want." So Pack Animal saddled up the mule and away they went. When he arrived in town, he tied the mule to a post just like in Westerns, and went into the bar. He had a few drinks and gossiped with the locals. When he walked outside to head back over the mountain, the mule was gone! Inebriated, he called to it, like you might a dog, "Here little mule. Here little mule." But the mule was nowhere to be seen.

Pack Animal had only one choice at this point, walk back to the farm across the mountain, unsure how the mule had gotten loose. When he arrived, there the mule stood by the barn door, waiting to be let in. It looked at him as if to say, "What took you so long?" Pack

Animal had a feeling that the farmer probably had a good laugh at his expense, certain his boss knew that the mule could untie the rope and would walk back to the farm.

The longer we talked, the cloudier the sky became. It was still early in the day, but the loft area of that shelter called to me. Lonnie was sort of okay with staying, while acknowledging the many miles we still had to Springer. By the time we were setup, everything outside the upstairs window was white!

In the early morning, we wished Pack Animal a good hike, and ventured out, the ground crusted in snow. Later in the day, we passed a trail maintainer who indicated that the Hurricane Shelter was just two miles or so past Dickey Gap. It was too cold to check the notes in my pack, so we trusted his info, but he was a little off on his distances. Hurricane Shelter was over five miles, which quickly turned our day into a nineteen-miler. By ourselves again, we set the tent up inside the shelter, hoping to ward off the frigid night.

34

VISITORS AT 5400-FEET

A sunny Monday morning brightened our spirits after the raw, bitter night. At Route 603, there was a grassy area to our left with a picnic table where we decided to have lunch. I took the sleeping pad off my pack and set it on the bench for a warmer seat for our bottoms, to ward off the lingering cold. While eating, a car drove down the road slowly, then stopped in front of us. The driver rolled down his window and called out, "Are you hiking the trail?"

Lonnie yelled back, "Yeah."

The man asked, "Do you know *Loup?*" We recognized the trail name, having run into him several times. *Loup,* the hiker had told us, was French for *Wolf.*

"Yeah," we both answered. I added, "He's ahead of us."

"No, actually, he's behind you now," the man answered. "I just had breakfast with him this morning. Just wanted to check if he'd come through. My wife and I hiked the trail southbound in 1990. *Loup's* my son and just graduated high school, and wanted to hike the trail, too."

I said, "We started our hike last year, but single-digit temperatures and deep snow at Rockfish Gap in Virginia forced us off the trail. Now we're back, trying to finish."

"I had to finish my hike the following year also. Well, thanks a lot. I'll find him soon enough."

The man added, "I'm joining him for a few days. We're hiking to the Old Orchard Shelter tonight, so I'll catch up to him somewhere."

While munching on my sandwich and chips, I pondered about him hiking in 1990, the same year as Molly and Geoff. In that moment I realized I didn't bring Molly's photo. Hadn't thought about it—too much excitement to get back on the trail. Couldn't even remember where I had put it. Lonnie and I never knew where we'd camp, but I did add, "We hope to get to the Thomas Knob Shelter."

Watching him leave, something troubled me from what he had said. Not sure what, though. Lonnie gave me a look, since one of our *rules* was to never tell anyone where we planned to camp.

After finishing our lunch on this cold day, we both felt that chill from eating, but maybe mine was from this man and what he had said, or my slip of confiding our campsite. I put the food items in my blue bag, picked up my pad and snapped it back on my backpack. We did our usual one arm lift to hoist the backpack and sling it up on our back, bending over slightly to get it high on our hips, then fastening the lower belt buckle, straightening up to adjust the pack to get it just right, then snapping the chest strap and tightening the shoulder straps.

We crossed the road and immediately started the 1500-foot climb up Pine Mountain, at 5,000 feet elevation. Just over three and a half miles to the top, the trail was steep at times, mostly meandering through pines. From the top of Pine Mountain, we descended, then climbed again, eventually arriving at the meadow of Grayson Highlands State Park four miles later. Gazing across the plain, I noticed little dots up ahead. After a few moments, I realized they were ponies —short, stout animals that had been introduced in 1974 to these open grasslands, allowed to run completely free. But they did not run, just stood waiting for our arrival, until I was close enough to pet one. Unfortunately, I did not have anything to feed it. It was apparent hikers fed the curious creatures, and the ponies waited patiently, but no goodies today. Not from us, anyway. In reality, feeding them, even petting them, is frowned upon and against park policy.

Bitter wind whipped around us as we climbed over rocky ledges, passing more pines. After another five miles, adding to an already arduous day, we arrived at the Thomas Knob Shelter. Not really wanting to stay in the structure, we searched until nearly dark for a suitable campsite. Finding none, we decided once again to tent inside the shelter, hoping no other hikers happened by. At an elevation of 5400 feet, we were only about four-tenths of a mile from a short trail leading to the top of the highest mountain in Virginia—Mt. Rogers, at 5,729 feet. The night was black and seamless as windy gusts roared across the mountain.

On this arctic night, lying on the floor of the Thomas Knob Shelter, nestled inside our tent, I was grateful for my down bag. Not long after Lonnie and I finished dinner, stowed our gear and snuggled down into our sleeping bags, we thought we heard talking beyond the tent, but it was hard to tell because of the wind. Visitors on this blustery night? It had been dark for at least two hours.

I saw lights coming first, then heard voices, sounding like two men talking to each other. Our tent was set up to one side, so I hoped there was enough room for these late-night wanderers. They talked quietly as they unpacked. Lonnie asked, "Do you have enough room?"

"Oh, yeah, sorry to bother you. We're good," a man's voice spoke up. "We were going to stop at the previous shelter, but felt we could make it to this one. I'm here with my son." It sounded like they were eating. I questioned if this could be the man who stopped and asked about his son earlier when we were eating lunch?

The man went on, "My wife and I hiked the trail twenty years ago, but we had to leave the trail because a couple was killed."

They continued whispering to each other with their headlamps splashing through the walls of our tent. I couldn't believe my ears. Did he say twenty years ago, a couple killed?

They sounded as if they had finished eating and setting up, and were settling into their sleeping bags.

I had to ask, "The woman…was that," I paused, almost afraid of the answer, but needed to know, "Molly LaRue?"

"Yes," he answered. He then kept talking, telling us what had happened.

He and his wife had just left Duncannon. They had taken their time climbing the mountain, navigating over all the rocks, and had looked forward to staying at the shelter. It was September 13, 1990. They'd been hiking southbound all the way from Mt. Katahdin in Maine. They were both doing well, excited about arriving at the halfway point near Boiling Springs, PA in two days. The couple took the blue-blazed trail down the hill to the shelter, but just before arriving, the man stopped. Something didn't feel right. He wanted to check out the shelter first, and told his wife to wait. (This in and of itself was odd; when you know there's a shelter up ahead, it's hard to contain the enthusiasm, especially when you see that blue-blazed trail with the shelter sign. You're practically running at that point, wanting to get the pack off your back, have a meal, and relax for the evening.)

The man and his wife had spent the night in Duncannon and were refreshed, so they didn't have that hiker urgency. Nevertheless, his wife felt that same uneasiness, and didn't argue. She waited. The man headed slowly around to the shelter. At first, he saw food and gear strewn about everywhere, as if previous hikers had been rude and inconsiderate. He turned to face the front of the shelter; a shock wave charging through him. Blonde hair, bloodied, lying over the edge of the shelter front. Overwhelmed, trying to hold it together, he knew the young woman was dead, and most likely murdered. Not far from her, was another body near the back of the shelter, a young man still in his sleeping bag, who authorities would discover had been shot to death.

The man told us, "My body shook all over. I couldn't move. I couldn't understand how such a thing could have happened!" He knew there was nothing he could do for this young couple. He ran back to his wife, and said, "Let's go. There're two people who've been murdered, a man, a woman, both young, dead, lying in the shelter."

His wife, though she had not witnessed the scene, struggled against her own disbelief.

"We've got to get back to Duncannon," he'd told his wife, then said nothing else. He told us that he'd thought about covering up the woman, but stopped since the police needed to view the crime scene. He feared for his wife and himself, searching in all directions as he followed her back to the trail, watching and looking all around for a potential attack. Finally, down the mountain, they arrived in Duncannon and headed to the police station.

When he first described what he'd seen, the police began firing questions at him. He cried out, "You've got to get someone up there to…" Tears came to his eyes, he choked up. "They're dead. Someone murdered them. Please, where's my wife?" The couple had been separated to recount their stories individually. The police continued questioning him.

"I was in disbelief," the man told us, speaking across the darkened shelter, us still in our tent, he and his son in their sleeping bags. He went on to say that even though officers had already been called to the scene, the persistent questioning made the man realize they suspected him. Now his shock turned to anger. He told us he shouted to the police, "You make it sound like I could do something so horrible as this!"

The police explained that they were just doing their job, but it took the man some time to calm down. Then he grew quiet, and chose to say nothing more. He eventually told the police in a calmer voice, "There are so many hikers out there; any of them could be this maniac's next victims. Find who did this. And please let hikers know." His thoughts went to that couple, who were still lying in the shelter, their hike never to be finished.

At the time, he and his wife had no idea who they were, though ironically, did know of the pair. They had often read their shelter journal entries and hoped they would catch up to them. They even looked forward to it. His wife had said later, "We knew we were going to catch Geoff and Molly. We followed them from Maine and when you follow someone for so long…it's like you already know them."[1]

Loup's dad continued with more details, telling us that the police had not let up on their interrogation of him. Their bodies were returned to Duncannon, but officials only found one backpack. Geoff's pack was missing. Evidently the killer had taken his backpack, which would be the search party's most critical clue to the killer's identity.

Reports of the murders went out over the airwaves, and witnesses who had thought they may have seen this person near the area started coming forth. After a composite drawing of the man was created, police scoured the trail and nearby towns. But the trail has its own means of communication. Hikers meet up with fellow hikers and then may not see them for days. However, one hiker leaves a note, and it gets passed along to others. News ran up and down the trail. Hikers jumped off, fearing that this murderer could still be out there. *Loup's* mom and dad left as well, headed home. Their hike was finished.

And now, years later, *Loup* was out here hiking, maybe to help erase this tragic event from the stories he heard throughout his youth *and* to create a new story of his own.

I simply said, "Molly was my cousin's daughter, and I'm hiking the trail to finish the hike for her." There was silence for a while. Maybe *Loup* and his dad were taking in what this could possibly mean as Lonnie and I were. The synchronicity of meeting the man who had found Molly and Geoff twenty years earlier was a shock to us, way beyond belief.

Lonnie sat up in the tent, unzipping his sleeping bag. I asked him what he was doing.

"I'm going outside for a minute." I thought about joining him, but in that moment, it felt as though we didn't need to be in each other's space.

"I've got it," I said to him as I reached across and zipped up the tent opening.

---

1. Liz Reisinger, "Crews' Murder trial takes court on trail odyssey", Sunday, The News-Sun, May 22, 1991.

Lonnie whispered, "Thanks," then moved out across the floor-boards, stepping down the stone steps. I lay back down in the stillness, thinking about Molly and this stranger. His words still hung in the air; he and his son, lying across from our tent. I couldn't get my mind to release Molly and what had happened to her so many years before in a shelter just like this one. The oddest thing occurred to me as I lay there wide awake; I started thinking about sushi. What an odd thought given the circumstances. I wondered if Molly liked sushi? I do not.

(Much later, I was talking with Jim, Molly's dad, and I asked him ,"Did Molly like sushi?" He said, "Well, when she would come home from college, she was always tired of dorm food. She wanted me to take her to any kind of Japanese or Asian restaurant and often ate sushi, the spicier the better.")

35

DAMASCUS & THE ROOT CANAL

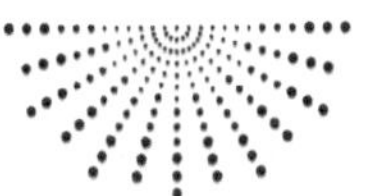

onnie and I packed up and left before Loup and his dad were ready. Loup's dad said he was going to be heading home that day. He didn't seem to have been impacted like we were. However, he'd had many years to process the horror of their death, as had his son.

Lonnie and I headed out, still stunned by this turn of events. After a short time, we came to the side trail to the top of Mt. Rogers. "Do you want to hike up there?" Lonnie said.

I shook my head. "Let's keep going," I whispered.

Both of us had eaten our cereal in silence, attempting to rationalize meeting the man who had found them. I felt uncomfortable, *even feared for my safety.* At times I felt I might just start crying. Was their murder more real to me now? Later when Lonnie and I talked, we realized we both had similar feelings. Mostly, we were incredulous.

At this point in our hike, our movements were almost robotic, moving forward doing what we'd been doing every day for the past month. Later that afternoon, our minds finally back on our hike (or so it seemed at the time), we came to a shelter near a road crossing. In Maine, we had seen many northbounders who arrived at a shelter, plopped down, pulled out their food bags, fired-up their stoves, cooked, ate, and packed up in what seemed like less than five minutes. On this day, Lonnie stopped at the Lost Mountain Shelter right off the trail, unpacked the stove, and had the water boiling by the time I arrived with our Mountain House meal in my pack. I handed him the meal, went to get water, and started filtering—our drill so well-rehearsed it took barely five minutes; we had become southbound *northbounders!*

A local man sat there with an older friend visiting from England who had wanted to hike on the Appalachian Trail. They had left their car at that road crossing. Lonnie and I ate, passing the food pouch back and forth, then rinsed our spoons, stowed our trash, and packed up, all the while answering questions about our hike.

Two miles later, we came to the Virginia Creeper Trail, an old rail-road bed that travels thirty-three miles from Abingdon to the Virginia-North Carolina state line, initially a Native American foot-path that early settlers, including Daniel Boone, used. Later we found a nice camping spot which would only leave about twelve miles to Damascus.

The next morning the climbs surprised us. They were tough, especially going over Feathercamp Ridge, then Iron Mountain. Close to Damascus, we were back on the Virginia Creeper Trail, the A.T. following it for about three hundred yards right into town.

Damascus is known for its Appalachian Trail Days May Festival. The event draws thousands of hikers and interested people each spring to celebrate the trail, and peruse all the latest trends in hiking gear and gadgets. On this cool, yet sunny Thursday afternoon, there were not many visitors and just a few other hikers. We found a bed and breakfast for the night and checked into our room. After showering, the local pizzeria, Quincy's, became our objective.

While waiting for our pizza, our bodies no longer moving at a frenetic pace, both of us sat in silence, the day's spirited hiking fading to the background of our minds. I still pondered all the variables that came together for us to meet the man who'd found Molly and Geoff. I wondered where Lonnie's thoughts were, if he was still affected, when he said, "I don't know if I can go on."

In some strange way, though I didn't feel the same as Lonnie did about ending our hike, I understood. Molly's death twenty years earlier had been a story that lived on the periphery of my life and that of my immediate family. It was tragic for her to die so young, but to me it was still abstract at best. There were few details about what had actually happened, and my mother had related what she knew, or at least I trusted that to be the case. But the man from the shelter, the one who had found their bodies, who had been questioned by the police, who testified in the murderer's trial, shared shocking and horrific details of their deaths I had never been privy to before. In the charged darkness of the shelter two nights earlier, the man told us that her partner had been shot three times in his sleeping bag, and had died immediately, while Molly had been stabbed repeatedly while being sexually assaulted. Obviously, I had never fully internalized Molly's harrowing ordeal, her partner lying there dead, the facts of her assault, all of it still spinning through my mind.

"This entire scenario has freaked me out," Lonnie added a moment later, his face drawn and blank. The pizza arrived a few minutes later, and we started eating through the silence.

"This pizza is so delicious, best on the entire trail so far," I finally said, needing to hear my own voice, something to break the spell.

"You're right, I agree. It's so good," he said. But after only a few more bites, he suddenly stopped eating, setting the slice of pizza on his plate. When I looked over, he was rubbing his jaw toward the back. A sudden pain in one of his upper molars. He tried to eat on the other side, but then could hardly move his jaw. The discomfort had intensified. Our Motrin and Tylenol were in the room. We took the pizza with us, and headed back to the B&B. He took the pills and placed ice on his cheek, but the throbbing continued.

"It feels like a damn abscess," he said, both angry and disappointed, and a bit worried. The next morning, a Friday, his tooth was a full-blown explosion of pain. He hadn't slept well, so he took more Motrin and Tylenol. Hiker hunger overcame both of us, needing something more than just cereal, even though Lonnie wasn't sure he could even chew. We headed to a breakfast café for pancakes and eggs, thinking maybe he could eat them, but he couldn't.

An hour later, he said, "I can't go on! I've got to see a dentist!"

He called his daughter, Britt, who lived near Asheville. She picked us up, already having called her dentist. He couldn't see Lonnie until Monday, but prescribed a painkiller that would help alleviate some of his discomfort. After a two-hour drive, we arrived at Britt's home, both of us much more relaxed. He took one pill the doctor had prescribed, and within an hour or so, the pain was gone! The rest of the weekend went by smoothly, to the point that Lonnie wondered if he even needed to have the tooth looked at.

"I feel great," he said at one point. "The pain is completely gone." He had also told me that he felt safer, calmer, just being off the trail. Maybe, it wasn't just the medication. We both considered later that his fear of being so vulnerable had overcome him to the point where he unconsciously created a way to get off the trail—*the need for a root canal.*

On Monday, Lonnie had the root canal and all seemed well. His tooth was better. The two of us discussed our fears and concerns for returning, especially for him. But then I wondered, will I create some kind of illness or excuse to get off the trail? I called my sister for support. She's always had a sense around strange kinds of things, so when I told her what had happened, and Lonnie's sudden abscess, needing an emergency root canal, she said, "You'll just have to wait and see how this affects you."

Then she added, "You will know when they (*Molly and Geoff*) no longer need you. Just be prepared for what could come."

My sister seemed to be suggesting that Molly could be connecting somehow from the other side. About then my thinking went off the rails; could they still be trying to move on and need something from us? A sensation hit me, that I've always heard, there is no *time* or *place* in heaven—for them it could be as if they had just died.

Things took a weirder turn, as I thought to myself, *Did my sister mean I could be killed, or both Lonnie and I could be?* She couldn't have meant that. Since that bizarre meeting at the Thomas Knob Shelter, we had been feeling a disquieting unrest, an underlying agitation neither of us could understand. We had moved forward, trying to "walk off" the anxiety. It seemed we were unable to hike fast enough to out-distance it, so maybe a full-stop was called for, a moment to delve deeper: *the need for a sudden root canal...*

36

THE JACUZZI ROOM

On Tuesday, November 16th, Britt drove us back to Damascus. We said goodbye, thanking her, then headed out, planning to return to her home in a week for Thanksgiving. We were both pumped, ready to hike. Perhaps knowing we would be off the trail again soon, made it easier to continue. After four miles, we entered Tennessee, our twelfth state.

Plenty of dark, impending clouds moved quickly across the sky toward evening. While I filtered water at Double Spring Gap, it started to rain. When the rain came harder, and not being sure when we'd find another campsite, we settled on a nice one right there at the gap.

Hurrying to get set up before we were soaked, we threw our gear inside helter-skelter and then jumped in behind it, quickly zipping the opening closed. Not our best decision: making camp in the rain. While we were erecting the tent, our gear sat on the ground getting drenched. Fortunately, our sleeping bags were only damp, buried deep inside our packs, which we then emptied under the vestibule, where things usually stay relatively dry.

After midnight, we woke to discover water pooling in the tub of our tent beneath our pads, seeping onto our sleeping bags, soaking the underside of them. By now the storm had blown out, leaving behind a full moon illuminating the fabric of our tent. With both of us unable to get back to sleep, we decided it was time to tidy up.

We put on our headlamps, took everything out of the tent—sleeping bags, all our gear, even the fly—hanging everything on the clothesline we'd strung between two trees. With the tent empty, Lonnie lifted it up and tilted it until all the water ran out. Waiting for the nice breeze to dry everything, we enjoyed the star-filled, tranquil late-night experience. After about an hour, with everything dried, we stowed our gear and looked forward to more sleep.

Long after daylight, we woke to fog.

We hiked up and down mountains, the mist eventually dissipating, the sun burning through. After descending Holston Mountain under a perfectly blue sky, the trail became a disabled-accessible pathway with a bench overlooking a scenic view of the valley down to Route 91.

Sitting on that bench, we warmed ourselves under the bright sun. On the other side of the road, we were delighted to discover trail magic in a bear-proof metal container provided by a nearby church group—water, soda, Moon Pies, and other goodies. We took a few of these treats, topped off our water bottles, and left revitalized. A wonderful surprise toward the end of our sixteen-mile day. A short distance later we came to a spring with a campsite near it.

The next day we yo-yoed over more of the Iron Mountain subrange for fourteen and a half miles, the trail eventually treating us to a view of Watauga Lake. We were excited to traverse the earthen Watauga Dam, which would take us to the shelter right on the shore of Lake Watauga; at least according to the notes. We got there only to find that the view from the wooden structure was completely clogged with trees and bushes, and the shelter itself was a fair hike to the water's edge, if you could even get there. But we stayed anyway. The next morning, descending to the lake's shoreline, we saw that there were camping spots beside the lake with gorgeous vistas, the rising sun shimmering on the water.

Leaving the lake and climbing for a time, we descended past Laurel Falls into the Laurel Creek Hollow, then headed down the steep walls of the depression, which caused us a few problems. It dropped me to the ground first, then Lonnie, twice. At the falls, with cliffs on both sides of the stream, we wondered how we'd get out. After a brief search, we saw that the trail rose right up the cliff for a tenth of a mile on steep rock-steps. It was exhausting.

The trail then followed an old, but fairly level, railroad bed moving through rocky cliff walls which had been blasted out for the railroad. Once again, I wondered how we would get out of this chasm. Just ahead, the trail left the roadbed and headed straight up the mountain again.

Here I learned that when the notes don't describe the climb, expect the worse. Grabbing roots and rocks to pull ourselves up this steep incline, we came to several overlooks where we could stop for a few minutes and catch our breath.

Later, signs along the trail warned hikers to *stay on the trail,* since some of the pathway was near private land. In 1990, local landowners feared the Forest Service would seize their property to create a buffer along the trail. That was not the case.

However, due to the preponderance of misinformation around the issue, some locals employed drastic measures to discourage hikers from passing through the area, such as hanging fishhooks from trees on invisible monofilament line above the trail to *snag* unsuspecting hikers. Recalling all the wonderful trail magic and scenery we'd encountered along this stretch of trail, I was saddened that something like that could have ever happened in this beautiful area.

The next day the trail was easier, smaller hills, lots of streams, and no rocks to navigate, even though we climbed White Rocks Mountain, topping out at 4,206 feet. After that, we came to Hardcore Cascades, a forty-foot waterfall, and a serene place to rest.

A short time later we came to a bench beside the trail dedicated to the memory of R. Frey Greer—his trail name, Vango. Eventually we came to our first view of Hump Mountain, part of the Roan Mountain balds. That night we camped above Elk River, eating our last couple of dinners, knowing that the next day would be a hostel-B&B stop.

Before completing our fairly easy hike to the hostel—a little over six miles—we took a break in an open field with an exceptional view of the valley below, as well as Hump and Roan Mountains. After our snack, we took inventory of our remaining food: four mustard packets, three M&M's, two CLIF bars. Good planning... or lucky break? On the trail it's hard to tell sometimes. At least we had a resupply box at the B&B.

We arrived around eleven and met our wonderful hostess, Mary, and her husband, Terry. The cozy hostel above the barn was down the hill from Mary and Terry's residence. It was pleasant, but we had already decided to splurge and stay in the Jacuzzi room in the main house. It just happened to be Sunday, which also meant—*NFL Football.*

Terry drove us to a convenience store down the road where we stocked up on tailgate food and drinks, at least non-alcoholic ones. Basking in the hot, bubbling jacuzzi, we watched football on the large screen TV next to our king-sized bed—*this is the life.* Maybe we were free of the fear that had tainted our hike just a few days before.

Monday morning, we decided to slack-pack the nineteen miles back to the B&B after Terry shuttled us to Hughes Gap. We would hike *north* again, over Roan and Hump Mountains back to Route 19E, something we hadn't done since Whitebeard shuttled us in the Shenandoah's. Hiking north for a southbounder doesn't break any *rules* of the trail, but it felt odd to us.

The steep slope from Hughes Gap reminded us of Maine, climbing 2,000 feet over boulders and roots, the narrow trail tunneling up though a thick copse of pine and spruce for over two and a half miles. The aroma of the evergreens kept our spirits up, seeming to make the climb easier. At one point I thought I saw a moose, the feeling of Maine so strong.

Seeing light above, we reached the open flat top of Roan Mountain and walked around the grassy field, stopping to read the weathered sign describing this old hotel, *Cloudland,* which had stood there from the 1880's till the early 1900's.

Cloudland was built as a twenty-room lodge of spruce logs, very rustic, almost like camping, until its popularity soared. That's when the owner, John Thomas Wilder, an industrialist and U.S. Army brigadier general in the Civil War, constructed a one-hundred and sixty-six room white-clapboard hotel on top of Roan. For twenty years, *Cloudland* served as a wonderful retreat for the wealthy of the South, who would visit for the summer and fall, arriving at the mountaintop via a cog railway train. They even had golf and croquet on the grassy bald. Inside, guests found spring beds, steam heat and plenty of fresh food. The local people thrived by supplying food, cooking the meals, cleaning the hotel, and... *selling spirits.*

The hotel sat on the border of Tennessee and North Carolina. Liquor was illegal in North Carolina, but for a time was allowed in Tennessee. Stories suggest a large painted stripe went right down the middle of the floor in the huge dining room. If you wanted to drink you had to be careful to sit on the Tennessee side. It's been said a sheriff sat there making sure of it.

Wandering around the open field, we imagined the festivities, the people and hubbub, noticing the last vestiges of Cloudland; small portions of concrete footers overgrown with weeds still marking the site. The day was warm with very little wind as we moved over Roan Mountain, then down through the conifers, where the trail followed the old cog railway path, nothing remaining but a wide, barren swath where the rails and deadmen had been removed.

Coming out of the woods at Carver's Gap, where Route 19E crossed over the mountains, we saw the signs for North Carolina to the east, Tennessee to the west. The North Carolina mountains appeared much larger than the ones on the Tennessee side. We were only in the woods again for a brief stint before we came out to the vast, wide-open terrain of the balds; the series of peaks serving as the border between the two states.

Viewing the distance between Little Hump and Big Hump, we were concerned about time, hoping to arrive back at the B&B before dark. The view reminded us of Saddleback Mountain in Maine, which took over two hours to cross. Fortunately, we had no problems, the hike to Big Hump taking about thirty minutes; the gentle trek free of all the hidden dips and valleys we had encountered on Saddleback.

After stopping for a lunch break near the summit of Hump Mountain, we enjoyed the amicable weather, and one last view of the wide-open space before heading down into the woods. While descending, we saw two deer hunters sitting off the mountain, but still on the bald. A short while later we spotted a reddish-colored horse in a distant field. It reminded me of the horse Daniel Boone was rumored to have lost up here one snowy day. Hence, the name, *Roan* Mountain.

We were so glad we chose to do this section without our heavy packs, making for a relaxed day. It was delightful, with great weather, and we even made it back to the B&B before dark. There we topped off our amazing afternoon with the Jacuzzi and Monday Night Football.

In the morning, Mary prepared another superb breakfast. Terry returned us to Hughes Gap, where we resumed out trek south. The forecast called for rain, and after about four miles, the weather folks were proven right. After numerous grueling hauls up the stair-stepping knobs of Iron Mountain in pouring rain, I said to Lonnie, "If I ever suggest hiking the A.T. again, just remind me of Iron Mountain!"

I was wet and exhausted from the strenuous climbs… and maybe just a bit soft from our B&B time. We came to the gap at Route 107 with a hostel close by, which meant the Cherry Gap Shelter was only three miles farther. We so looked forward to getting to the shelter, changing into warm, dry clothes, eating a hot meal and waiting out the rain, then moving on. We still had sixteen miles to Erwin and knew we wouldn't get there that day.

Molly and Geoff made it to Gambrinus Restaurant, where PA Rt. 309 crosses over Blue Mountain, "At that moment, eight days before they were found murdered along the trail near Harrisburg, their thoughts were not on the many miles that lay ahead, but on a hot meal and a cold beer....Heidi Ginder, of Lehighton, who waited on Hood and LaRue the evening of Sept. 5, said they were "sweet people; calm and quiet."

She described Hood as thin with short, curly dark hair. LaRue was slender with brown hair pulled back into a ponytail,...They sat down to a dinner of German sausage and a few beers, and dessert of chocolate cake,... The couple did not appear to be in a hurry, said Ginder, unlike many hikers who are anxious to finish the journey.

"They weren't like pushing ahead." Ginder said. Hood and LaRue were looking forward to camping out that night, she said, and were given permission to camp behind the restaurant. They were also warned to sleep clear of the trash container because it was frequently visited by a bear.

The hikers' entry in the restaurant log book reflected their moods. They wrote, "Clevis and Nalgene, in for a cold beer and good food! What a treat now we'll sleep with the bears."[1]

At the shelter were four hikers, their gear spread out over the entire wooden floor and picnic table. They hardly said a word when we arrived. We gathered from their discussion they had just come from the hostel at the gap. We had always found everyone so friendly and willing to move over to make room, but these four did *nothing* to give us space.

Lonnie went to get a little water to hold us for our next climb. The notes indicated a spring at Deep Gap, where we planned to pitch our tent, but we wanted to eat something first, maybe a hot meal to get us there. Instead, with very little room to get our cooking gear out of the drizzle, we stood at the edge of the picnic table eating the last of our cold pizza from the night before. Ready to depart the unfriendly reception, we picked up our packs and headed back to the trail, the four kids never acknowledging that we even existed.

Climbing Unaka Mountain was tough, about a 1500-foot climb over two miles, but we kept going. The notes said it reminded hikers of Maine, and it did, especially with all the spruce trees. I had a tearful meltdown as I climbed, still upset that we couldn't rest longer at the shelter, but I kept putting one foot in front of the other.

The top of the mountain at 5,180 feet, was gorgeous, thick with

---

1. Martin Pflieger & Scott Bieber, *'Ill-fated Appalachian Trail Hikers paused at Route 309 Restaurant'*, The Morning Call, September, 1990.

huge spruce trees swaying in the wind. After having been so put off by the energy of the kids at the shelter, I was relieved to be swept up in the sounds from the dancing trees, helping return my calm. Much of the trail gives off discernible vibrations of peace and serenity, which we sometimes overlook.

Dropping down off Unaka, we watched the sky open up, brilliant golds and violets. The rain had passed leaving behind a gorgeous sunset, a thick pad of bluish clouds blanketing the valley below. Not having found the spring, we continued on. By the time we reached Beauty Spot, an open field at 4500 feet, it was dark… the night impenetrable, with foggy mist rushing past in the howling wind.

White blazes on posts were our only guide, but finding them in the thick soupiness with our headlamps proved difficult, visibility no more than ten feet. We followed the rutted path for about a mile, trusting we were on the trail. Near the top, the trail turned and headed back into the woods. I knew from the notes we would be descending, and since there were very few campsites listed, and with the fog so thick, we settled on the first spot we found where we could conceivably make camp, a small, weedy slope with just enough of a clearing to wedge in our tent.

Now, with barely a liter of water between us, we knew cooking a meal was out of the question. And there'd be no more water for five more miles. After shedding our damp clothes, we climbed into our sleeping bags and ate two tuna sandwiches each, conserving our precious water. Still no hot meal, just wind screaming across the open field, shaking our tent, lulling us to sleep.

In the morning, with the sky clear, the Beauty Spot, which had seemed like some dismal, foreboding planet the night before, was now transformed into an inviting open field with full view of the valley, and a nice, flat campsite just a few feet from us! We'd have ten miles to think about the experiences from the day before as we headed into Erwin.

Hiking down the mountain, the clouds hovered over the valley, a splendorous picture even with power lines dissecting the view. Our water situation improved greatly when we arrived at a spring next to the trail. Curley Maple Gap Shelter would be our next stop, for a relaxed lunch, and then the final couple of miles into Erwin. Britt and her husband had left a car at a hotel in Erwin, so we were able to pick it up and drive back to their home for Thanksgiving.

It rained on the Friday after Thanksgiving, so we decided to wait until Saturday to get back on the trail. We also thought perhaps we'd skip the section from Erwin to Hot Springs since we had done that on our shake-down hike. We were growing concerned about hiking through the Smokies, especially with December closing in.

HAIR-COMBING MAN

Britt graciously took us to the trailhead in Hot Springs, since we did decide to skip the previous section from Erwin. Now we were officially in our thirteenth state, North Carolina, even though we had been skirting back and forth across the NC/TN border in the last segment.

At Hot Springs I went into the outfitter's store to pick up the permit for the Smokies while Lonnie waited with his daughter. The clerk informed me that we had to stay in the shelters, where no tents were allowed. I went outside and told Lonnie. He was frustrated about this, even suggesting we skip the Smokies completely, not something I wanted to do. I didn't care about staying at shelters, but I did like sleeping in our tent. Regardless, it was still disappointing that we couldn't hike the way we'd been doing all along. Then Lonnie balked about needing a permit, since we'd been hiking for so long with no rules. I wasn't so bothered by that, but these new developments left us both irritated and upset with each other.

After Britt left, Lonnie moved up the trail ahead of me, and I didn't care. We were not talking. It was a strenuous climb, with several crests. Usually, he waited for me at each one, but not today. I kept climbing and could not catch up to him. Didn't even see him. At that point, though, I cared less if I saw him or not. Of course, we shared all the gear, so we needed each other to set up the tent and cook our food, but at that point, I thought, *Whatever.* Anger can make you feel and think things that really don't make sense.

As I continued up the mountain—now a good hour since we'd left the trailhead, and with no sight of Lonnie—I came upon a man I hadn't seen on the trail or in town. He was to my left, above me, standing on the ridgeline in the weeds, facing up the mountain, maybe fifty feet above the trail. From my vantage point, I could see his profile, where he was combing his long, light brown hair, which reached down to the middle of his back. For whatever reason, I was spooked; it was baffling seeing this man combing that hair, staring out at nothing; no backpack, no tent, no hiking gear at all that I could see.

A chilling dread swept through me. Just then, the craziest notion seized me; I was convinced the hair-combing man had *murdered* Lonnie. I expected to see Lonnie's body on my right lying in the leaves, discarded somewhere down the side of the mountain. Moving up the trail, I climbed toward that ridgeline tense with fear. When I reached the crest, the trail continued up the mountain, away from the man, putting him now behind me. I didn't look back but kept moving upward, searching the dead leaves and underbrush for Lonnie's body.

My movements became stilted, fearing at any moment the hair-combing man would be upon me. I kept ascending. Still no sight of Lonnie. I dared to look back, but did not see anyone. No one was following me. I hoped the stranger was gone. Maybe he was still down on that ridge combing his hair. I knew I hadn't imagined him. I wondered where Lonnie could be.

Then I realized how terrified Molly and Geoff must have been. The fear and ultimate death they suffered. For me it was all in my head, with no physical changes, only emotional ones. My body stopped. I sat down, feeling weak, unable to move. Lonnie nowhere in sight. I remembered my sister's words: *You will know when they no longer need you. Just be prepared for what could come.*

I spoke to them out loud, "I'm going to finish this hike for me, now. You can move on." It felt real to me, these words and thoughts going through my head, but I wondered if this debate related to them at all—was this about *my* hike or *theirs*—was I meant to feel this angst and if so, why?

Something swept through me, the fear releasing its hold. I was suddenly aware of my breathing, which had become easier. I stood and continued up the mountain. After a few minutes I saw Lonnie standing on the trail, looking toward me, waiting. I quickened my pace, even ran, right into his arms. As best as two people can hug with cumbersome packs and other paraphernalia, we embraced. Tears poured from my eyes. I just held onto him.

He said, "Are you okay?"

I answered, "I am now."

I wasn't ready to tell him what I had experienced. Molly and Geoff were in every corner of my mind; imagining their fear, their agony, their last breaths, as I clung to Lonnie. We had two hundred miles left to Springer Mountain in Georgia. I felt that when we climbed that final mountain, they would be there with us somehow.

The day was cold and windy, yet I felt a peculiar calmness as we arrived on the summit of Bluff Mountain. Later, at the Walnut Mountain Shelter, we ate our meal and went to bed, neither of us talking about what had really transpired our first day back on the trail after Thanksgiving; with me realizing I had so much to be thankful for.

Climbing Max Patch took longer than expected. We stopped at the Roaring Fork Shelter where we had lunch and a short break before continuing on toward the summit. Max Patch, at 4,629 feet, was spectacular. Being Sunday, with road access nearby, family groups had gathered on this open field mound, luxuriating on sprawled blankets, enjoying the stunning 360-degree vista. Children ran and played like little sprites bouncing along the grassy field, with dogs chasing behind.

Visitors to Max Patch have been enjoying this superb mountaintop for over a hundred and fifty years. It began in the 1800s when early settlers cleared this land for grazing animals. The name, Max Patch, may have come from a family with a Mc prefix who either owned the land or managed it, spelled Mac's or Mack's in the beginning. But by

1875, the name Max stuck, the mound referred to as Max Patch Mountain, or Max Patch Gap.

However, there was another tale about how the mound received its name. I prefer this more light-hearted story, that there was once a horse that loved to escape and run to his favorite patch to graze and feel the cool breeze and soak up the sun. The horse's name was Maximilian, resulting at first in Max's Patch, then finally, Max Patch.

In the 1920s, this patch became a great place to land airplanes, treating passengers to soaring adventures through the breathtaking mountains. Now, a hundred years later, families still flock to this bit of earth to revel in the beauty surrounding this special sweep of land.

We left Max Patch around two, knowing that the Groundhog Creek Shelter was nearly six and a half miles away. Amazingly, we went over the hills so quickly, we arrived and made camp by 4:15. The campsite had lots of clear, cold water at the stream, and bear cables to hang our food.

On the bald of Snowbird Mountain, we had our first view of the Smokies—clouds hung over the peaks, with the mountains creating their own weather. Reaching Davenport Gap, I was confused by which road led to the Standing Bear Farm Hiker Hostel, (now called Bear Farm Hiker Hostel) where we had a food box.

We almost hiked right by it, since I forgot the guidebook notes were written for *northbounders.* Fortunately, a sign for the hostel on a rock by the dirt road kept us from straying, directing us two-tenths of a mile up the road. Heading there, rounding a curve in the dirt road, a small black bear sprinted across in front of us and disappeared into the woods. Only the second bear we'd seen during the entire hike. Maybe he was saying, *Welcome to the Smokies!* After arriving at the hostel, dusky clouds started rolling in. This gave us concern about entering the Smokies the next day as planned.

It was only one in the afternoon, and already we had decided to spend the night. People at Max Patch told us lousy weather was coming, and the dismal cloud cover seemed to confirm the forecast, so we would decide in the morning what to do.

Curtis and his wife, Maria welcomed us to their hostel, a unique retreat wrapped in the lap of surrounding mountains. Exploring the grounds we came upon the unusual hiker shower stall. Constructed of beer bottles tipped on their sides and set in concrete, the walls glowed with the rarefied light of stained-glass windows. Curtis told us that one summer, with the help of some hikers, they tackled the shower wall crack, rebuilding it with jettisoned beer bottles in a rainbow of colors cemented together. They even managed to form an A.T. symbol with beer bottle ends in the midst of this notable design.

Sleeping in the cabin at the hostel, our plan was to get up early and head out. However, that morning Curtis was quick to tell us a nasty rainstorm was heading right toward the Smokies. We decided to wait a while at the hostel. By 8:30 that morning, the storm still hadn't arrived and Curtis told us it had stalled just west of Knoxville. There were six thru-hikers who had arrived the night before, and were preparing to leave. Since the weather was balmy, in the sixties, we also decided to head out. We packed up and were eating breakfast in the kitchen when it started to pour. The sky glowed with an ominous greenish-gray hue.

When the rain let up, it felt too late to head into the Smokies, so instead we opted to slack-pack the two and a half miles from Davenport Gap back to the hostel. Curtis dropped us at Davenport where we easily hiked back to the hostel, mostly downhill, once again heading north.

That afternoon, the sky still threatening, Maria drove us to Newport, TN twenty miles away, where we stayed at the Motel 6 that night. The weather, though overcast, was still warm, and we questioned our decision to delay our start into the Smokies. Even so, conditions seemed ripe for a huge storm.

Out on the trail, there are no wrong decisions, or so we told ourselves, giving our philosophy further thought. By late afternoon, the storm slammed the Smokies. The rest of the day it poured, high winds, temperatures still in the sixties. From the hotel, we sloshed through two parking lots in the dark to have dinner at Shoney's. Hopefully, we'd have an early start on the trail in the morning with no rain.

By six am the sky was slate-gray, though the rain had finally stopped. We checked the weather; the forecast called for clear skies by noon. From our motel window, that didn't seem possible. Curtis picked us up at eight and took us to Davenport Gap. As we said our good-byes, a few snowflakes floated down from the steely sky. It wasn't hard climbing, but with the snow intensifying, we questioned our decision to hike the Smokies in December. If the forecast for blue skies by noon was wrong, we could easily find ourselves in a foot of snow. Or more.

SIBERIAN WINTER

$\mathcal{A}$s we climbed, the snow fell to a half inch, then three inches, but by the time we reached the ridge crest, to our delight, the sun appeared. There was a patch of blue shining through, then a little more until finally, right around noon, just as predicted, we had full sun with an intense azure sky. The front had definitely brought colder temperatures, yet the sunshine was soothingly warm. The beauty of the Smokies came alive for us—spectacular, glistening crystals on snow-coated trees, making for a very special day. We did the first eight miles to Cosby Knob Shelter so quickly, we decided to move on. The next seven miles took much longer, though; lots of rocky sections with snowmelt running down the trail.

At Tri-Corner Knob Shelter, being by ourselves, we pitched our tent inside, despite the rules. When we were at the Motel 6 in Newport waiting out the storm, I reread the trail notes, which said thru-hikers could tent if the shelter was full, as long as it was on an already flattened area. But considering the time of year, and the weather, we figured there'd be no other hikers. A blue tarp hung along the front edge of the shelter for added protection, separating us from the cold wind. During the night I heard an animal walking outside, figuring it was a deer. In the morning there were tracks, which looked more like a bobcat.

Hiking over a narrow mountain crest, we met two older guys and six girls with a *dog* coming from the opposite direction. But seeing that dog surprised us, since dogs were *not* allowed in the park. It seemed we weren't the only ones bending the rules.

The next night we found a hiker at the Icewater Shelter. Don, from Tennessee, had come in from Newfound Gap, to give the outdoors a try for a few days. It seemed odd to us that he would choose to come to the Smokies in December to try his hand at backpacking. When we arrived, he was walking around the front of the shelter, as if not knowing what to do with himself, or maybe just trying to keep warm. We set up, this time just outside the structure, but under an over-hanging portico. By the time we finished making camp and chatting with Don, it was dark, and I could tell he was *really* happy we were there.

The next morning felt like a Siberian winter, the temperature dipping into the low twenties, maybe lower. Don had slept on the shelter floor in his sleeping bag, telling us he froze most of the night. Now, with a fire going, he was attempting to warm up. Though the fire was inviting, we wanted to get going, and said good-bye and wished him well on his journey.

Later that morning we met another natural impediment to winter hiking—ice. Descending to Newfound Gap, we found sections of ice on the trail that made the long downs tedious and tiring. At one point I sat on the ice, too afraid to walk across it, sliding down the trail on my bottom, the base of my backpack dragging along the ice helping to slow my progress. Still a little scary with a fairly steep slope to my right.

A short while later, I was following Lonnie when he slipped and fell, twisting his body as he slid down the mountain, trying to find purchase on the slippery slope with his trekking poles.

"Are you okay?" I asked, hurrying to him as he was trying to turn around to get up.

"I think so."

Stuck precariously on his back, head first ten feet down the mountainside, he was unable to get up, gravity trapping him. He checked himself for injuries, undid his pack, then grappled with the poles to get himself turned around.

"Yeah, I seem to be. I think I *ginked* my left knee a little, but I'm okay." He turned, righted himself, and crawled up to the trail dragging his pack. I couldn't believe how fast he'd gone down. We proceeded cautiously, toward the gap.

Route 441 cuts through the Smokies at Newfound Gap, with the town of Cherokee on the eastern North Carolina side, and Gatlinburg, Tennessee to the west. The sun, now bright in the sky, made the gap a perfect place to rest and have lunch. We were shocked to find the parking area clogged with cars and buses, throngs of people milling about. Several women from a tour bus wandered over to ask what we were doing, the smell of their perfume reaching us before they did. Being in the woods so long, our senses had become more acute, the fragrance of their perfume a bit cloying. We smiled and explained that we were hiking the A.T. One woman took our photo, but I wasn't sure why. Maybe to her we were some kind of mountain oddity.

We welcomed the quiet of the trail, but navigating the ice was exhausting. It wasn't long before I slipped, coming down hard on my elbow and bruising it.

Climbing Mt. Love, we maneuvered over more rocks, being careful to find the dry ones, trying to avoid the slippery footing. Around four we arrived at the highest point in the park, Clingsman Dome. At an elevation of 6,643 feet, it is the third highest mountain east of the Mississippi River, named in 1859 for Thomas Lanier Clingman, a U.S. Senator from Asheville, NC.

In September of 2024, the mountain was restored to its original Cherokee name, Kuwhoi, which means "mulberry place," honoring the Cherokee people.

The elaborate spiraling concrete lookout area was completely void of people. No one. Apparently, the seven-mile access road from Route 441 was closed, denying tourists admittance to this spectacular viewing area. But it was an hour till sunset, so we couldn't linger long, knowing we had two and a half miles to the Double Spring Gap Shelter.

Near the shelter, we stopped when we heard a weird noise. We looked up in the trees, thinking it was above us, but then it seemed to come from in front of us, sounding like the drumming of wings. We moved forward, with me in the lead. I stopped just before the clearing of the shelter and whispered, "Look over there."

Lonnie asked, "Where?"

"Right in front of the shelter."

It was a huge turkey, standing, as if waiting for us. I snapped a few photos as we advanced. The turkey did not move. Right by the shelter, the turkey pecked at the ground, within four feet of us. It continued to eat, then preened its feathers, but did not move away.

Lonnie kept saying, "This is not good." Especially when I opened the plastic bag to take out the water filter, and the turkey jumped up on a log by the fire pit within two feet of where I sat. We believed this *wild* turkey had been fed before. Fortunately, it did not pester us, a gentle and patient bird, but it received no treats this evening. I remembered the turkey with her babies that had attacked me while walking near our mountain home. Fortunately, this was not the season for little ones.

"Don't worry, it will leave to roost in a tree as soon as the sun goes down," I said.

"How do you know that?" he said, not buying any of it.

"I raised chickens," I told him, thinking that should assuage his concerns, him being such a city guy, but he just glowered at me like I had two heads. Because of my experience with chickens, I did feel I had more experience with turkeys; at least it made sense to me, a fowl is a fowl. And after dark, we didn't see it again, but Lonnie didn't seem to notice.

The air wasn't quite as cold as the night before, but still below freezing. We set up in front of the shelter, under the roof, the elevation 5,507 feet. Lonnie had brought his track phone on this second hike and, amazingly had service. He talked to Tom, our friend, who had offered earlier to pick us up once we finished the Smokies. Lonnie arranged for him to meet us in two days at the Fontana Dam Visitor's Center, where the trail led across the dam of this sprawling reservoir after leaving the Smokies.

Tom had told Lonnie there was a chance of rain. However, the next morning the sun prevailed, affording us awesome views. Later though, the sky turned gray, and as we began our descent, sleet and *snain* pelted our jackets. With six more miles to the Derrick Knob Shelter, we quickened our pace watching the sky turn threatening over the mountain ahead. By the time we arrived, it was all snow. We sat at the picnic table behind the blue tarp covering the front of the shelter, deciding what to do. Even out of the snow and wind, it was still super cold; I couldn't stop shivering, sitting in this bleak shelter. We recalled the night we had made camp in the rain a few weeks earlier, our gear getting drenched, and wishing we had kept going.

So now we could add "snowing" to the *Keep Moving* decision.

We were still twenty-two miles from Fontana Dam where we would meet Tom the next day, too far to hike in one day under these conditions. In lieu of lunch, we hurriedly ate a bar and scooped peanut butter out of the plastic jar. Since we did not have phone service now, it was impossible to change the plan with Tom. I hoped my shivering would stop as we left the shelter.

This was one of those days when no plan sounded good. I just wanted to be warm. We passed several gaps and climbed to the east peak of Thunderhead Mountain. Then crossed the fairly level Rocky Top with no view, only a white wall of falling, wet snow. By this time my gloves were soaked, and I questioned, with the snow mounting, how I would get them dried for the next day's hike. A chill had already burrowed inside me, and I wasn't sure if I could get warm again. Darkness arrived and we still had three miles to the Russell Field Shelter.

The snow had turned back to *snain,* the night quickly turning colder and wetter. We put on our headlamps, and just kept moving forward with little visibility when fog moved in.

Arriving at the shelter, I was so glad to be there, though the situation with the snow and cold was distressing. We mulled over our options, deciding to pitch the tent under the extended roof next to the picnic table. We couldn't imagine anyone else coming through tonight and felt it was a good decision to keep the tent somewhat protected.

By now the fog was so dense we couldn't see more than two feet. Just to go to the bathroom, we had to continually call out to each other so we didn't get lost. In the heavy snow and fog, our headlamps were useless, only serving to illuminate the drifting particles, making it easy to lose our bearings.

Secured inside our tent, we still had the problem of wet gloves. Lonnie's were soaked like mine, but he had an extra pair. I did not, and worried how I'd keep my hands warm the next day. We started our meal of pasta primavera. Once we poured the boiling water into the pouch, we used the opportunity, while the meal cooked, to pass the warm pouch back and forth to help our slowly thawing hands.

Sitting in our sleeping bags, taking turns eating from the hot meal, we discussed what we could do to dry our gloves. Lonnie came up with an idea—take a pair of spare socks, placing one sock inside each glove to sop up the excess water, then remove the sock and place the gloves under our body, allowing our body heat to do the rest. It wasn't a tried-and-true technique, but hopefully, by morning, they'd be dry enough to get us through the day. After removing the socks from my gloves, I placed the gloves under my bottom, me nestled in my sleeping bag. Oh, they were so cold and wet at first, but I knew I'd get used to it. It took quite a while to warm up with those soggy gloves under me.

The wind ripped at our tent all night, the snow drifting up against it, the fog relentless, like a black shroud around us. But we were finally warm, our bellies full. We had gone sixteen and a half miles that day, and sleep came easily. By morning not only were my gloves dry enough to get me down the mountain, but the storm had passed.

When we left the shelter, with thirteen miles to Fontana, we hiked beneath a gray sheet of sky, windy, and piercingly cold. We trudged through snow the entire day, with levels in several drifts up to ten inches deep, but usually on the trail only a few inches. We knew it could have been a lot worse.

Nancy and Lonnie in the Great Smoky Mountains National Park in the snowstorm. (Photo: Lonnie Busch)

We stopped at the Mollies Ridge Shelter for a short rest. Legend says this ridge was named for a Cherokee maiden named Molly, who was searching for a lost hunter, perhaps her beloved, and as she moved across this land she froze to death before she could find her way out.

After passing the side trail to the Shuckstack Tower, we knew the trail would start its descent toward Fontana Lake. However, we never anticipated how this drop of 2100 feet over four and a half miles would feel to our legs and knees. We were used to ups and downs, but this challenging grade gave us trouble, especially for Lonnie; the knee he bruised from his fall near Newfound Gap was *talking* to him.

Halfway down, I had to stop, rest my legs, and eat peanut butter bread, but Lonnie just wanted to get down the mountain. It was somewhat nice standing there, hitting pause on the long steep grade, observing Fontana Lake far down below us.

At last, we reached the bottom and left the snowy landscape behind. As we crossed the dam, we stopped to peer down at the huge chutes, the dizzying drop to the bottom making my knees weak. At 480 feet, Fontana Dam is the tallest in the eastern United States. It took almost three million cubic yards of concrete to build, completed in 1945.

Even though the flurries continued at the dam, the ground was bare, and too warm for snow to lay. The visitor center was closed, but the bathrooms were *open.* And *heated!* What a wonderful bonus standing in this bathroom, recalling how just hours earlier I'd been freezing.

We ate snacks and Cokes we'd bought from the outdoor vending machines (which incredibly were working), peeking out occasionally at the parking lot to see if Tom and his wife, Sandy, had arrived.

Lonnie started wondering if they would come, if Tom had forgotten the plan. A short time later we heard a car pull up. We grabbed our gear and burst through the door. Tom came to a stop as we rushed his car, more than a little giddy to see them. It's so great when a plan comes together! They were our constant trail angels, driving us all the way to Waynesboro in October two months earlier to begin this second leg of our southbound hike.

After a nice meal at a Mexican restaurant with our friends, they drove Lonnie and me to a motel where we started figuring out the last stretch of our hike. For the next two days we ate a lot, relaxed in the motel, did laundry, resupplied, and concocted a plan to get home after our hike, which would involve dropping one of our cars with a friend who lived near Springer Mountain. With the plan set, it was time for banana splits.

The weather was turning more brutal, and it didn't seem to be letting up just because we were heading farther south. The next eighty miles of North Carolina we had hiked numerous times as part of our preparations for the journey, so, due to weather, we decided to skip it and head to Deep Gap, since we were technically section hikers now. From there we would finish the last four miles of North Carolina, then enter our last state, Georgia.

NO GRADE GREATER THAN FIFTEEN DEGREES

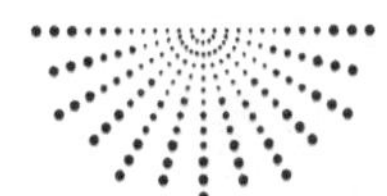

After taking Lonnie's car to a friend's place in Georgia, we drove back to our home and waited for Tom to pick us up and drive us to Deep Gap, several miles south of Standing Indian Mountain. After thanking him, we headed out for the last leg of our journey. The air didn't feel that cold, most likely because of our hustle up to the ridge from the gap.

Upon reaching Muskrat Creek Shelter, while setting up the tent inside the structure, we realized the temperature had dropped significantly, a chill spreading through us. All finished, we laid down in our sleeping bags and were chagrined to find that the crisp air had penetrated the floor of our tent, into our bags, through the spaces in the shelter floor boards, sweeping up under the structure's platform. Putting our tent outside on the ground may have been a better choice.

The next morning we headed to the Georgia border, our fourteenth and last state, and almost missed the border sign. The faded wooden sign was attached to a tree just past Bly Gap. Funny how when we finished our first state, Maine, we both celebrated, but now, with *both* of Lonnie's knees throbbing, he had walked right by it, and wasn't interested in going back for a photo.

The knee he injured on the ice before Newfound Gap was still painful. Now his other knee was giving him problems, starting toward the end of the Smokies with the long down from Shuckstack to Fontana Dam. When you hurt one knee, you begin to coddle it, which puts more stress on the healthy knee, until both become stressed. He had tended to them at the motel in Franklin, but to no avail. Sitting on a log eating lunch, I looked over the trail notes. There were places to leave the trail at several gaps with main roads. This news seemed to energize Lonnie, the knowledge that there were places to leave the trail put his mind at ease. By the time we finished lunch, his knees had actually stopped hurting.

The next day we journeyed up four major mountains, all above 4,000 feet. In the Smokies, the notes had indicated that there was *no grade more than fifteen degrees*, but in Georgia, it seemed as if there were no grades *less* than fifteen degrees, with difficult hiking all day. Despite that—Georgia was beautiful, especially in the winter with countless views.

We climbed to Kelly's Knob, then Tray Mountain. On the climb up Tray, Lonnie was ahead when a bear dashed across the trail about thirty yards in front of me. It was the third bear we'd seen on our hike, though Lonnie missed this one.

We went over Rocky Mountain, then started our last climb up Blue Mountain, the Blue Mountain Shelter a mile past the crest. The spring at the shelter was just a trickle, but with Lonnie's ingenuity, creating a little dam, we soon had our portable bucket filled. For the entire hike we've been using a fold-up vinyl bucket that held two gallons of water. It was lightweight, and once folded, fit neatly into a plastic pouch about four inches square that Lonnie had attached to his pack belt.

In high school Molly wrote a story, illustrating the text during her college years. The book was eventually called, the Reds. the Yellows. the Blues.—a story of differences between people and how some are able to see past them. Her little book carries an important message, ending with:

"And time and life went on and on. And the people on the little white island talked and thought and laughed and argued and cried and worked and loved. And the little island gained their love and their colors and grew. And everyone and everything just lived."

Molly loved art, but also wrote poetry, and always with an eye for nature and the outdoors:

"Blue Flower"
Strolling through the woods one day...
I came upon a clearing—
Overflowing with flamboyant flowers
It appeared to be a sea of yellow.

Skipping about the field,
Something caught my eye;
It was a lone blue flower,
Among the multitudes of golden ones
Blue, beautiful blue.

About art, she wrote:
There's lots of "stuff" (feelings, ideas, memories, colors, shapes...) in me—
Stuff that's hard to put into words --- art's easier.
I can be quiet on the outside
While my stuff inside is pretty
Loud. My art is some of This noise. I'm glad there's art.

Growing up in Signal Mountain, Tennessee, Geoff could explore the nearby forest, river, and many trails. His mother remembers him being very active in the Boy Scouts, even going to the Philmont Scout Ranch in New Mexico. She says, "He wanted to work in nature, teaching kids. He was outdoors all the time." He studied at the University of Tennessee: Chattanooga graduating with a degree in Outdoor Recreation Education. Before meeting Molly, he had rock-climbed in Colorado, experienced winter camping in Minnesota, and taught climbing at Philmont.

In their journal, he wrote, "What a day for the naturalist. First, along the stream bank, we saw a turtle hatch (their egg shells are paper thin.) Later we saw a moose, our first one after several days of tracks." GH

Molly's dad said, "Molly loved every minute of being outdoors." When she was just twelve years old, she went on a church backpacking and mountain climbing adventure. That may have started her with this wonderment around nature.

Both Molly and Geoff experienced Outdoor Leadership schools before they met. Their experiences and love of nature, along with their desire to help kids, is what brought them together.

That night, Old Man Winter blasted us again as we ate dinner. We crawled shivering into our sleeping bags, but after a while, we were toasty warm. The tent was definitely warmer sitting directly on the ground, no air sweeping under us. When I saw lights approaching, realizing it was Friday night, I chuckled to myself. It never failed! The hikers walked by the shelter, but didn't stop. Seeing late-nighters, especially on cold nights, I often wondered where were they going? We had set up our tent away from the shelter, so they probably didn't even know we were there.

With an early start the next morning, we were getting closer to that final destination—Springer Mountain. More ups and downs, climbing precipitous mountains, struggling down steep slopes. I now understood why so many northbound hikers arrived in Franklin with knee problems.

The day was long, eighteen miles. It felt good to finally arrive at Neels Gap. The afternoon sun tried to poke through the mounting clouds. Another storm brewing.

Mountain Crossings Hostel and store were popular haunts for hikers at Neels Gap, where the trail actually passed between buildings via an outdoor breezeway. We knew we wanted to stay, but weren't sure about being at the hostel. After asking the store clerk about nearby lodging, we were directed to the Blood Mountain Cabins about a hundred yards down the road, each unit with its own kitchenette.

They sounded awesome, so after a phone call about availability, we headed down the hill. It looked like snow coming, so perhaps this was a good decision. Our cottage proved perfect—warm, roomy, and yes, a nice kitchenette. Unfortunately, we didn't have anything to cook, but we didn't care. Sleeping on a soft bed made it ideal.

The next morning, Lonnie decided to make toast in the toaster with our flat bagels. He put two in the toaster and left for a moment to pack his gear. When I started smelling something, I stopped what I was doing and went into the kitchen.

The toaster was smoking, flames shooting out of it!

In the same moment, Lonnie rushed from the bedroom and turned it off, then unplugged it to be sure, saving us from burning down our *perfect* cottage. It brought to mind the misuse of our camp stove in the shelter so long ago during our shake-down hike.

Regaining our calm after this little mishap, we packed and started walking up the road to the trail, a fresh padding of snow on every-thing, the sky promising more at any moment. The climb up Blood Mountain was a struggle. Even though it was well below freezing with snow falling, Lonnie was soaked with perspiration, the two-mile-1800-foot climb a chore.

And the throng of day hikers was a shocker, especially given the conditions, numerous folks in puffy jackets navigating around us and our huge packs, talking and laughing.

At the crest we crossed over various flat rocks, where there were supposed to be fantastic views, but for us, nothing but clouds and a curtain of snow. When we reached the Blood Mountain Shelter, we were stunned to see at least twenty people standing around outside, with more folks milling about inside.

The Blood Mountain Shelter, built by the Civilian Conservation Corps in 1937, was made from local stone with no open front, but a solid door. All the day hikers were dressed in brightly colored ski jackets, scarves, and mittens. We had never seen so many people along the trail and couldn't understand the attraction. Then it hit us; for people in Georgia, this snow was unusual, even miraculous, maybe! And everyone wanted to be a part of it. Except for Lonnie, who was exhausted from the climb, freezing, and dealing with an upset stomach. And there we were with our ragged gear and dirty clothes, not sharing the gaiety of the moment. Nevertheless, there was no way to stop and get warm at this shelter. Time to move on.

The snow continued throughout the morning into the afternoon. Tired and hungry, and feeling weak from the long climbs, I needed to eat something other than bites of an energy bar. The snow was coming heavier now, almost a blizzard, but I stopped anyway, announcing that I needed to eat something, much to Lonnie's irritation.

He was beyond frustration, with the climbs, the weather, and the rawness of the day, not to mention the crowds, and chilled from his own sweat. I took off my pack and pulled out the bread and cheese to make sandwiches, manipulating them as best I could while setting everything on top of my pack which was sitting on the snowy ground. When I opened the mustard packets, Lonnie said, "Why are you bothering with those?"

It was stupid on my part, but in the process of trying to put some on the bread, I got mustard all over myself. Moments before this mishap, I had mentioned, "Once we finish this hike, why don't we hike the Pacific Crest Trail?" We had heard about it from other hikers who talked about the PCT, a 2,650-mile trail starting at the Mexican border, through California, Oregon, and Washington, ending at the Canadian border. It was poor timing on my part, mentioning the PCT.

"Jeez, Nance! We haven't even managed to finish this one, yet!"

Standing there, him freezing cold and feeling sick, I had no compassion for his plight. I even thought to myself, "I'll just hike that trail by myself!" We finished eating, then hiked on, snow falling, anger flaring, Lonnie still sweating like crazy, and freezing from his wet clothes. Silence sat between us like a bad dream.

We arrived at Woody Gap and Route 60, with several cars in the parking lot. Only twenty miles from Springer, *so* close to that final mountain, our destination and goal, but the hypothermic weather was winning, the chill overcoming Lonnie. People lingered by their cars, most likely folks from nearby cities, who seemed ecstatic about the snow. Near the road was a restroom, one door for men, the other for women. We crammed into the men's side, which only accommodated one person at a time, to talk about what to do *and* get out of the cold.

Lonnie said, "I've got to get warm. I'm soaked and just don't know how I can go on."

"Do you want to get off the trail?" I asked him.

He stood there a moment, contemplating, then answered, "I know I can't go on hiking this way."

"Well, I think this road goes to a town." I had the notes out searching how far it would be. "It seems the best thing is to get to a motel, stay the night and see what's going on tomorrow. Does that sound good to you?"

"Yeah, now we just have to find a way to get someplace warm."

His chill was getting worse, and when that happens, it's hard to warm up while still out in the cold, hypothermia always a dangerous possibility. When we opened the door, there was a man waiting to use the restroom, surprised to see the two of us coming out. He went in and closed the door, while we stood outside still discussing our situation. Our voices must have been loud enough for him to hear, because when he came out, he said, "Do you need a ride somewhere?"

Once again, just when we needed something, someone appeared to help. But later I thought, that didn't happen for Molly and Geoff; no one came to their aid and rescue. I said to this gentleman, "Yes, could you take us to the nearest motel?"

Within a few minutes we were in his car, the heater blasting, us almost floating down the mountain. In the morning, the temps were in the single digits, the wind outside the room howling. We learned that the freezing weather would continue for the next several days.

In 2009 we had delayed the finish of our hike a year due to brutal temperatures and deep snow. Now, the idea of postponing this hike to finish at a later date during better weather was not an easy one. We called Debbie, my friend who lived nearby where we had left Lonnie's car. She came to the motel and soon Lonnie and I were once again headed home to wait out the finish of our Appalachian Trail Adventure—the last twenty miles.

KEEP YOUR HANDS CLEAN

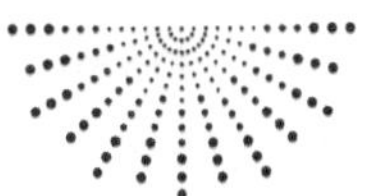

December of 2010 and January of 2011 were freezing cold with continuous snowstorms. We decided to wait for better weather to finish our last twenty miles. On February 13, 2011, with warming temps, the weather sunny and pleasant, we headed back to Woody Gap where we had stopped a few months earlier. These last miles seemed to go quickly, only needing one night in our tent.

On February 14, 2011, we hiked to the top of Springer Mountain, where we had our final hot chocolate and mini-donuts. We sat there munching our goodies, both of us quiet, realizing we were at the end. I thought of Molly and Geoff, their hike and its tragic ending. It was hard to picture such a terrible fate for them, when Lonnie and I had had such an enriching experience, even with the bumps along the way. Being outdoors day after day, immersed in the grandeur of nature, the revitalizing influence of fresh air and movement, they had hiked nearly half the trail, and I can't imagine they ever gave a moment's consideration to their hike ending under such horrific circumstances. Who would?

For us, there was a feeling of *now what?* When we returned home it would be similar to our experience the year before; wandering around the house, lost and unable to focus. But the last time, we always knew we'd be returning to finish these last twenty miles. We didn't have that now. A thru-hiker always has a goal in mind, either finding camp, getting to the next town, refilling with water, or maybe just to see how many miles he or she can hike in a day, but finishing the trail is a true end. No goal for the next day, a maelstrom of mixed and conflicting emotions; excited to be finished, yet sad at the same time.

We were both experiencing a sort of glum melancholy, when a young hiker appeared, with a brand-new backpack and a smiling face. A northbounder. He had come up the trail from Amicalola Falls State Park, where most north-bounders began their hike. The approach trail, the first eight miles from the park aren't even part of the Appalachian Trail; it doesn't begin until hikers reach Springer Mountain.

Buoyant and fresh, and filled with anticipation, he saw us and bounded over to chat. As he plopped down on the ground, we both noticed his clean clothes, his pack neat and tidy, and brand-new trail runners. Starting a hike with brand new shoes can be problematic, causing painful blisters, as I experienced at the beginning of our hike.

But his gear seemed squared away, making me think he'd been given pointers about packing, warned against carrying too much weight. Excess weight, especially starting out, can cause injuries, even prematurely ending a hike. Some hikers never make it past Neels Gap. It's rumored that some northbound hikers, so disenchanted with the whole enterprise, leave their gear behind at Neels Gap, calling it quits forever. But Matt's excitement for the hike, his broad smile, bright eyes and effervescent attitude, would most likely carry him a long way, if not all the way to Katahdin!

Matt wanted to know about our hike. We emphasized how many adventures he would have, people he would meet. Not just other thru-hikers, but day hikers, and people in towns, tour buses loaded with curious people, and especially all the trail angels who would appear just when he needed them. Finally, when it was time for Lonnie and me to finish *our* hike, Matt asked one last question: "What is the one piece of advice you would give me?"

We both paused, looking at the other, the tumblers in our heads clicking through the infinite number of possibilities, when Lonnie blurted out: "Keep your hands clean!"

It seemed a ridiculous thing to say, given that there were so many recommendations to consider, but Lonnie knew there were many things that could end a hike, and getting sick didn't need to be on the list. On our own hike, Lonnie and I had been amazed by how quickly our hands and fingernails became disgustingly grimy, germ magnets, at times making us afraid to touch our own food. Lonnie reached into his pocket and handed Matt his hand sanitizer. Matt accepted it graciously, with a heartfelt smile, and was on his way. As we watched this exuberant young man start up the trail, there was a part of both of us that wanted to follow him; his beginning marking our end.

With our young hiker friend gone, us sitting in our own silence, I thought of Molly and Geoff. For Lonnie and me, in 2010, to have met the man near the summit of Mt. Rogers in Virginia who had found them in the Thelma Marks Shelter in 1990, was inconceivable! Not to mention disconcerting. *How and why had our paths crossed?*

Maybe someday I'll understand why our two journeys had come together twenty years apart. Maybe it happened so I would tell their story. Or maybe it was meant as a reminder of just how extraordinary and synchronistic life can be? Then again, I may never know the reason.

But… it happened.

The following is on Molly's gray granite gravestone:
"A life shared with children, art and nature."

EPILOGUE

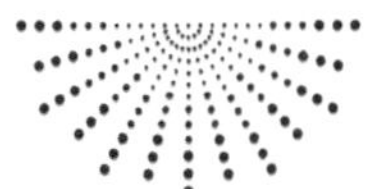

$\mathcal{U}$pon completing her southbound hike, Nancy spent months, which turned into years, wanting to write Molly's story, but not knowing where to start. Finally, her muse showed her the way, spurring her on to complete this intertwining story of two hikes, Nancy's and Molly's, and how they overlapped twenty years apart.

Before Nancy finished the Appalachian Trail, she was already imagining a hike of the Pacific Crest Trail, which begins at the Mexican border, winds up through the mountains of the west coast, ending in Canada, the northern most terminus, 2,650 miles later.

She, and her partner Lonnie, pursued that venture on April 17, 2014, hiking 2,000 miles of the PCT the first year, with concerns over rattlesnakes, desert heat, and heights neither had ever imagined climbing. Just like beginning the A.T., they found ways to deal with all the potential obstacles.

Wildfire trail closures, ankle issues, and a broken elbow necessitated finishing their hike in three parts over as many years. Finally, on September 25, 2016 in a snowstorm, they reached the Canadian border, their final goal!

And Nancy did finally hike and camp by herself on the Appalachian Trail and had an awesome experience.

So what's next? The Continental Divide Trail?

We'll see...to be continued.

AFTERWORD

By Molly's father,
   Jim LaRue

Shortly after her death, one of her closest college friends sent my wife and I a note that said she thought Molly, the artist, was now creating sunsets each day for us and there has not been a day since that we have checked the western skies, exclaiming when there is a beautiful sunset, and laughingly remarking that Mol had taken the day off due to heavy cloud cover that made the sunset impossible on that day. My wife, no longer living, has joined Molly in her sunset paintings.

> There's lots of stuff…feelings, ideas, memories,
> colors, shapes…in me. Stuff that's hard to
> put into words…art's easier.
> I can be quiet on the outside while my stuff
> inside is pretty loud. My art is some of this
> noise. I'm glad there's art.

My daughter Molly wrote these words for a display of her senior project at Ohio Wesleyan University. The display was a set of large junk yard dogs that she had welded together from parts she scavenged from metal scrap yards. Male students would take the dogs during the night and hide them in women's rest rooms and outside the doors of the university president and deans.

In her senior year in high school her art teacher asked her class to enter a US Postal Service contest to have school students design a stamp. She entered and there were more than a half million other entries. Molly's stamp won!

She wrote a children's book while at Ohio Wesleyan titled: the Reds. The Yellows. the Blues. I published it a few years ago and it is available at Amazon.com.

A few days before Christmas 2005, I was called by the County Prosecutor for Perry County, PA, the county where Molly and her friend Goeff were murdered. He indicated that the murderer who had been sentenced to two death sentences was given a new trial on appeal because he was considered to have been poorly represented. The Prosecutor said the county could not afford a new trial and the defendant had agreed to not proceed with the trial if his sentence was changed from death to life without parole. I was asked whether I would agree and I enthusiastically agreed. I was also asked if I would like to say anything to the defendant. Though I had no clue what I might say I decided to agree to go and speak to him. I had just a few days to prepare. Below is the statement I shared with the defendant.

FORGIVENESS STATEMENT
December 21, 2006

Paul, early in the morning of September 13, 1990, you tortured, raped and murdered my daughter, Molly. The hole in my heart from her loss remains.

But, I am here today because I am very pleased that your death sentences have been replaced with life imprisonment without chance of parole. However horrible your actions, I do not believe in the death penalty which is an act of vengeance, even if it is state authorized. Vengeance is never an answer to anything. It only breeds more violence and more retribution.

And so, Paul, I am here today to offer you forgiveness for what you have done.

I wish that you and I can now find peace.

What do I ask of you for this offering of forgiveness? Nothing! It is freely given.

But I do offer you a suggestion. With the death penalty no longer hanging over you, I hope that you will be able to find significant meaning in your life. Your mind and spirit can never be imprisoned. There are a growing number of serial killers in the country. My family has always believed that discovering the pain and fear that caused the violence could foster understanding and make us all more genuinely human. I hope you will consider accepting counsel from those who can help you understand what caused you to commit acts of violence and how you might help other troubled people.

Molly had decided to devote her life to working with troubled children, like you certainly were. She was determined to find out why these kids acted out in terribly violent ways. She was convinced that if you could reach them at an early enough state of their development, they could find their way through the circumstances that seemed to be driving them to violent ends.

She would have wanted that for you.

Paul, I think it would be great if you could pick up where Molly left off, starting with yourself. Help the Mollys of this world learn who you are and try to enlist the help of other inmates to help in this effort. You are a gold mine of critical information that needs to be unearthed.

I can assure you Paul, that Molly will be with you every step of the way because that is how much she cares!!

Peace be with you. Peace be with you.

Jim LaRue, Molly's Dad

ACKNOWLEDGMENTS

I am so thankful for the support and talent of Lonnie Busch. He not only is my loving partner, and publisher, but helped in many ways for this book to come to life. His encouragement and assistance all through this process—listening to me work out the storyline, adding the right phrase or word, the many edits, even when I said, *Would you read it one more time*—I am grateful. Without his literary skills as a writer and author, this book would not have been written.

I am especially grateful to the Maine Appalachian Trail Club and the Appalachian Trail Conservancy staff whose members assisted me with answers to my numerous questions. They included Andrew Downs, Brian King, Karen Lutz, Lester C. Kenway, Janice Clain, and Hawk Metheny. Thanks to you all.

A very special thank you goes to my cousin, Jim LaRue. His kindness in sharing stories of Molly and cooperating with my questions and especially, for patience through all the aspects of the writing and publishing, and to finally seeing this story complete, ready to be shared.

Also, a very special thank you to Geoff's mom, Glenda Hood, who shared her thoughts and memories with me. It took some time for me to find her, but she sent her new address to Molly's dad, Jim, at just the right moment. I then was able to share with her this story.

Also, thank you to my college friend, Avis, who read the first draft and gave many thoughts that were so helpful in the editing process.

And thanks to our friends who supported our hike. Tom and Sandy helped us get to and from the trail. Graybeard Beaver, whom we met on the trail, our 'troubadour' in Washington D.C. and in the

Shenandoah's. Another friend, Regina, who welcomed us in New York City, becoming our city trail angel during the Halloween celebration. The late Ed Peers, who transported us to and from the trail for a wonderful Thanksgiving, having told us he'd pick us up wherever we were on the trail. My storytelling friend in Georgia, Deb, who graciously let us leave our car at her home for when we completed our hike.

Thanks to our family who supported us in various ways. My brother, Dick and his wife Bonnie, gave us a ride to the train station, then later, returned us to the trail. Jessica, my niece, who gave us a fond farewell in the Philadelphia train station before we headed to Maine. My sister Sandra, who picked us up from the trail and gave us a wonderful fun-filled eating and laughing weekend, then camped out with us at the Blue Rocks Family Campground. Lonnie's son, Eric and his wife, Karen, who transported us from the trail for a family wedding as well as my graduation from East Tennessee State University. Lonnie's daughter, Brittany, and her husband, Nate, who took us in during the twelve-inch snowstorm. Britt also supported us in Southern Virginia, Tennessee and North Carolina.

And to all the trail angels who showed up just when we needed assistance. They came to our rescue, supported us with rides to and from the trailhead, shared their insights, and some generously provided delicious snacks and drinks.

And to all the others who helped with our journey—Thank You!

ABOUT THE AUTHOR

As an elementary teacher for over 23 years, Nancy used story to teach the concepts. In 1998 she left the classroom—to be a storyteller with no idea where that would take her. Teaching ESL in South Korea, exploring the vastness of Australia, Thailand, and even driving a U.S. rental car through Mexico, all along the way, stories found her.

Then she discovered long-distance hiking: completing the Appalachian Trail and the Pacific Crest Trail, and with those hikes, many more stories—even writing this book about her A.T. hike.

Nancy holds a master's degree in storytelling from East Tennessee State University, and has shared her stories in numerous venues across North Carolina and Georgia. Another performance, "Tales from the Trail," is a collection of stories from each of her two hikes.

In "Grandma Gatewood Returns," Nancy is in character as Emma Gatewood, who in 1955, became the first woman to solo thru-hike the entire Appalachian Trail. Nancy tells through Emma's voice, bringing to life Emma Gatewood's amazing journey.

Nancy is currently president of the NC Storytelling Guild, a member of NSN and the Asheville Storytelling Circle.

nancyreeder.com